Hiking Zion and Bryce Canyon
National Parks

HELP US KEEP THIS GUIDE UP TO DATE

Every effort has been made by the authors and editors to make this guide as accurate and useful as possible. However, many things can change after a guide is published—trails are rerouted, regulations change, techniques evolve, facilities come under new management, and so on.

We would appreciate hearing from you concerning your experiences with this guide and how you feel it could be improved and kept up to date. While we may not be able to respond to all comments and suggestions, we'll take them to heart, and we'll also make certain to share them with the authors. Please send your comments and suggestions to the following address:

Globe Pequot Press
Reader Response/Editorial Department
PO Box 480
Guilford, CT 06437

Or you may e-mail us at: editorial@GlobePequot.com.

Thanks for your input, and happy trails!

Hiking Zion and Bryce Canyon National Parks

A Guide to Southwestern Utah's
Greatest Hiking Adventures

Third edition

Erik Molvar and Tamara Martin

FALCONGUIDES

GUILFORD, CONNECTICUT
HELENA, MONTANA
AN IMPRINT OF ROWMAN & LITTLEFIELD

For Jamie for his love

FALCONGUIDES®

Copyright © 2005, 2013 Rowman & Littlefield
A previous edition of this book was published by Falcon Publishing Co. in 1997.

FalconGuides is an imprint of Rowman & Littlefield.
Falcon, FalconGuides, and Outfit Your Mind are registered trademarks of Rowman & Littlefield.

Photos by Erik Molvar unless otherwise credited.
Maps by Roberta Stockwell © Rowman & Littlefield

ISSN 1554-1916
ISBN 978-0-7627-8276-5

Printed in the United States of America

Contents

Overview

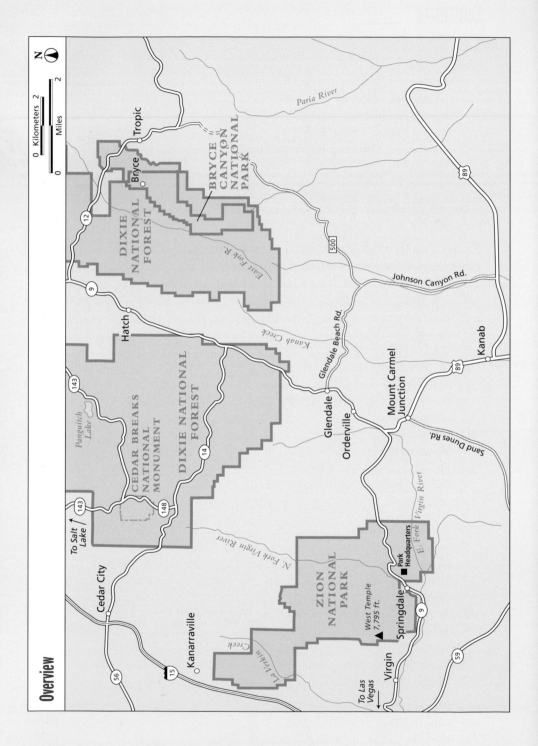

N

0 Kilometers 2

0 Miles 2

Paria River

Tropic

Bryce

BRYCE CANYON NATIONAL PARK

89

DIXIE NATIONAL FOREST

12

East Fork R.

500

Johnson Canyon Rd.

9

Hatch

Kanab Creek

Glendale Beach Rd.

Kanab

143

CEDAR BREAKS NATIONAL MONUMENT

Panguitch Lake

Mount Carmel Junction

89

148

DIXIE NATIONAL FOREST

14

Glendale

Orderville

Sand Dunes Rd.

143

To Salt Lake

N. Fork Virgin River

E. Fork Virgin River

Cedar City

Kanarraville

ZION NATIONAL PARK

Park Headquarters

56

15

La Verkin Creek

West Temple 7,795 ft.

Springdale

9

Virgin

To Las Vegas

59

ACKNOWLEDGMENTS

First of all, we would like to thank the residents of Long Valley for their outstanding hospitality during the course of our research. Myrna Cox and her family, of Glendale, were particularly helpful in our search for a place to live. Thanks also to Cleve and Lorene Esplins and to the Chamberlains for sharing their fascinating stories with us. Kent Traveller of Dixie National Forest and Steven Robinson of Cedar Breaks National Monument were wellsprings of information about their respective areas. Thanks also to Rod Schipper of the Bureau of Land Management's Kanab office for his geological insights. Dan Habig of Zion National Park provided interpretive information for this book, and Jerry Davis oversaw the review process for that part of the book. Special thanks to Steven Floray of the Zion Museum for tracking down the origins of the Left Fork dinosaur tracks. Thanks to Paula Henrie of Bryce Canyon National Park for reviewing the Bryce Canyon section. We would also like to thank our respective families, particularly Kathy, James, John, and Ginger, for their never-ending patience, support, and love throughout all of our adventures.

INTRODUCTION

The southwestern corner of Utah offers some of the most fascinating and awe-inspiring landscapes in the desert Southwest. Towering cliffs and slickrock canyons, with colorful spires and natural arches, exist here on a scale that dwarfs the works of humans and provides a humbling timescale by which to measure our own histories. Half a billion years in the making, this land was laid down in seas and lakes and dunes and then thrust skyward to be sculpted by the ceaseless efforts of wind and water. Here the visitor finds refuge from the fast-paced modern world, in a country little changed for a thousand years.

The geology that underlies Zion and Bryce National Parks is the product of millennia of sediment deposition. Over time sediments that collected at the bottoms of lakes and seas, on flat valley floors, and on vast desert dunefields were buried in layers called strata, in which geologists read the tale of the Earth's history. This southwestern region has one of the great undisturbed sequences of stone in the world, stretching from the 10,000-foot heights of the Markagunt Plateau down to the bottom of the Grand Canyon, at 2,400 feet above sea level. The rock layers form a stairstep series of ledges and cliffs known to geologists as the Grand Staircase.

The top layer of the Grand Staircase is made up of the freshwater limestones that weather out into the crenellated walls and striking pillars of Bryce Canyon and Cedar Breaks. It is a relatively young sedimentary layer, having been laid down between thirty-six and fifty-eight million years ago at the bottom of the vast Claron Lake system, which stretched northeast as far as present-day Wyoming. As shells and skeletons of freshwater animals disintegrated on the lakebed, they formed the limy calcium carbonate that cements the stone together. This cement dissolves easily in water, making the rock of this stratum (called the Claron Formation) weak and subject to erosion. It forms pillars called hoodoos where a harder stone lies atop the more erosive limestone: As the limestone around the hard rock cap melts away, only a slender column sheltered beneath the caprock remains intact. The Claron Formation is rich in iron and manganese. When exposed to the atmosphere, these minerals oxidize; the iron compounds form reddish colors, while the manganese compounds lend a purple or lavender cast to the stone (hence the Pink Cliffs).

The next major stratum in the geologic staircase is the Carmel Formation, a layer of shale that was laid down when shallow seas covered the region. This marine shale lacks the iron oxides and manganese that make the Claron limestone so colorful; instead, it appears as a dull gray. This formation gives rise to the Gray Cliffs, which make a long belt around the Upper Kolob Terrace in Zion National Park. Although the Gray Cliffs are a major geologic feature, few park visitors see them.

Below the Gray Cliffs lies a deep layer of sandstone, formed from sediments deposited as windblown dunes in a barren desert. This formation, known as Navajo sandstone, is more than 2,000 feet thick in places, and it forms the famous White Cliffs of Zion Canyon. The sandstone is mainly uniform in texture, but a discerning eye will notice that there is a great deal of cross-bedding in the stone, where changes in prevailing winds layered the sand at varying angles. The Navajo Formation is prone to vertical cracks or joints, by which water can seep into the bedrock and hasten erosion. Because the joints are vertical, stone falls away from the walls in blocks, leaving behind sheer rock faces. The upper layers of the Navajo Formation have been leached by groundwater, which carried away all of the iron compounds and left the stone bone white.

The lower layers of the Navajo sandstone have retained their iron and are a rusty red. Together with the Moenave Formation, which underlies it, the lower Navajo forms the Vermilion Cliffs that can be seen to the south of Zion and Bryce Canyon National Parks.

Beneath the Moenave lies the Chinle Formation, with a hard layer of conglomerate at its bottom that forms a caprock protecting the weaker layers below it. This caprock of conglomerate forms the top of buttes and mesas above the Moenkopi Formation. The Moenkopi is banded with orange and white layers, creating the "painted desert" of southwestern Zion. In other areas the Moenkopi is a chocolate brown and makes up the Chocolate Cliffs.

At the bottom of it all is the Kaibab limestone, laid down in a saltwater environment about 260 million years ago. This formation can be seen in the Hurricane Cliffs, east of Zion. Though the Kaibab limestone forms the oldest rock layer in the Bryce and Zion area, travelers who move farther south will find that it forms the upper rims of the Grand Canyon. Here, the most ancient strata in the Grand Staircase have been exposed by the relentless downcutting of the Colorado River.

This geologic wonderland was preserved at the beginning of the century by far-sighted conservationists. Today southwestern Utah attracts visitors from around the world who come here to enjoy the natural wonders and the boundless freedom of the Utah backcountry.

Weather

Southwestern Utah encompasses low deserts, arid uplands, and high, subalpine forestlands. There is no time of year when good hiking opportunities cannot be had.

Winters are cool and rainy at the lower elevations, but the high plateaus are typically locked in deep snowdrifts from November through April. Despite the snow, Bryce Canyon National Park is open year-round. Some of its day-hiking trails may remain passable throughout the winter, but deep snows collect in other areas. The park also has marked cross-country skiing trails that are distinct from its hiking routes. These trails loop through the forests atop the plateau, and some offer views of the hoodoos and canyons for which the park is known. This guide does not cover these ski trails, but information about them can be obtained at the Bryce visitor center.

Cedar Breaks and the rest of the Markagunt Plateau are completely snowbound and inaccessible to hikers during the winter. The uplands of Zion National Park typically are closed to entry during winter, although the Zion Canyon area remains open. Water temperatures are usually too low during winter to allow wading for extended periods.

The hallmark of spring is melting snow, and streams in this otherwise desert region become swollen with runoff. Many of the canyon hikes become impassable as a result of spring flooding. The high country is still snowbound at this time, although the Kolob Terrace of Zion National Park begins to open up in late April. The low deserts receive much of their annual rainfall in the spring, when they burst into a colorful display of blossoms. However, the moist soils of the low desert are prone to sticky mud at this time, which makes cross-country hiking an unpleasant activity—as well as one that can damage the environment. Spring is an excellent time to visit Bryce Canyon: Its cliffs and hoodoos are even prettier with a light dusting of snow.

Summertime brings the peak of visitation to the area, and crowds are commonplace in the most accessible parts of the national parks. Sweltering daytime temperatures make hiking at midday toilsome, especially in the lower elevations. Confine your hiking to early morning and evening hours to avoid the worst of the heat. Savvy hikers retreat into the shady depths of the canyons or up to the breezy subalpine country atop the plateaus to beat the heat. The region experiences dry weather through the first half of summer, but late August is known for torrential thunderstorms that can trigger flash floods in the slot canyons and create spectacular waterfalls on the cliffs. Lightning strikes along the rims of the Bryce Canyon and Cedar Breaks amphitheaters are also a serious hazard at this time.

Autumn is perhaps the best time of year to visit the region. Temperatures are warm during the day with frigid, crystal-clear nights. Water levels in the canyons are low at this time, and the water temperature remains fairly constant until late October, when it begins to plummet. As a bonus, travelers along the waterways are treated to colorful displays as the maples and cottonwoods shed their leaves, and visitors to the high country can take in the brilliant gold foliage of the aspens. The highest plateaus enjoy cool autumn weather but generally remain snow-free until mid-October. The lower terraces and canyon bottoms are warm and temperate at this time. Temperatures in the low desert of southwestern Zion become tolerable in late October.

Hiking in Arid Lands

Hiking in the Southwest poses challenges that are encountered nowhere else. Much of southwestern Utah's public land is free of trails, and hikers may have to rely on their map and compass skills to find their way. The defining feature of the region is "slickrock," in which vast expanses of sculpted sandstone have been scoured bare by wind and water. As its name suggests, slickrock can be very slippery when it gets wet. Trails and routes that cross slickrock will be marked only with cairns, if they are marked at all. Hikers who travel through canyons should remain constantly aware that it is much easier to climb up a slickrock face than it is to descend one. Local residents are routinely called away from their jobs and families to rescue hikers who ventured up onto ledges from which it was impossible to descend.

Perhaps the most obvious challenge in desert hiking is the extreme weather. During the hottest parts of the day, the temperature can reach 120°F several feet above the floor of the low desert. Summer hikers should wear broad-brimmed hats, long-sleeved shirts, and baggy pants to protect themselves from the intensity of the desert sun. Cover exposed skin with sunscreen lotion. Take a lesson from the local wildlife and hike in the cool of the mornings and evenings, and rest in the shade during the heat of the day.

The desert air wicks moisture away from the body at an amazing rate, and active hikers should plan to drink about a gallon of water per day. Desert water sources may run dry for part of the year and often contain exotic microbes that can cause intestinal disorders. Always carry enough water to meet your daily needs, and filter all surface water to remove the harmful microbes.

Many desert-dwelling animals have evolved poisons, and they may bite or sting when provoked. The rattlesnake is the most notorious of these, although its reputation for aggressiveness is undeserved. This nocturnal predator will flee when given a chance, and it rarely bites unless it is surprised or cornered. To avoid snakebites always watch where you put your hands and feet and avoid reaching into dark places or overturning boulders. This practice will also help you avoid scorpions, most of which have painful stings. Scorpions like to hide in dark, moist places; hikers who leave their boots outside overnight may be in for a nasty surprise in the morning.

Desert hikers must be particularly careful not to upset the ecological balance of desert communities. Many plants and animals live on the edge of their capabilities, and any added stress may result in death. Give a wide berth to nesting birds, animals with young, and wildlife that is using a water source. Feel free to watch these wild inhabitants of the desert, but do so at a respectful distance so that your presence does not disturb them. Finally, hikers who are traveling in the low desert or piñon-juniper scrubland should watch for biological soil crusts and avoid walking on them. These crusts are dark and granular and contain algae and other microbes that come alive following rains. A major source of nutrients for desert soils, they form a crucial link in the web of desert ecosystems. Biological soil crusts are very fragile and may not recover for decades after being trampled.

Sharing the Trail

Visitors should expect to encounter a wide variety of user groups in southwestern Utah, particularly on Bureau of Land Management and National Forest lands. This magnificent wilderness is a magnet for outdoor folk and solitude seekers of all descriptions. In the interest of a safe and pleasant wilderness experience for all, exercise consideration and good manners when meeting other parties on the trail. Respect for others is the cornerstone of the traditional western ethic, a code still in force in the backcountry areas of Utah. Backpackers must share the trail with stock users and mountain bikers in many areas. The following commonsense guidelines will help backcountry travelers avoid a bad experience when encountering other visitors.

Pack and saddle stock have the right-of-way on the trails wherever they are allowed. Because pack and saddle stock are less maneuverable than foot travelers,

Cairns, piles of stones placed to mark the route, mark the trail below the north face of Cathedral Mountain, Zion National Park.

hikers should yield to horse parties when the two meet on a trail. In such a situation, the best thing that a hiker can do is to hike up the hillside above the trail for at least 20 feet and allow the stock to pass. It often helps to talk to the animals in reassuring tones as they pass by. This keeps the animals from panicking and tangling up the pack string.

Mountain bikes are not allowed on most trails in national parks and designated Wilderness areas. Bikers who use traditional hiking trails where permitted should proceed slowly and with caution, especially when approaching blind corners. Always bike at a speed that allows instant braking if an unexpected obstacle or traveler appears in the path. Bike users should yield the right-of-way to horse users, and hikers and backpackers should yield the trail to both horse users and mountain bikers.

How to Follow a Faint Path

Many of the most popular treks in this corner of Utah exist only as primitive routes that may not be marked at all. Visitors to backcountry areas should have a few elementary trail-finding skills in their bag of tricks, in case a trail peters out or a snowfall covers the path. A topographic map and compass, and the ability to use them, are essential insurance against disaster when a trail takes a wrong turn or disappears completely. A few additional tricks, noted below, may aid a traveler in such a time of need.

Maintained trails in southwestern Utah are typically marked in a variety of ways. Signs bearing the name and/or number of the trail are present at some trail junctions, although weathering and inconsiderate visitors sometimes remove these plaques. These signs rarely contain mileage information, and where they do, the information is often suspect. Along the trail several kinds of markers indicate the location of maintained trails. In forested areas cuts in the bark of living trees, known as blazes, are made immediately beside the path. In spots where a trail crosses a gravel streambed or bare slickrock, piles of rocks called cairns mark the route. These cairns are typically constructed of three or more stones piled atop one another, a formation that almost never occurs naturally.

In the case of an extremely overgrown trail, markings of any kind may be impossible to find. On such a trail the techniques used to build the trail serve as clues to its location. Well-constructed trails have rather wide, flat beds. Let your feet seek the flat spots when traveling through tall brush, and you will almost always find yourself on the trail. Look for check dams and other rock-work on the trail that may have been put in place to prevent erosion. Old sawed logs from previous trail maintenance can be used to navigate in spots where the trailbed is obscured; if you find a sawed log, then you must be on a trail that was maintained at some point in time. Switchbacks are also a sure sign of an official trail; wild game travels in straight lines, and horsemen traveling off-trail seldom bother to zigzag across hillsides. Previous travelers can also leave clues to the location of old trails; watch for footprints or hoof marks as you travel.

When attempting to find a trail that has disappeared, ask yourself where the most logical place would be to build a trail given its source and destination. Trail builders tend to seek level ground where it is available, and they often follow the natural contours of streamcourses and ridgelines. Bear in mind that most trails avoid up-and-down motion in favor of long, sustained grades culminating in major passes or hilltops. Old trailbeds can sometimes be spotted from a distance as they cut across hillsides at a constant angle.

Zero-Impact Camping Techniques for Arid Lands

Many backcountry areas in southwestern Utah do not have established camping areas. As a result, backpackers have unlimited options in choosing a spot to bed down. Along with this freedom comes the responsibility to leave the camping site exactly as it was found. It is easy to see that if even half of the backcountry campers left evidence of their passage, Utah's backcountry would soon be dotted with damaged campsites. Travelers should inspect their campsites when they leave and camouflage any spots that have been impacted. Pack out what you brought in with you, and pick up any trash that may have been left by less-considerate campers.

Campsite selection is a key component to an enjoyable backpacking trip. Choose a level spot that is already free of vegetation so that it doesn't have to be cleared. Flash floods are a very real threat to desert campers; even under blue skies, a rainstorm 20

Dunes offer a good traveling surface. Footprints will soon be erased by the wind.

miles away can send a wall of water down a dry wash in minutes. Be sure to pitch your camp on high ground, well away from streamcourses. When traveling along a major canyon, do not camp in the mouth of a side canyon or across from its mouth: Flash floods that roar down tributary canyons typically expend much of their force in the area near the canyon's mouth. Finally, seeps and permanent streams are a critical feature of wildlife habitat. Camp at least 200 yards away from such water sources so that the animals will be undisturbed, and as a result you will get a good night's sleep.

Campers should move their camp every night so that their impacts are not concentrated in any one spot. Soils of the low deserts and scrub woodlands are particularly vulnerable to compaction. Compacted soils do not absorb water as well, and this leads to an increase in runoff. This in turn hastens soil erosion and leaves less water for desert plants, which may die as a result. By moving camp frequently, hikers will not compact the soil as severely, and the damage they do can be repaired by the activities of burrowing animals and insects. In addition, a human presence that is only temporary will be less likely to disturb behavior patterns of local wildlife.

There is something magical about having a campfire in the desert, with stars scattered across the infinite heavens like so much sparkling dust. Campfires can have major impacts on the desert community, however, and campers who build them should practice minimum-impact techniques so that their fire-building activities do not scar the landscape. To build a zero-impact fire, dig a pit 6 inches deep in mineral soil. Do not surround the pit with rocks; these will only get scorched and will not stop a fire from spreading in any case. Gather dead and downed twigs of small diameter (these will burn completely and leave no charred stumps). When your fire is spent, make sure the ash is cool to the touch, then bury it with the original soil. Scatter twigs sparsely across the site to camouflage it. Campfires are illegal in some areas, and firewood may be hard to find in others. Come prepared by bringing a lightweight backpacking stove in place of a campfire for all your cooking needs.

Finally, wilderness sanitation may be one of the next great problems facing land managers in southwestern Utah. Few outhouses are found in the Utah backcountry; thus, hikers must practice zero-impact techniques while having a bowel movement. When relieving yourself, select a site that is far from any stream, spring, or wash that might become contaminated. Dig a "cat hole" 4 to 6 inches deep in mineral soil, relieve yourself, and cover the site with soil. An even better solution is to carry a "poop tube" lined with paper bags to pack out any of your solid wastes. Such a tube can be constructed of a short length of PVC pipe, with screw-on caps at either end. This inexpensive, lightweight solution may represent the wave of the future in these arid lands.

For more information about zero-impact camping, visit the Leave No Trace website at LNT.org.

Flash Floods

In an area where soils are thin and bare rock covers much of the landscape, flash floods are an ever-present danger. Southwestern Utah is deeply scored with a network of spectacular chasms that bear mute testimony to the erosive power of the floodwaters. Floodwaters grow in magnitude rather than dispersing when they enter slot canyons, and any living thing that stands in the way of the water is sure to be swept away. Although no foolproof method can guarantee your safety in a narrow canyon, hikers can take three basic steps to reduce the chances of being caught in a flash flood.

First, assess the potential danger before you begin your trip. If rain threatens or a moisture-laden weather system is expected to pass through, do not venture into narrow canyons. Zion National Park uses the Flash Flood Warnings issued by the National Weather Service as a barometer to gauge risk and will close narrow canyon hikes during periods when a Flash Flood Warning is in effect. At other times, visitors are expected to check the weather forecast and make their own decisions regarding acceptable levels of risk.

The second step in avoiding death by flash flood is to continually reevaluate the potential for floods as you hike. Remember that a flood can occur under a clear blue sky if a downpour is in progress many miles away. Watch the skies for changing weather, and climb to safety or abort your hike if the clouds roll in. As you walk, watch the canyon walls for a muddy film and stranded driftwood that mark the high-water line during previous floods. Constantly scan the terrain for escape routes by which you can climb to safety above this high-water level. Also, keep your ears open. Flash floods make a muted roaring sound as they roll down a canyon, giving a few minutes' warning of the impending wall of water. An unaccountable roaring from upstream, often accompanied by a brisk and sudden wind, indicates the approach of floodwaters. Climb immediately to high ground.

The third step to surviving in a flood-prone environment is to know how to escape floodwaters if they overtake you. The best course of action is to climb out of harm's way, but the sheer walls found in many slot canyons often make it impossible to climb above the water. If you cannot escape by climbing, seek out a side cleft where you can hide from the full fury of the floodwaters. Large boulders can also be used as shelter from floods—wedge your body behind the lee side of the rock so that you will not be swept away by the initial surge. Remember that floating debris is as dangerous as the water itself; if you are knocked unconscious, you will certainly drown.

Also remember that a timely rescue is unlikely in the event of a backcountry flood. Be prepared to rescue yourself and your companions in an emergency. Carry a supply of extra food when hiking in backcountry canyons in case you are trapped for several days by floodwaters.

Planning Your Trip

Reading this guidebook to the Zion and Bryce region is a good start, but wise hikers will gather as much current information as possible before starting out on a wilderness expedition. Permits are not required for expeditions into most of Utah's public lands, although they are required for backpacking and some day hikes in the national parks. It is always wise to check in with a local ranger station to get the latest report on trail conditions. Ask for the trail supervisor or recreation planner, who will be well prepared to answer your questions. A list of addresses and phone numbers for these ranger stations is provided in Appendix A at the back of this book.

Backpackers will need to do additional research. Overnight camping within Cedar Breaks National Monument is not allowed. Designated backcountry camping spots occur only in Bryce Canyon National Park and parts of Zion. For the more popular hikes in Zion, it is recommended that visitors obtain wilderness reservations in advance through the online reservation system. Where established campsites do not occur, backpackers should practice minimum-impact camping techniques, as outlined earlier in this chapter. In wilderness humans are passing visitors and should leave no trace of their passage to mar the wilderness experience for others.

The key to a quality hiking experience is good planning. Hikers who underestimate the distance or time required to complete a trip may find themselves hiking in the dark, a dangerous proposition at best. An experienced hiker traveling at a fast clip without rest stops can generally make 2.5 miles per hour on desert terrain, perhaps more if the distance is all downhill. Novices and hikers in poor physical condition generally have a maximum speed of 1.5 miles per hour. Expect even slower hiking speeds over wilderness routes, on steep terrain, and on treks that require wading. Each hike is accompanied by an estimated hiking time, calculated using an average speed of 2 miles per hour. And note that these rates do not include stops for rest and refreshment, which add tremendously to a hiker's enjoyment and appreciation of the surroundings. Higher elevations can also pose some hazards, such as exposure to bad weather, thinner air, and even altitude sickness. If you feel any effects of altitude sickness, descend to a lower elevation immediately.

Eight miles a day is a good goal for travelers new to backpacking, while old hands can generally cover 10 miles comfortably. We recommend traveling below top speed, focusing more attention on the surrounding natural beauty and less on the exercise of hiking itself. In addition, desert heat and aridity make it unwise to push one's limits.

How to Use This Guide

The primary intent of this FalconGuide is to provide information that will help hikers choose backpacking trips according to their desires and abilities, as well as a detailed description of each trail, interpreting its natural and historical features. This guide is intended to be used in conjunction with topographic maps, which can be purchased at ranger stations and at local gift and sporting goods stores, or through the US Geological Survey, PO Box 25286, Federal Center, Denver, CO 80225. The USGS has stopped making the larger fifteen-minute map series and now publishes only seven-and-a-half-minute maps. Additionally, several fine topographic maps of larger areas have been published by various private organizations and are available in local stores.

In this book each trail description begins with an outline describing the physical characteristics of the trail for quick and easy reference. A general description of the trek comes first, followed by distance and the approximate hiking time. Extended trips cannot be reached by road, while wilderness routes represent abandoned trails and cross-country routes where the only indication of a trail might be an occasional cairn. This description is followed by information on the best season for attempting the trail, which may be influenced by summer heat, winter snows, and/or wet season flooding.

Next is a difficulty rating. The rating can be interpreted as follows: Easy trails can be completed without difficulty by hikers of all abilities; hikes rated moderate will challenge novices; moderately strenuous hikes will tax even experienced hikers; and strenuous trails will push the physical limits of the most Herculean hiker.

Difficulty ratings may be followed by star symbols. These indicate difficulty in following the trail. Trails with one star may have had a well-defined tread at one point but have become overgrown in places. It might be necessary to follow cairns for short distances. This rating also applies to canyon routes in which the intended direction for the trek is fairly obvious. If you pay close attention to where the trail is ultimately headed, you should not have much difficulty following these routes. If the difficulty rating is followed by two stars, then the trail may be faint or even nonexistent for long stretches. Hikers must refer to a compass and topographic map frequently on such hikes.

Water availability along the trail is described next, according to its reliability. Even perennial, or year-round, water sources may dry up during drought years, and intermittent sources hold water only during the wet months. Wise hikers bring their own water rather than relying on natural supplies.

Next, for some hikes, are comments on trail hazards and recommended equipment to bring along. These are followed by the appropriate seven-and-a-half-minute quadrangle topo maps for each featured hike, which are listed in plain type. Maps published by sources other than the USGS appear in italics. The managing agency responsible for the area is then listed under jurisdiction, and a brief set of directions for finding the trailhead rounds out the statistical section. GPS coordinates are included for trailheads.

A detailed interpretive description of the trail—including geologic and ecological features, historical sites, campsites, and other important information—follows. We have included supplemental photographs to give the reader a visual preview of some of the prominent features along the trail.

An elevation profile accompanies almost every trail description, providing a schematic look at the major elevation gains and losses that hikers will encounter during the course of the trip. The overall representation is an approximation; do not depend on the profile alone to lead you through the hike.

In all of the profiles, the vertical axes of the graphs show the distance climbed in feet. In contrast, the horizontal axes show the distance traveled in miles. It is important to understand that the vertical (feet) and horizontal (miles) scales can differ between hikes. Read each profile carefully, making sure you read both the height and distance shown. This will help you interpret what you see in each profile. Some elevation profiles may show gradual hills to be steep or steep hills to be gradual. Elevation profiles are not provided for hikes with little or no elevation gain.

The key points at the end of each hike provide a mile-by-mile description of landmarks, trail junctions, and gradient changes. The official distances of the land management agency are presented for all trails that had them at press time. Where official distances were unavailable, they were developed using an instrument called a planimeter, which measures two-dimensional distances on a topographic map. These distances were then corrected for altitude gain or loss. The resulting mileages should be looked upon as conservative estimates because they may not account for small-scale twists and turns or minor ups and downs.

Map Legend

═══15═══	Interstate Highway	✕	Airport
═══89═══	US Highway	⌣	Bridge
═══9═══	State Highway	▪	Building/Point of Interest
═══500═══	County/Forest Road	▲	Campground
═══════	Local Road	⊥⊥⊥	Cliff
═══════	Gravel Road	⫶	Gate
═══════	Unimproved Road	🅿	Parking
•─•─•─•─•	Power Line	⌣	Pass/Gap
⊢───────⊣	Tunnel	▲	Peak/Summit
▬▬▬▬▬▬	Featured Trail	⊞	Picnic Area
─ ─ ─ ─ ─	Trail	⬛	Ranger Station
··············	Off-Trail Route	◪	Scenic View/Viewpoint
─ ·· ─ ·· ─	State Line	⟋	Spring
∼∼∼∼	River or Creek	○	Town
∼ ∼ ∼	Intermittent Stream	①	Trailhead
⬭	Body of Water	❓	Visitor/Information Center
▬▬▬▬	National Forest/Park	⋛	Waterfall
▭▭▭▭	National Wilderness Area		
▭▭▭▭	State/County Park		
▭▭▭▭	BLM Lands		
⫽⫽⫽⫽	No Camping		

Zion National Park and Surrounding Lands

Zion National Park encompasses the landscape of high plateaus, deep canyons, and sheer monoliths surrounding the North Fork of the Virgin River. It is a relatively small park that receives heavy visitation, particularly the day-hiking trails within Zion Canyon. Most park trails and routes can be hiked in a single day, and few corners of the park are out of range for day trekkers. Backpackers will find it difficult to plan a Zion trip of more than two days without running into a road. The longest possible extended trip in the park combines the La Verkin, Hop Valley, Wildcat Canyon Connector, West Rim, Observation Point, and East Rim Trails. This trek requires five to seven days to complete.

The story of Zion National Park began more than 200 million years ago, when dinosaurs roamed much of North America. This corner of the continent was a barren desert at that time, buried deep in dunes of windblown sand that resembled the modern-day Sahara. These great dunefields later solidified into stone to form the Navajo sandstone formation. This formation is more than 2,000 feet thick in places, and it forms the spectacular monoliths, slot canyons, and towering walls of Zion Canyon. The upper layers of the Navajo Formation were cleansed of iron oxides by groundwater and became bone-white, while the lower layers of sandstone retain a distinctly rusty cast. Much later, the sand dunes were covered over by freshwater lakes and shallow seas, which contributed sediment to form the rock layers that top the Navajo sandstone.

A major uplift occurred in this region about ten million years ago, creating the Colorado Plateau. The area that was to become Zion National Park rose thousands of feet above its previous elevation, and rivers that once wandered aimlessly across featureless plains began to cut downward into the uplifted bedrock. They sculpted the deep gorges and narrow slot canyons that now attract visitors from around the world. At the same time, a period of volcanic activity began, forming the cinder cones and lava flows that can be seen atop the Kolob Terrace. This period of volcanism ceased less than a million years ago, a mere eyeblink in geologic time.

This unique landscape has become a haven for wildlife and unique plant communities. Zion Canyon offers the most diverse flora and fauna, featuring lush riparian

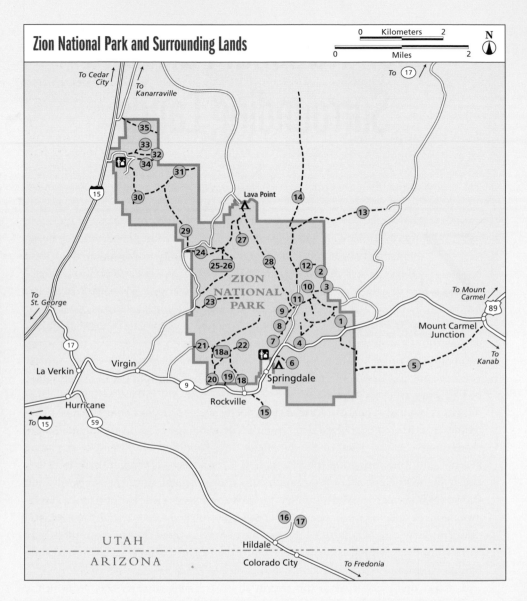

habitats, a rich array of birds, and a burgeoning population of mule deer. The canyon comes alive at night, when ring-tailed cats and foxes emerge from their hiding places to prowl the valley floor, night-blooming sacred daturas unfurl white petals to the night breeze, and porcupines sally forth in search of forage. Springs and seeps along the canyon walls support lush hanging gardens that are home to the endemic Zion snail, which is found nowhere else in the world. Above the rims are vast expanses of arid scrubland where mountain lions and golden eagles still reign supreme. The southwest corner of the park is home to a low desert community that is as beautiful as it is forbidding.

The earliest inhabitants of the Zion country are classified by archaeologists within the Basket Maker culture, forerunners to the Anasazi people. They grew maize, squash, and beans on the alluvial soils of the floodplains, and they built huts and granaries beneath the overhanging rock of the canyons. Little evidence of their labors remains.

Two Spanish missionaries named Escalante and Dominguez explored this area in 1776 while searching for an easy route between Santa Fe, New Mexico, and Monterey, California. When these first Europeans arrived here, they found the land inhabited sparsely by the Paiutes, a tribe that suffered from constant depredations at the hands of fiercer neighboring tribes. Jedediah Smith, the preaching mountain man, was the first American to arrive on the scene, passing through in 1826 on his way to California.

Settlement of this country came with the arrival of Mormon pioneers in the 1860s. The new arrivals were inspired by the striking landscape of their new home and called it "Little Zion." Names of landmarks often have religious references, many of which can be traced to early explorer Frederick Vining Fisher, a Methodist minister. The Mormons who settled here cultivated a friendly relationship with the neighboring Paiutes and built homesteads within Zion Canyon and along the streams that flow westward from the Kolob Terrace. The remains of a few old corrals are all that remain from the pioneer period. Zion Canyon was recognized as a geological wonder by the early settlers, and in 1909 the area was set aside as Mukuntuweap National Monument (*mukuntuweap* means "straight canyon" in Paiute). This preserve was expanded and christened Zion National Park in 1919.

The modern park can usefully be divided by elevations into two geographic zones. The canyon bottoms lie beneath the cliffs of the Navajo Formation, while the Kolob Terrace encompasses the plateau above the rimrock. Access to Zion Canyon is via UT 9, about 22 miles east of Hurricane and 25 miles west of Mount Carmel Junction. The main park campground and visitor center are at the mouth of the canyon. A scenic spur road ascends the canyon to access trailheads and the Zion Park Lodge. Since this area receives heavy use, the National Park Service has closed the road to private vehicles and now provides access by free shuttles. Currently, private shuttles transport hikers to the upper trailhead for The Narrows.

Hikers can reach the plateaus east of the canyon by trail from the Zion Ponderosa Ranch Resort, on the road to Navajo Lake. The western part of the Kolob Terrace is accessible via the paved Kolob Reservoir Road, which departs from the highway at the town of Virgin. A primitive campground and a fire lookout manned by rangers can be found atop Lava Point. At the western edge of the Kolob Terrace are the Kolob Canyons, surrounded by spectacular towers of stone. Access them by a paved road from I-15; a small visitor center here is permanently staffed by rangers.

Like most national parks, Zion requires a wilderness permit for overnight trips. Formerly free of charge, these permits are now available for a fee from the main visitor center or the Kolob Canyons Visitor Center. Additionally, permits for many wilderness sites can be reserved on the official Zion National Park website (see

Appendix A). For most trails and popular routes, visitors must obtain reservations for designated campsites. In remote parts of the wilderness where campsites have not been designated, travelers must select their own site (choose one that is not easily damaged) and erase all traces of their visit when they leave. Camping is prohibited within a quarter mile of springs, which are critical areas for desert wildlife. Other no-camping areas are marked clearly on maps in this book with striped gray shading. Camping in The Narrows, the Southwest Desert area, West Rim, Hop Valley, and along La Verkin Creek is limited to designated campsites, which are assigned at the visitor center. Day hikers who attempt the entire hike of The Narrows also must have a permit, a system that has been enacted for the Left Fork day trip as well.

Zion Canyon and the Eastern Approaches

The most famous monoliths and highest cliff walls in the region surround Zion Canyon, shading a riparian lowland of outstanding ecological diversity. This area also attracts the greatest numbers of tourists. Temperatures in the canyon can reach 100°F at midday, and summer visitors are advised to hike in mornings and evenings. Most hikes in the canyon are paved, with limited opportunities for exploration—most treks here are short day hikes. More primitive trails cross the high plateaus to the east, offering backpacking opportunities that take in the spectacular rimtop overlooks at the canyon edge. Permits for day hikes through The Narrows and for overnight backpacking trips can be obtained at the main visitor center outside the town of Springdale. Two highly developed auto campgrounds near the visitor center can accommodate a large number of visitors but fill up early during the peak season. Springdale offers a broad spectrum of supplies and services to satisfy most needs.

The last of the White Cliffs in The Barracks hike (hike 5)

The Zion Canyon Shuttle

Private automobiles are no longer allowed to drive up Zion Canyon; instead, the Park Service has instituted a shuttle service equipped with natural-gas-powered trams. The primary starting point for the tram is the main visitor center just east of Springdale, but during busy periods (when the visitor center parking lot is likely to be full), you can catch the tram at various marked points in the town of Springdale itself. There is no charge for the shuttle service, but riders are still required to pay the park entrance fee. The tram stops at Zion Canyon trailheads and points of interest four or more times each hour, from early morning to late evening. This shuttle service is fast and convenient, with plenty of room for backpacks. The clean and quiet trams have improved the visitor experience remarkably from the traffic jams and parking snarls that formerly characterized this marquee area.

1 East Rim

A day hike or short backpack from Zion's East Entrance over a high plateau to intersect the Observation Point Trail

Distance: 7.8 miles (12.6 km) one way
Hiking time: About 4 hours
Best seasons: April–May, September–November
Difficulty: Moderately strenuous*
Water availability: Stave Spring is reliable; a seep in Cave Canyon is intermittent.

Topo maps: The Barracks, Springdale East, Temple of Sinawava; Zion National Park (Trails Illustrated)
Jurisdiction: Zion National Park. See Appendix A for more information.

Finding the trailhead: Drive west on UT 9 from Zion National Park's East Entrance for 150 yards to reach a paved road that runs north past a ranger residence. The trailhead is at the end of this short spur road. GPS: N37° 13' 55.848" / W112° 52' 34.890"

The Hike

Hikers can complete the East Rim Trail in a long day, or undertake it as a backpack with an overnight stay atop the plateau or in the upper reaches of Echo Canyon. The trail starts in the arid slickrock country near the East Entrance and then climbs atop a wooded plateau for some excellent views before wandering away from the rim. Spectacular scenery accompanies the trail during its descent through Echo Canyon. The Observation Point Trail is the most popular exit route, offering a steep and scenic descent for an additional 3.6 miles to reach the Zion Canyon Road near Weeping Rock.

The trek begins on an old dirt road that follows the dry wash of Clear Creek between widely spaced cliffs of Navajo sandstone. This is a barren landscape, with bare shoulders of slickrock rising amid a sparse growth of ponderosa pines. The roadbed eventually bends northward into the narrow canyon of Cave Creek and begins to climb. Steep, wooded slopes are broken by bands of rock in this small tributary canyon. A spring at the bottom of the gulch can be reached only by a steep descent across unstable slopes; it should be regarded as an emergency-only water source.

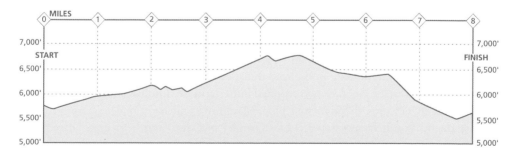

A rocky rib guards the Clear Creek valley.

The old roadway climbs above the Navajo Formation and then turns south atop the rimrock high above Clear Creek. This part of the trail offers superb views down the Clear Creek drainage at Checkerboard Mesa and its more massive neighbor to the west. A checkerboard pattern has been worn into the faces of these cliffs by erosion: Wind has scoured horizontal striations along the boundaries of different strata of sandstone, while runoff has carved deep lines along vertical cracks or "joints" in the stone.

The track runs westward along the rimrock and then makes a long detour north as it skirts the vertical cliffs of Jolley Gulch. A shallow descent to the dry watercourse carries travelers to a dramatic pour-off that overlooks the smooth walls of the gulch below. The old road then climbs into the arid hilltops, where a scrub woodland of piñon pine and Utah juniper grows from thin, dry soil. The route soon swings northwest, allowing distant views of two wooded buttes and then finds its way into a loose woodland of old-growth ponderosa pine. Manzanita and bare gravel surround the pines on the south-facing slopes, while Gambel oak and swards of grass share the understory on moist sites.

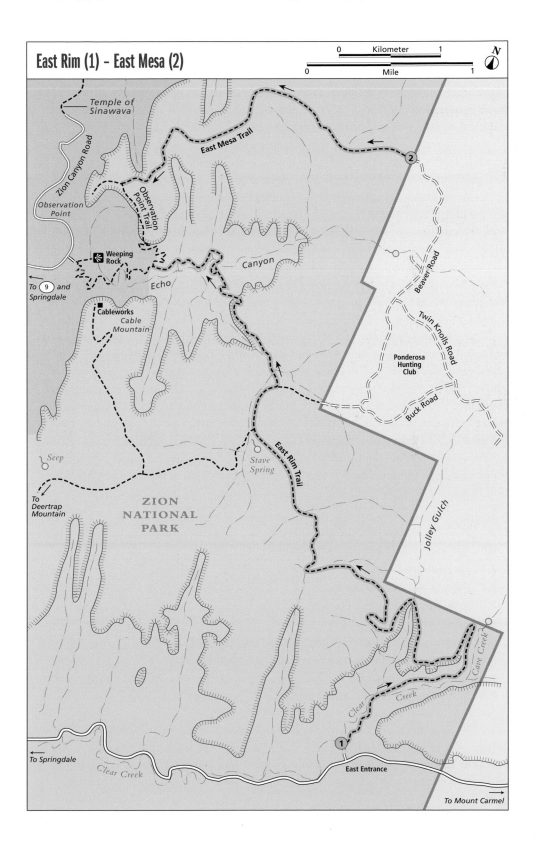

East Rim (1) – East Mesa (2)

0 Kilometer 1
0 Mile 1

N

Temple of Sinawava

Zion Canyon Road

East Mesa Trail

2

Observation Point Trail

Observation Point

Weeping Rock

Echo Canyon

To 9 and Springdale

Cableworks
Cable Mountain

Beaver Road

Twin Knolls Road

Ponderosa Hunting Club

Buck Road

Seep

Stave Spring

East Rim Trail

To Deertrap Mountain

ZION NATIONAL PARK

Jolley Gulch

Cave Creek

Clear Creek

1

To Springdale

Clear Creek

East Entrance

To Mount Carmel

After crossing the crest of the hills, the trail makes a long and gradual descent into the watershed of Echo Canyon. The upper reaches of this drainage feature rolling woodlands, and near the bottom of the grade a short side path leads southward to Stave Spring. Water trickles freely and dependably from a pipe at this site, providing the most reliable source of water on the East Rim.

Upon leaving Stave Spring, the trail follows the gulch downhill to reach a broad sage flat. In the midst of the sagebrush, there is a well-marked junction with the trail to Cable and Deertrap Mountains. Bear right as the main trail makes its way down a gentle slope. The path to the Ponderosa trailhead soon breaks away to the right while the East Rim Trail angles downhill toward the head of Echo Canyon. The canyon rims soon drop away to the left of the path, and flat benches along the tops of the cliffs afford vistas of the sheer, white walls below. Ponderosa pines grow from every chink and shelf where a seedling could possibly take root. The trail follows the rimrock for 0.5 mile and then zigzags steeply down the face of the cliffs. Along the way hikers get outstanding views of Echo Canyon, with Cathedral Mountain and Angels Landing framed by its mouth.

The cliffs soon give way to a steep, north-facing slope where lofty pines thrive in sandy soil. This slope ultimately plays out onto a finger ridge with a sunnier exposure, and several sandy pads here might accommodate a small tent. The path crosses a side canyon and then works its way around onto east-facing slopes. Finding the route is a bit challenging as the path crosses bare slickrock marked only by cairns. Hikers must negotiate several steep friction pitches before the path turns east and ascends the final distance to the Observation Point Trail.

From here travelers can make the steep descent to Zion Canyon Road at Weeping Rock or can ascend another 900 feet to the East Mesa Trail at the base of Observation Point.

Key Points

0.0   Trail leaves parking area near East Entrance.

1.0   Mouth of Cave Canyon

1.7   Overlook of Clear Creek basin

2.6   Jolley Gulch

5.3   Stave Spring

5.4   Junction with trail to Cable and Deertrap Mountains. Bear right.

5.8   Junction with spur trail to Ponderosa Hunting Club trailhead. Turn left.

7.5   Floor of upper Echo Canyon

7.8   Trail ends at junction with Observation Point Trail.

2 East Mesa

A day hike offering access to Observation Point

See map on page 21.
Distance: 3 miles (4.8 km) one way
Hiking time: About 1.5 hours
Best seasons: April–May, September–November
Difficulty: Easy

Water availability: None
Topo maps: Temple of Sinawava; Zion National Park (Trails Illustrated)
Jurisdiction: Zion National Park. See Appendix A for more information.

Finding the trailhead: From Zion National Park's East Entrance, drive east on UT 9 for 2.4 miles to a junction with a paved road that runs north toward Navajo Lake and The Narrows trailhead. Turn left onto this paved road, and after 5.3 miles it arrives at the Zion Ponderosa Ranch Resort. Don't forget to sign in and out of the book in the mailbox at the gate. Pass through the main entrance and drive west on the main route, which is Twin Knolls Road. The road ends at a T intersection; turn right and follow Beaver Road northward. This road deteriorates into a primitive track, which ultimately swings west to enter Zion National Park at the beginning of the East Mesa Trail. GPS: N37° 17' 42.229"/W112° 54' 1.734"

The Hike

This trail provides a shorter and easier route to Observation Point and, in contrast to the paved trail from Weeping Rock, is open to horses. The path begins by running west from the national park boundary through an open stand of ponderosa pine. This country burned in patches during 1995, clearing much of the underbrush. Lightning strikes are common atop the high plateaus of Zion, and the plant community found here is well-adapted to periodic burns. Ponderosa pines have thick bark that protects them from the flames, and their seedlings do well in the sunny openings created by fires. Manzanita is a fire-adapted shrub that benefits from periodic burns by colonizing the new openings in the forest.

The first views of the hike are northward, and they feature the lofty Pink Cliffs of the Virgin Rim, which rise to 10,000 feet along the northern horizon. These cliffs are made up of freshwater limestone that is colored by oxides of iron and manganese. Below them is the Gray Cliffs band, an older layer made of shale deposited in a marine environment.

After 1.5 miles the trail approaches a low knoll. Side paths diverging to the right are bound for overlooks of Mystery Canyon. The White Cliffs found in this canyon are of the same Navajo sandstone that makes up the walls of Zion Canyon.

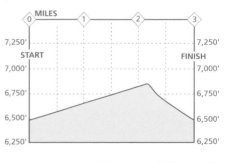

This formation, even more ancient than the marine shales of the Gray Cliffs, was laid down as windblown sand dunes during the Jurassic Period.

The main trail soon swings southwest, revealing views of Echo Canyon as well as the lower reaches of Zion Canyon itself. The West Temple rises prominently above its rim, capped with a thin band of reddish limestone. The trail strikes the south rim of a nameless cleft that joins the Virgin River just below The Narrows, offering excellent views of the White Cliffs. Upon crossing a low saddle, the trail passes several sandy camp spots and then makes a brief descent to meet the Observation Point Trail 0.2 mile from its terminus.

Key Points

0.0 East Mesa trailhead

3.0 Trail ends at junction with Observation Point Trail.

3 Cable Mountain

A day hike or short backpack from the eastern boundary of Zion National Park to Cable Mountain with an option to Deertrap Mountain

Distance: 3.1 miles (5 km) one way
Hiking time: About 1.5 hours to Cable Mountain
Best seasons: April–May, September–November
Difficulty: Moderate
Water availability: Stave Spring is reliable; a seep along Deertrap Mountain Trail is intermittent.

Topo maps: Springdale East, Temple of Sinawava; Zion National Park (Trails Illustrated)
Jurisdiction: Zion National Park. See Appendix A for more information.

Finding the trailhead: From Zion National Park's East Entrance, drive east on UT 9 for 2.4 miles to a junction with a paved road that runs north toward Navajo Lake and The Narrows trailhead. Turn left onto this road. After 5.3 miles the road arrives at the Zion Ponderosa Ranch Resort. Visitors are expected to register at the small mailbox at the Ponderosa Gate (sign in and sign out). Turn left at the entrance, which puts you on Twin Knolls Road. Drive west on this road for 0.8 mile, then turn left onto Buck Road. Bear right at the first junction and continue for 0.4 mile to a major split. Bear left here, following signs for Cable Mountain. The last few hundred yards require high clearance as the road (now called West Pine Street) descends a rocky grade and crosses a wash before entering the park again at the trailhead. Be sure to close the gate behind you so that livestock cannot enter the park. GPS: N37° 16' 4.50"/W112° 53' 56.53"

The Hike

These trails offer day trips to two lofty viewpoints on the upper rim of Zion Canyon. Both overlooks can be visited in a long day trip of 10.4 miles. Cable and Deertrap Mountains can also be reached by means of longer and more strenuous routes via the East Rim Trail from the East Entrance or by combining the Observation Point Trail with the northern end of the East Rim Trail. Each overlook point rewards the hiker with outstanding views into Zion Canyon. The historic cableworks atop Cable Mountain is a fragile structure, and visitors should not climb onto it. This description highlights the hike to Cable Mountain.

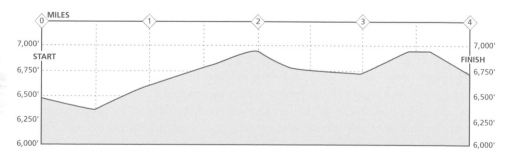

The old cableworks atop Cable Mountain

The trek begins in an open woodland of ponderosa pine just beyond the Zion Ponderosa Ranch Resort, but the trees soon open up into sagebrush meadows that gently slope away toward the head of Echo Canyon. In the midst of the meadows, the path is joined by the East Rim Trail; turn left for Cable and Deertrap Mountains. After a brief and gentle uphill trek, the trail to Cable and Deertrap Mountains veers right at a junction and the East Rim Trail splits away to the left. About 100 yards up the East Rim Trail is Stave Spring, the only reliable source of water along the route. A small pipe releases a steady trickle of water into the draw. This water source is important to local wildlife, and camping is not allowed within 0.25 mile of it.

Back on the Cable and Deertrap Mountains Trail, hike westward, climbing steadily through a mixed scrubland of juniper, piñon pine, and Gambel oak. A few old ponderosa pines rise above the scrub, and some of them bear the scars of old forest fires. Mature ponderosa pines can often survive fires of moderate intensity because their thick and corky bark shields the living cambium from the flames. The pines recede as the trail continues to gain elevation at a steady clip. A sage flat marks the top of the grade, and here the path splits at a well-marked intersection.

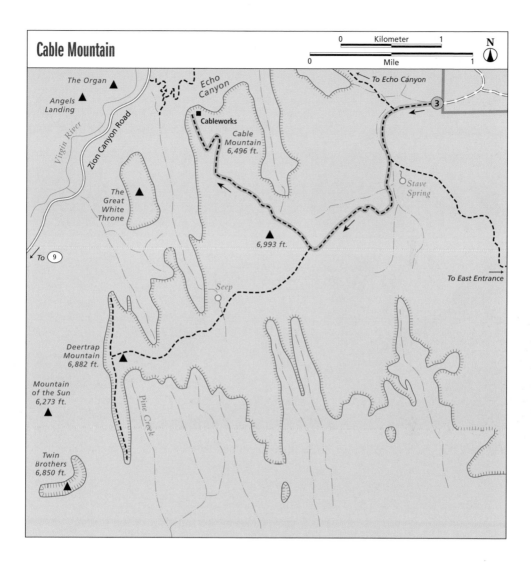

0   Kilometer   1

0   Mile   1

N

The Organ ▲

Angels ▲
Landing

Virgin River

Zion Canyon Road

Echo Canyon

To Echo Canyon

3

■ Cableworks

Cable
Mountain
6,496 ft.

The
Great ▲
White
Throne

▲
6,993 ft.

Stave
Spring

To 9

Seep

To East Entrance

Deertrap
Mountain ▲
6,882 ft.

Mountain
of the Sun
6,273 ft.
▲

Pine Creek

Twin
Brothers
6,850 ft.
▲

The Cable Mountain Trail bears northwest from the junction, climbing gently to the rounded crest of the uplands. The slope falls away to the north, revealing a sweeping vista that encompasses the lower terrace of the Markagunt Plateau. Several minor ridges rise Sphinx-like in the middle distance, while the pink cliffs of the Virgin Rim soar on the northern horizon to elevations exceeding 10,000 feet. Beyond this point the path glides downward among clumps of manzanita and juniper. The descent quickens as the uplands resolve themselves into a broad promontory that juts into the empty void of Zion Canyon, guarded by sheer cliffs of white sandstone.

The path ultimately finds its way out onto the tip of the promontory, a point named Cable Mountain after the cable tramway that was built here by pioneers. The tramway carried sawlogs from the heights of the plateau to the Virgin River and was

The Mountain of the Sun and West Temple as seen from Deertrap Mountain

in use between 1904 and 1926. What remains of the tramway structure is extremely fragile and hazardous; help to save it from collapse by staying clear of the timbers.

The upper cableworks stands remarkably intact at the edge of a sheer precipice that overlooks the Big Bend of the Virgin River. Occupying the center of this entrenched oxbow are The Organ and the more massive Angels Landing. The pale cliffs of Cathedral Mountain rise behind these two stout pillars. To the north is the broad gulf of Echo Canyon, bounded by smooth walls of alabaster sandstone.

Key Points

0.0   Zion Ponderosa Ranch Resort trailhead

0.3   Junction with East Rim Trail. Turn left.

0.7   Stave Spring junction. Trail to Cable and Deertrap Mountains splits away to right (west).

1.8   Trail splits. Turn right for Cable Mountain or left for Deertrap Mountain.

3.1   Terminus of Cable Mountain Trail

3.9   Deertrap Mountain Trail reaches rim of Deertrap Mountain.

Deertrap Option

This option to a second high viewpoint will take you 3.9 miles (6.3 km) from the start to the top of Deertrap Mountain. Hiking time one way is about 2 hours. Follow the Cable and Deertrap Mountains Trail to its junction with the Deertrap Mountain Trail as it glides downhill and soon finds itself following the rimrock above the head of Hidden Canyon. The path swings southward upon reaching a broad clearing filled with low-growing manzanita, and several gullied paths lead downward to a small seep at the bottom of the draw. Stay left for the main trail, which ascends gently toward the low mesa that rises to the southwest. A brief but vigorous climb leads to its crest, and after a brief journey through the scrub, the trail descends to regain its original level. During the descent, a window in the plateau reveals southward views that feature the red-rock badlands of Parunuweap Canyon. For a better look bushwhack southward for 150 yards from the sagebrush saddle at the foot of the next mesa.

The main trail climbs over the top of this second mesa and then charts a steep, eroded track down to Deertrap Mountain. As the trail arrives at the rim of Zion Canyon, the Mountain of the Sun sits immediately below and the stalwart Twin Brothers rise to the south. Across the canyon are the West Temple, The Beehives, and the Court of the Patriarchs.

Paths run in both directions along the rimrock; the shorter and better-defined northern trail runs 0.4 mile to an overlook at the northern tip of the promontory, providing views of Angels Landing and the reddish spires of the Temple of Sinawava guarding the entrance to The Narrows. The Great White Throne hulks to the north, capped with a delicate crown of red and yellow stone that comprises the Temple Cap formation.

The southern trail is a rough pathway (0.6 mile) that follows the edge of the rim, and it soon devolves into an overgrown game trail. The route gets tricky as it passes the foot of some undercut cliffs and then gets easier as it runs out onto flat, grassy savannahs that cap a narrow stone promontory. From its tip, views encompass the East Temple and the Twin Brothers, as well as the wind-sculpted wilderness of stone that makes up the upper drainage of Pine Creek.

4 Canyon Overlook

A short out-and-back day hike to an overlook of lower Zion Canyon

Distance: 1 mile (1.6 km) round-trip
Hiking time: About 0.5 hour
Best season: March–November
Difficulty: Moderate
Water availability: None

Hazards: Cliff exposure
Topo maps: Springdale East; Zion National Park (Trails Illustrated)
Jurisdiction: Zion National Park. See Appendix A for more information.

Finding the trailhead: From the Zion Visitor Center, drive east on UT 9 for 5 miles. The trailhead is just beyond the first tunnel. GPS: N37° 12' 44.163" / W112° 56' 24.753" W

The Hike

This short but scenic trail runs to a high overlook immediately above the Great Arch, commanding vistas of the lower reaches of Zion Canyon. Interpretive brochures found at the trailhead explain the plants, animals, and geological features found along the route.

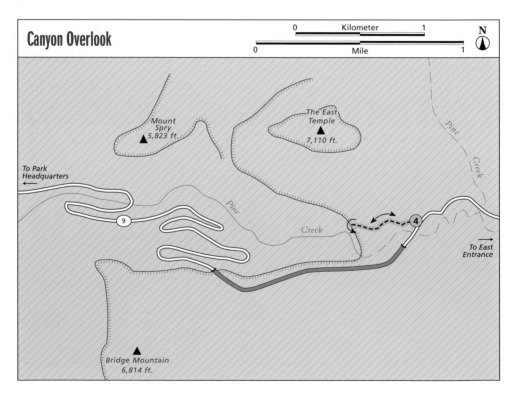

The path initially climbs a series of stairsteps and then traverses across the upper walls of the deep slot canyon of Pine Creek. The path passes beneath several overhangs and in a few spots offers uneven footing above dropoffs; proceed with caution. The path ultimately emerges onto a hilltop covered with hoodoos, or pillars of eroded stone. It then weaves across the slickrock and between piñon pines to reach Canyon Overlook, a spectacular vista point. East Temple looms to the north, while to the west spreads a panorama highlighted by Bridge Mountain, the West Temple, the Towers of the Virgin, and the Streaked Wall. Travelers carrying binoculars can glass the cliffs to the south for desert bighorn sheep, which have been reintroduced into Zion National Park.

Key Points

0.0 Trailhead on UT 9
0.5 Canyon Overlook

The East Temple as seen from Canyon Overlook

5 The Barracks

A wilderness route down the East Fork of the Virgin River through spectacular canyon country, then out via a difficult scramble over a poorly marked route

---

Distance: 18.4 miles (29.6 km) overall
Hiking time: About 9 hours
Best seasons: May–July, September–October
Difficulty: Moderate* for Parunuweap Canyon; strenuous** for Checkerboard Mesa exit route
Water availability: Numerous springs flow into the river above and below Mineral Gulch; Rock Canyon usually has water, and the East Fork of the Virgin River flows permanently through the canyon (although it is silty and contaminated with agricultural runoff).

Hazards: Flash flood danger, scrambling over steep terrain
Recommended equipment: Wading staff, gaiters
Topo maps: Mount Carmel, The Barracks, Springdale East; Kanab (BLM)
Jurisdiction: Bureau of Land Management, Kanab Field Office; Zion National Park. See Appendix A for more information.

Finding the trailhead: From Mount Carmel Junction drive south on US 89 for 0.5 mile to reach a gravel road that drops westward into the bottoms of the East Fork of the Virgin River. Follow this road for 0.9 mile to reach a gate that marks the beginning of lands leased to The Barracks Ranch. Park outside this gate. The Checkerboard Mesa exit route emerges at a pulloff on UT 9, 0.5 mile west of Zion National Park's East Entrance. GPS: N37° 11' 37.876"/W112° 41' 55.926"

The Hike

This route follows the East Fork of the Virgin River into Parunuweap Canyon, one of the most spectacular and unknown canyons in southwestern Utah. The upper reaches of the canyon are open and fairly arid, while The Barracks' lower end is made up of slot canyons with towering walls. The cleft lay along John Wesley Powell's route during his explorations of the early 1870s. Powell's party took several weeks to lead a string of pack mules through the canyon, working its way past obstacles such as Labyrinth Falls, now considered impassable without mountaineering gear.

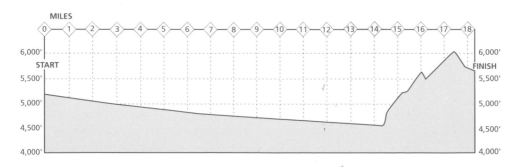

Powell christened the canyon Parunuweap, a Paiute term that translates as "Roaring Waters Canyon."

Today the upper reaches of the canyon are administered by the Bureau of Land Management, while the lower reaches fall within Zion National Park. The National Park Service has closed public access to the part of the canyon that falls within Zion as a pristine research area. This stretch of canyon contains sensitive prehistoric ruins from the Basket Maker culture and in any case requires mountaineering gear to negotiate. Park rangers have pioneered an exit route that climbs out of the canyon at the national park boundary and emerges at Checkerboard Mesa, allowing a one-way trip through the BLM-administered upper reaches of the canyon.

These upper reaches are under consideration as a potential Wilderness Area, which would be closed to bicycles and motor vehicles. Special regulations for the area are also under consideration, including quotas on visitors, limits on party size, and user fees. Check at the BLM ranger station in Kanab for an update on regulations before attempting the route. This area is primitive and remote, and visitors should practice zero-impact camping techniques to preserve its wilderness character.

From the parking area the route initially follows the improved gravel road along the East Fork of the Virgin River, making one ford as it passes across state lands leased to The Barracks Ranch. There are several gates across the road; shut each one after passing through. The grassy bottoms of the valley floor are overlooked by scrub-covered mesas, where piñon pines and junipers grow atop drab cliffs of sandstone. The road ultimately reaches a block of private property (no trespassing!) and the route veers left, following a jeep track down to the riverbed. Hikers will make numerous shallow fords as the route proceeds westward.

The deep cleft of Monument Hollow soon appears to the north. A final fence gate leads onto BLM lands. Just beyond it, Yellowjacket Canyon joins the valley from the south, guarded by the Meeks Cliffs.

As the main valley widens, the cliffs that guard it rise higher, tinted with yellow and streaked with reddish iron leached out of the iron-rich layer of freshwater limestone that overlies the main formation. The walls themselves are composed of the upper strata of Navajo sandstone. Geologists believe that the upper layers of the Navajo Formation are light-colored because iron oxides present in the sand were leached out by groundwater before the rock solidified. This same formation makes up the spectacular monoliths of Zion Canyon. Here it forms cliffs that are 500 feet high, rounded and sculpted by wind erosion.

The old jeep track makes the fastest walking, but wilderness ascetics will find that the watercourse also provides easy traveling. Grassy benches surround the river on both sides, but these soon disappear as the canyon narrows. Bay Bill Canyon enters from the south amid rounded knolls of red stone, representing the lower, iron-rich layers of Navajo sandstone. Just beyond the mouth of this side canyon, the jeep trail climbs southward toward Elephant Cove. The remainder of the route follows the riverbed as it penetrates deeper into Parunuweap Canyon. The riverbanks are now choked with brakes of seep willow and cattail.

The White Cliffs soon march away to the north, leaving the river to meander through older, reddish shoulders of sandstone. These mounds soon rise to form low cliffs, with springs of clear water flowing from their bases. The river passes a number of potential campsites and negotiates three separate sets of narrows before arriving at the mouth of Mineral Gulch. This canyon can be recognized by its vertical walls surrounding a mouth that joins the valley on the same level as the river, rather than having an elevated mouth.

Mineral Gulch is well worth a side trip and features four sets of narrows. The first, brief set may contain deep pools of water even when the upper reaches of the wash are dry. These narrows open into a wide spot that offers several shallow caves to explore. The second narrows lie beyond this opening, more impressive than the first. The most spectacular scenery is contained within the third set of narrows, with its overhanging walls that block out all but a tiny sliver of the sky.

As the river leaves Mineral Gulch behind, the cliff walls recede, giving way to an open bottomland frequented by cattle. Note the drift fence across the major (but nameless) wash that enters from the south. The old Poverty Trail descends to the river opposite the fence. This wide and dusty track is a traditional route used to drive cattle down from the arid benchland into the rich bottomlands of the canyon floor. The cliffs soon close in again, augured by a triangular pinnacle with a keyhole through it that rises to the north of the river. The highlight of this section is a sharp oxbow bend overlooked by a towering cliff of red stone. Beyond this point the walls again back away, and the canyon devolves into a puzzle of incoming washes and wooded bottoms interrupted by rocky bluffs. It is toward the end of this section that Rock Canyon enters from the south, bearing a fairly dependable trickle of water.

Beyond the mouth of Rock Canyon, the walls rise again, sheer to the south but grooved and uneven to the north. A river oxbow carves a deep undercut into the north wall of the canyon, and beyond it lies a smooth wall to the south, polished by the wind and tinted with delicate streaks of color. The cliffs reach higher as the river makes its way downstream. Some of the alcoves have been entirely overgrown by canyon grape, a parasitic vine that climbs atop standing trees and shrubs in its effort to reach the sunlight. Just before reaching Poverty Wash, the river passes through several profound narrows, the second of which features a slot canyon entering from the south that invites further exploration.

Poverty Wash itself bears a trickle of water into the canyon from the north, as the river steepens in gradient beyond its mouth. In some spots the river runs over bare bedrock, which makes for some rather deep pools. The only major obstacle of the hike is found in this section: Fallen boulders constrict the river channel, forming fast runs with deep pools below. To avoid a swim, cross to the south bank and climb into a steep rift for about 50 feet, then drop through a narrow tunnel behind a stone

Narrows in Parunuweap Canyon just below the Powell plaque ▶

The Barracks

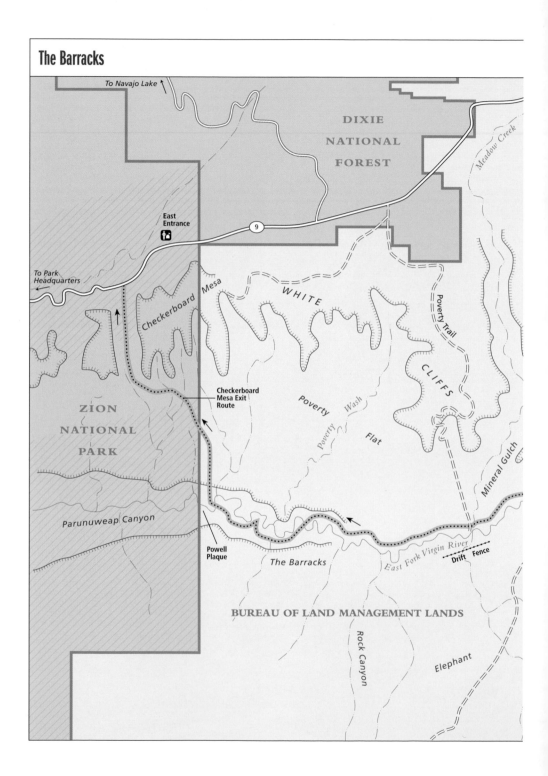

To Navajo Lake

DIXIE

NATIONAL

FOREST

Meadow Creek

East
Entrance

9

To Park
Headquarters

Checkerboard Mesa

WHITE

Poverty Trail

CLIFFS

Checkerboard
Mesa Exit
Route

Poverty   Wash

ZION

Poverty

Flat

NATIONAL

Mineral Gulch

PARK

Parunuweap Canyon

Powell
Plaque

The Barracks

East Fork Virgin River

Drift   Fence

BUREAU OF LAND MANAGEMENT LANDS

Rock Canyon

Elephant

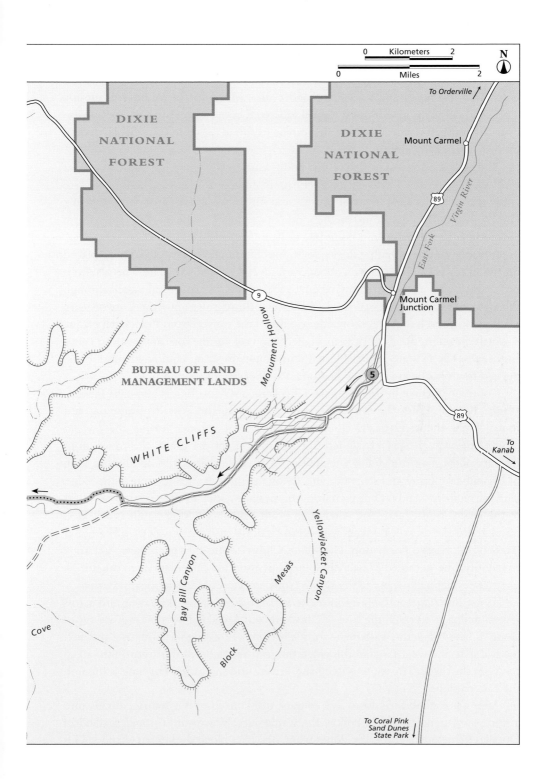

To Orderville ↑

DIXIE
NATIONAL
FOREST

DIXIE
NATIONAL
FOREST

Mount Carmel

89

Virgin River

East Fork

9

Monument Hollow

Mount Carmel
Junction

BUREAU OF LAND
MANAGEMENT LANDS

5

89

To
Kanab

WHITE CLIFFS

Bay Bill Canyon

Mesas

Yellowjacket Canyon

Cove

Block

To Coral Pink
Sand Dunes
State Park ↓

N

0   Kilometers   2

0   Miles   2

monolith. It is choked with fallen rock and is a tight fit; hikers may have to remove their packs in several spots. The last couple of camping spots are within 0.5 mile below this obstacle.

A side canyon known variously as "Misery Canyon" and "Fat Man's Misery" soon enters from the north, and a deep pool and a sulfur spring can be found at its mouth. This side canyon is a little-used rappel-and-swim route into Parunuweap Canyon from the north. It is a beautiful slot that can be explored for up to 0.5 mile depending on one's scrambling ability.

The walking gets easier below this point, as the cliffs soar high above the river to block out the sky. These narrows ultimately emerge at a horseshoe bend where sandy niches are cloaked in a riot of trees and shrubs. Look for cairns that mark the Checkerboard Mesa exit route on the inside of this bend—which is the approximate location of the unmarked east boundary of Zion National Park.

A plaque commemorating the explorations of John Wesley Powell has been placed on the north wall of the canyon about 50 yards below the exit route. The plaque is not easily found unless you know where to look. Powell's expedition passed through the area in 1872 and took two weeks to descend through Parunuweap Canyon with a full string of pack mules. A short side trip down the canyon from the Powell plaque is worth the effort; the walls close in, higher than ever, for the final approach to Labyrinth Falls. The falls are impassable without mountaineering equipment, and access beyond them has been closed by National Park Service regulation.

Continue the hike by following the Checkerboard Mesa Exit Route (aka Powell-Plaque Route). From the horseshoe bend just before the Powell plaque, the exit route climbs almost vertically along a weakness in the stone, bearing the traveler upward through the prickly underbrush. At the top of the grade, the route drops into a shallow draw and follows it upward to a saddle that overlooks another loop of Parunuweap Canyon. Turn west here, following the cairns to the top of the ridge. The cairns are few and far between from this point on; stick to the ridgetop, and skirt to the west for easier traveling when high points rise ahead. After a mile of trackless travel across the slickrock, hikers will see the reddish stone give way to white upper layers of the Navajo Formation. The White Cliffs rise ahead in plain view; take time to identify Checkerboard Mesa by its enormous, rounded cliffs that rise to the northwest. The route will penetrate the White Cliffs just west of Checkerboard Mesa.

As the low ridgetop trails off into a series of shallow draws, skirt westward across several drainages to reach the base of Checkerboard Mesa. Follow the wash westward along its base. When the wash turns northward into a box canyon, climb over the next low ridge to the west. Beyond this ridge the next ravine leads northward into a gap between the mesas. The route is steep and brushy, and the easiest traveling is high on the eastern slope.

After a hot climb turn down a steep track that runs from the drainage divide into a northward-trending gulch. Follow the watercourse downward through a stand of Douglas fir, detouring onto the slopes when obstacles block the stream channel. This drainage ultimately opens out near UT 9 and has several deep water pockets at its mouth. Contour northeast along a ledge in the rounded stone to reach UT 9, then follow the road eastward a short distance to reach the parking pullout that marks the end of the hike.

Key Points

- **0.0** Hike begins at gate across road.
- **0.1** Road fords East Fork of the Virgin River.
- **1.0** Gate across road. Turn left onto jeep track to the riverbed.
- **1.8** Mouth of Monument Hollow
- **2.3** Yellowjacket Canyon enters from the south.
- **3.7** Bay Bill Canyon enters from the south.
- **7.4** Mineral Gulch enters from the north.
- **7.7** Old Poverty Trail reaches canyon bottoms from the north.
- **9.4** Rock Canyon enters from the south.
- **12.2** Poverty Wash enters from the north.
- **14.0** Misery Canyon enters from the north.
- **14.2** Powell plaque and Zion park boundary. Turn north for steep initial pitch of Checkerboard Mesa exit route.
- **16.7** Base of Checkerboard Mesa
- **17.4** Pass behind Checkerboard Mesa.
- **18.4** Route reaches UT 9.

6 The Watchman

An out-and-back hike into the foothills below The Watchman and Bridge Mountain

Distance: 2 miles (3.2 km) round-trip
Hiking time: About 1 hour
Best season: April–October
Difficulty: Easy
Water availability: None

Topo maps: Springdale East; Zion National Park (Trails Illustrated)
Jurisdiction: Zion National Park. See Appendix A for more information.

Finding the trailhead: Head north from Zion National Park's South Entrance and take the first right toward The Watchman Campground. Park in the visitor center lot and walk to the trailhead. GPS: N37° 12' 3.60"/W112° 59' 11.46"

The Hike

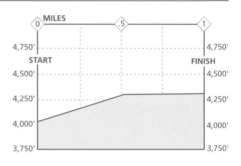

Climbing into the foothills beneath Bridge Mountain and The Watchman, this short trail begins on a set of wooden steps leading northward up a small knoll. Stay on the main trail, avoiding side trails created by a large population of mule deer. The official trail is about 3 feet wide and traverses the base of the first knoll toward the National Park Service residential areas. The vegetation in this area is characterized by a scrub woodland of juniper and piñon pine with sagebrush in the sunny openings.

The path then turns east and proceeds up the base of Bridge Mountain via a series of long switchbacks. Hikers will view overhanging cliffs and stratified rock layers along the trail as they ascend across the stone walls. In addition to views of Bridge Mountain and The Watchman throughout the hike, travelers can look westward across the Virgin River for a fine vista of the Towers of the Virgin, and also south toward the town of Springdale.

At the top of this trail, a loop path crowns the foothill. This short loop provides several good perches from which to view surrounding geological wonders.

Key Points

0.0 Trailhead
1.0 The Watchman viewpoint

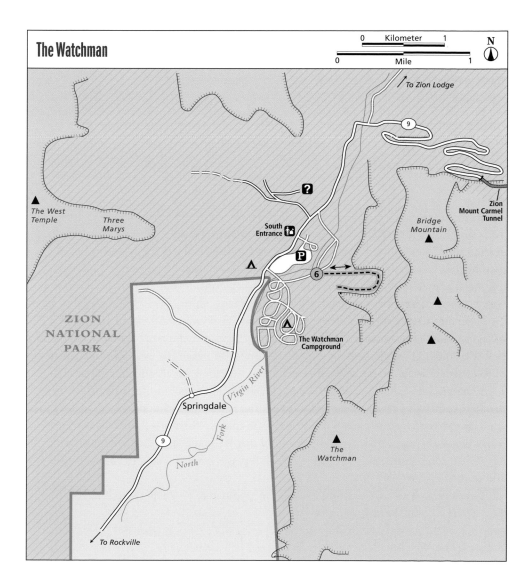

The Watchman

0   Kilometer   1
0   Mile   1

N

To Zion Lodge

9

The West
Temple

Three
Marys

?

South
Entrance

Zion
Mount Carmel
Tunnel

Bridge
Mountain

P

6

ZION
NATIONAL
PARK

The Watchman
Campground

Virgin River

North Fork

Springdale

9

The
Watchman

To Rockville

7 Sand Bench Loop

An out-and-back day hike through arid uplands in lower Zion Canyon

Distance: 3.4 miles (5.5 km) round-trip
Hiking time: About 2 hours
Best season: September–May
Difficulty: Moderate
Water availability: The Virgin River always has water, but it is silty.

Recommended equipment: Gaiters
Topo maps: Springdale East; Zion National Park (Trails Illustrated)
Jurisdiction: Zion National Park. See Appendix A for more information.

Finding the trailhead: Take the Zion Canyon tram to Court of the Patriarchs viewpoint, 2.2 miles up Zion Canyon Road. The hike starts from the viewpoint. GPS: N37° 14' 14.14" / W112° 57' 45.35"

The Hike

This sandy trail loops onto an elevated bench on the far side of the Virgin River, visiting the Court of the Patriarchs and the Streaked Wall along the way. It is heavily used by park concessionaires for horse tours, so hikers should be prepared to share the trail with heavy horse traffic during the peak season (April through October). For this reason rangers do not recommend the trail as a hiking route.

From the Court of the Patriarchs viewpoint, walk westward down the service road and past a large water tank to reach a footbridge over the river. Turn left on the far bank. The trail wanders up into the sagebrush meadows in the center of the Court of the Patriarchs. Immense monoliths of ancient stone rise on all sides, giving visitors a humbling perspective on their own significance. There is another junction here; turn left and cross a small streambed to begin the Sand Bench Loop.

The trail then begins a steady climb and soon splits to form the loop. This description follows the right fork first, but the loop can be hiked in either direction with equal ease. As it climbs, the west fork of the trail passes beneath the foot of sheer walls and rugged towers.

The trail tops out on a sandy alluvial fan populated by deep-rooted sagebrush. The Streaked Wall looms ahead on the near side of the canyon, while the ragged walls of The Watchman are visible farther down the valley. The trail then glides down onto a flat bench at the foot of the Streaked Wall, where tilted rocks rise among the piñon pines and juniper. A rest area and corral mark the southern end of the loop.

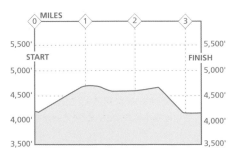

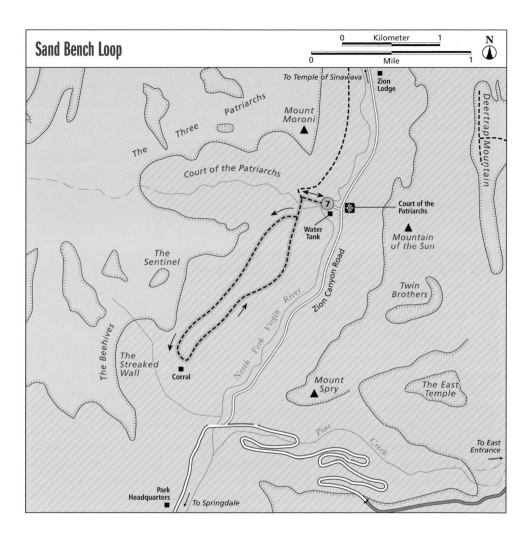

Sand Bench Loop

0   Kilometer   1

0   Mile   1

N

To Temple of Sinawava

Zion Lodge

Patriarchs

Three

The

Mount Moroni

Court of the Patriarchs

7

Court of the Patriarchs

Water Tank

Mountain of the Sun

Deertrap Mountain

The Sentinel

North Fork Virgin River

Zion Canyon Road

Twin Brothers

The Beehives

The Streaked Wall

Corral

Mount Spry

The East Temple

Pine

Creek

To East Entrance

Park Headquarters

To Springdale

From here the trail runs northward, skirting the edge of an escarpment high above the river. Superb views of the East Temple, the Twin Brothers, and the Mountain of the Sun accompany hikers for the remainder of the trek.

Key Points

0.0   Court of the Patriarchs viewpoint. Follow service road to river.

0.1   Footbridge over North Fork of the Virgin River

0.3   Trail junction. Turn left for Sand Bench Loop

0.9   Sand Bench Loop splits. Take right fork.

2.5   Trails rejoin to complete the loop.

3.4   Court of the Patriarchs viewpoint

8 West Bank of the Virgin River

A day hike along the Virgin River, from the Court of the Patriarchs viewpoint to the Grotto trailhead

Distance: 2.6 miles (4.2 km)
Hiking time: About 1.25 hours
Best season: Year-round
Difficulty: Easy
Water availability: The Virgin River always has water, but it is silty.

Topo maps: Springdale East, Temple of Sinawava; Zion National Park (Trails Illustrated)
Jurisdiction: Zion National Park. See Appendix A for more information.

Finding the trailhead: The trail begins at the Court of the Patriarchs viewpoint, 2.2 miles up Zion Canyon Road (take the tram). It ends at the Grotto trailhead, at mile 3.2 on Zion Canyon Road. GPS of start: N37° 14' 14.14"/W112° 57' 45.35"; GPS of finish: N37° 15' 28.592"/W112° 56' 58.601"

The Hike

Following trails along the west bank of the Virgin River, this short hike provides an alternative to the scenic drive for visitors who prefer to experience nature outside their cars. The trail is level and easy, but it is heavily traveled by horse parties between the Emerald Pools trailhead and the Court of the Patriarchs. Nonstop views of Zion Canyon are found all along the route, and the lowlands along the river are excellent places to spot birds and, in twilight hours, mule deer.

From the Court of the Patriarchs viewpoint, follow the service road west past a large water tank to reach a bridge over the Virgin River. After crossing the bridge, turn left and follow the trail into the center of the Court of the Patriarchs. Views are stunning beneath the giant monoliths of Navajo sandstone that line this deep alcove in the wall of Zion Canyon.

Continuing on, hikers will reach an unmarked trail junction at the edge of a grassy hill; turn right as the path climbs to an arid knoll and passes the remains of an old corral. The trail levels off here and follows the river northward. Due to the gradient of the river, hikers will reach the river bottoms without any noticeable loss of altitude. The bottomlands are robed in a riparian woodland of cottonwood and box elder. Mule deer often appear on the far bank of the river during the twilight hours. This is also the habitat of the elusive ring-tailed cat, which hides beneath rock overhangs by day and ventures forth to forage at night.

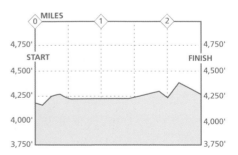

The Spearhead and the summit of Mount Majestic rise above the bottomlands of Zion Canyon.

The trail follows the river upward as the bleached summits of Mount Majestic and Cathedral Mountain rise beyond the reddish spire called The Spearhead. After a corral across the river marks an end to the horse traffic, a bridge spans the river, allowing hikers access to the Emerald Pools trailhead. The trail now becomes wide and paved. Foot traffic is heavy as the route climbs steadily before dipping into the stone amphitheater that bears the Emerald Pools. Spur trails climb to the upper pools, while the main trail runs around the edge of Lower Emerald Pool, with its rock overhang, delicate waterfalls, and hanging gardens. Bear right and follow signs for the Grotto trailhead as the trail threads its way through these picturesque rock gardens to reach a fine viewpoint at the bowl's edge.

The path then traverses northward, staying above a low cliff of Springdale sandstone, which is older than the Navajo Formation that overtops it. The Great White Throne presents its alabaster profile above the far bank of the river as the trail covers the final distance to a bridge that leads to the Grotto trailhead.

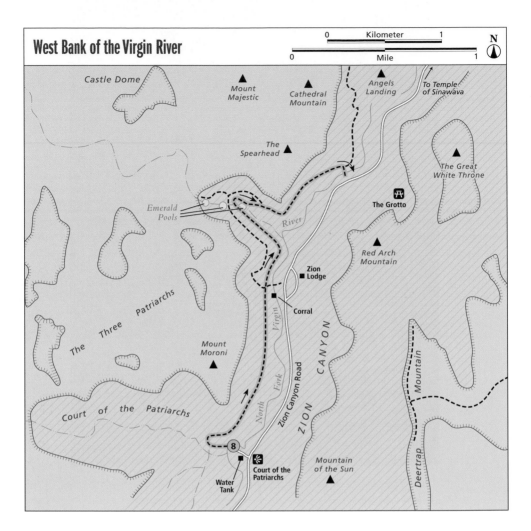

West Bank of the Virgin River

Castle Dome

Mount Majestic

Cathedral Mountain

Angels Landing

To Temple of Sinawava

The Spearhead

The Great White Throne

The Grotto

Emerald Pools

River

Red Arch Mountain

Zion Lodge

The Three Patriarchs

Corral

Virgin

Mount Moroni

Zion Canyon Road

North Fork

ZION CANYON

Court of the Patriarchs

8

Water Tank

Court of the Patriarchs

Mountain of the Sun

Deertrap Mountain

Key Points

0.0   Court of the Patriarchs viewpoint. Follow service road to river.

0.1   Footbridge over the North Fork of the Virgin River

0.3   Trail junction. Turn right for West Bank Trail.

1.3   Horse ford to corrals on east bank of river. Trail to Middle and Upper Emerald pools climbs to left. Keep going straight.

1.4   Footbridge with access to Zion Lodge

1.9   Lower Emerald Pool

2.0   Junction with trail to upper pools. Bear right.

2.6   Junction with Angels Landing/West Rim Trail. Cross bridge to finish the hike at the Grotto trailhead.

9 Emerald Pools

A network of trails of varied lengths to the Lower, Middle, and/or Upper Emerald Pools

Distance: 1.9 miles (3 km) round-trip with options
Hiking time: About 0.5 hour–1.25 hours
Best season: March–November
Difficulty: Easy (Lower Pool); moderate (Upper Pool)

Water availability: Emerald Pools have a permanent supply of water, but hikers are asked to bring their own drinking water.
Topo maps: Temple of Sinawava; Zion National Park (Trails Illustrated)
Jurisdiction: Zion National Park. See Appendix A for more information.

Finding the trailhead: From the Zion Visitor Center, take the Zion Canyon tram to Zion Lodge. The trailhead and parking area are on the west side of the road opposite the lodge. GPS: N37° 14' 58.265" / W112° 57' 27.448"

The Hike

There are three Emerald Pools—Upper, Middle, and Lower—and visitors may choose from as many trails: a short, 1.2-mile round-trip loop to the Lower Pool; a 1.9-mile round-trip visit to the Middle and Lower Pools; or a 2.5-mile round-trip hike to all three. The paths to the Lower and Middle Pools are wide sidewalks and easily traveled. The Lower Pool is accessible to people in wheelchairs if they have assistance. The optional trail from the Middle Pool to the Upper Pool is more difficult. This path is no longer maintained and is classified by the National Park Service as strenuous, with its uneven sand and rock surface and moderate to strenuous grade.

While visiting this area bear in mind that the National Park Service has spent considerable funds to restore and protect these pools. Contribute to this effort by refraining from bathing in or walking through the water.

From the parking area cross the bridge to the west side of the Virgin River, where a trailhead sign is located. Hikers who wish to travel directly to the Lower Pool can take the sidewalk to the right. The Middle Pool Trail is no longer a trail, but the Middle Pool can still be reached via Lower Pool Trail or Kayenta Trail. Those wishing to visit the Middle and Upper Pools should follow the path that climbs to the left. The trail description here follows the rocky path that climbs toward the Middle and Upper Pools.

The trail briefly parallels the Virgin River. Portions of the path have been paved with concrete. The trail up to the Middle Pool is

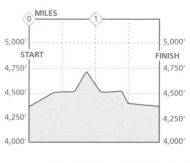

Along the trail to Middle Emerald Pool SHUTTERSTOCK

lined with box elder, juniper, bigtooth maple, and Gambel oak. As it progresses up the slope, the trail presents views of formations such as Lady Mountain, The Spearhead, Mount Majestic, Red Arch Mountain, Deertrap Mountain, and the Great White Throne rising above Zion Canyon.

The Middle Pool occupies a large, open area surrounded by slickrock. Pools of water have collected from the trickles above. At the edge of the main pool is a long drop-off leading down to Lower Emerald Pool. From this vantage point visitors can look out over canyon bottoms filled with a lush deciduous forest.

Traverse the Middle Pool area to find a small trailhead sign that marks a narrow path to the Upper Pool. This short, 0.3-mile trail is no longer maintained by the park staff. The trail is uneven and rocky and climbs up a moderately strenuous grade. The Upper Pool itself is surrounded on three sides by sheer cliffs and closed in on the fourth side by a boulder foothill. Maple trees shade this natural amphitheater, making this one of the most peaceful day-hike destinations in Zion Canyon.

To get from the Middle Pool down to the Lower Pool, follow the well-worn path to the north. This trail turns east and splits: The higher trail runs toward the Grotto Picnic Area, while the lower path heads to Lower Emerald Pool. The trail to Lower Emerald Pool descends quickly along stone steps peppered with sand. Looking down toward the pool, visitors will see a large alcove with a fine veil of water dripping over its edge and into a large mirror surrounded by Gambel oak, maple, and box elder.

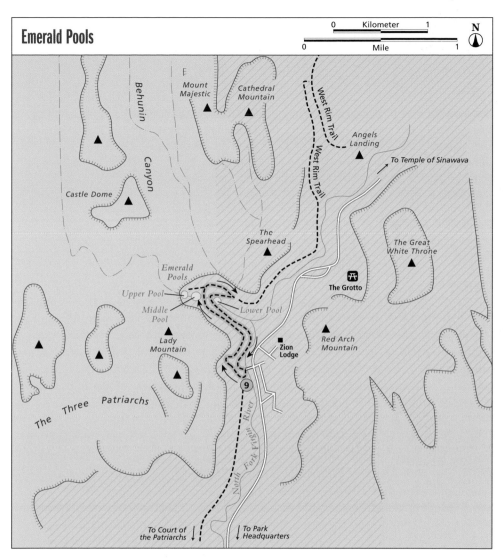

Emerald Pools

0 Kilometer 1
0 Mile 1

N

Behunin Canyon

Mount Majestic

Cathedral Mountain

West Rim Trail

West Rim Trail

Angels Landing

To Temple of Sinawava

Castle Dome

The Spearhead

The Great White Throne

Emerald Pools

Upper Pool

Middle Pool

Lower Pool

The Grotto

Lady Mountain

Zion Lodge

Red Arch Mountain

The Three Patriarchs

North Fork Virgin River

9

To Court of the Patriarchs

To Park Headquarters

Follow the trail as it winds beneath the alcove past the pool before returning to the trailhead on the far bank of the Virgin River.

Key Points

- **0.0** Trailhead for Lower Pool. Turn left to begin loop trip.
- **0.9** Middle Emerald Pool; junction with trail to Upper Emerald Pool (*Option:* This 0.3-mile trail is moderately strenuous.)
- **1.2** Junction with trail to Lower Emerald Pool and trail to Grotto Picnic Area. Turn right to visit the lower pool and return to trailhead.
- **1.3** Lower Emerald Pool
- **1.9** Trailhead

10 Angels Landing

An out-and-back day hike to the summit of Angels Landing

Distance: 4.4 miles (7 km) round-trip
Hiking time: About 2 hours
Best season: March–November
Difficulty: Strenuous
Water availability: The Virgin River always has water, but it is silty.

Hazards: Cliff exposure
Topo maps: Temple of Sinawava; Zion National Park (Trails Illustrated)
Jurisdiction: Zion National Park. See Appendix A for more information.

Finding the trailhead: The trail begins at the Grotto trailhead, 0.6 mile beyond Zion Lodge on Zion Canyon Road (accessed via the tram). GPS: N37° 15' 28.592"/W112° 56' 58.601" W

The Hike

This trail provides a spectacular day trip for well-conditioned hikers who have no fear of heights. It receives heavy use, so chances for solitude are slim. Beyond Scout Lookout, the trail becomes an uneven route across sheer cliffs, with chains bolted into the rock face to serve as handrails. This part of the route can be extremely slippery and dangerous when wet or icy and should be avoided unless dry conditions can be depended upon. It is not a good place to take young children in any weather.

The trail begins by crossing a bridge over the Virgin River and then turns north at a junction with the Kayenta Trail. Following the river, the path passes through a riparian woodland of cottonwood and box elder, with canyon grape and tamarisk growing in the understory. Tamarisk was originally brought to the Southwest as an ornamental plant, but it soon escaped from cultivated areas and now crowds out native shrubs in many desert wash environments. Angels Landing looms ahead, with the mouth of Refrigerator Canyon tucked between this monolith and the west wall of Zion Canyon.

The trail climbs vigorously to reach the elevated mouth of Refrigerator Canyon and then levels off as it enters the cool inner recesses of the cleft. Cool-climate plants

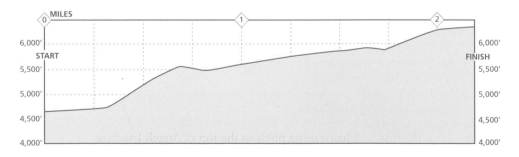

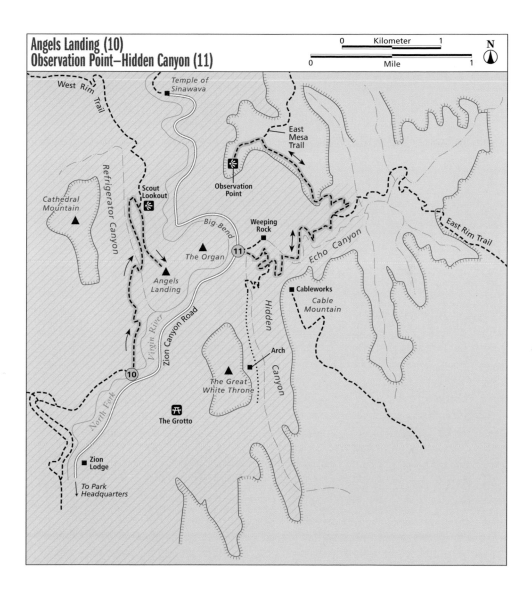

such as bigtooth maple and white fir thrive in the shade of the canyon floor, and the vertical walls of red sandstone are pocked with grottos and overhangs.

As the path nears the head of the canyon, it begins a strenuous ascent of the east wall. A series of twenty-one switchbacks has been built cunningly into a rift in the wall here and bears the traveler upward at a calf-burning pace. Known as "Walter's Wiggles," these carefully crafted stoneworks are regarded as one of the engineering marvels of the park. Soon after reaching the top of the switchbacks, the path makes a gradual ascent to a sandy pad called Scout Lookout. It occupies the saddle behind Angels Landing, offering aerial views into Zion Canyon for travelers who lack the stomach for the final and hair-raising pitch to the top of Angels Landing.

The West Rim Trail climbs northwest from Scout Lookout, while the Angels Landing Trail bears southeast. It follows the spine of a knife-edge ridge, with heavy chains attached to the rock to serve as handrails along most (but not all) of the drop-offs. Hikers must make a steep scramble to surmount the first knob, followed by an unprotected walk across a narrow saddle that is flanked by sheer drop-offs. One truly gets a feeling of walking on the razor's edge here. Climbing then resumes, aided by more handrails and footholds hewn into bedrock. This is the long and final pitch to the summit.

There are no guardrails on Angels Landing, where gnarled piñon pines grow from impossible toeholds above the dizzying void. Occupying the center of the Big Bend of Zion Canyon, the summit commands a spectacular 360-degree panorama of rugged spires and towering walls. Highlights include the Great White Throne, Red Arch Mountain, and the entrance to The Narrows.

Key Points

0.0 The Grotto trailhead

0.1 Footbridge over North Fork of Virgin River and junction with West Bank trail. Turn right for Angels Landing.

1.1 Trail enters Refrigerator Canyon.

1.8 Junction with West Rim Trail at Scout Lookout. Turn right for summit of Angels Landing. Footing becomes treacherous.

2.2 Angels Landing summit

The knife-edge ridge to the summit of Angels Landing
SHUTTERSTOCK

11 Observation Point

A long day hike from the floor of Zion Canyon to the top of Observation Point

See map on page 51.
Distance: 8 miles (12.8 km) round-trip
Hiking time: About 4 hours
Best season: April–October
Difficulty: Moderately strenuous
Water availability: None

Hazards: Cliff exposure
Topo maps: Temple of Sinawava; Zion National Park (Trails Illustrated)
Jurisdiction: Zion National Park. See Appendix A for more information.

Finding the trailhead: The trail begins at the Weeping Rock trailhead at mile 4.4 on Zion Canyon Road, reached via the Zion Canyon tram. GPS: N37° 16' 15.08"/W112° 56' 18.12"

The Hike

This popular trail offers a long and steep climb from the floor of Zion Canyon to the rimrock that soars high above it. There are excellent views all along the way, featuring the lower reaches of Zion Canyon, a brief firsthand look at the narrow slot of Echo Canyon, and views of the cliffs above upper Echo Canyon during the final climb. Observation Point itself is perched high above Zion Canyon and is the most accessible of the rimrock overlooks that line the canyon wall. (***Options:*** Hidden Canyon offers an intriguing 1-mile-total side trip into a secluded hanging canyon. The East Rim Trail joins the route at its midpoint, offering the possibility of an extended backpack. Observation Point can also be reached by a shorter and easier [though less scenic] route via the East Mesa Trail.)

The trail begins by zigzagging vigorously up an amphitheater carved out of the wall of Zion Canyon by the river. On the far side of the river, a gooseneck of rock juts from the far canyon wall, with lofty Angels Landing rising from its base and a smaller formation known as The Organ occupying its tip. This formation vividly displays the effects of an incised meander. Before the uplift of the Rocky Mountains and the Colorado Plateau, the Virgin River wandered lazily across a flat plain,

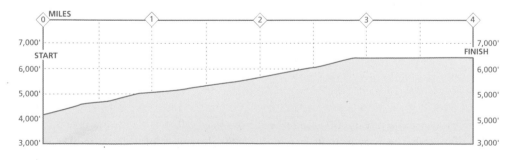

with a channel characterized by loops and oxbows. About fifty million years ago, uplift began.

As the bedrock rose, the river cut down through it with ever-greater speed, entrenching the existing loops and oxbows even as the water flow sped up. The sinuous course of the canyon, which doubles back on itself and forms stone goose-necks, owes its origin to the rejuvenation of an old river when the uplift increased its gradient.

As the trail continues upward, the alabaster walls of Cathedral Mountain appear above the far side of the river. The sheltered alcove that bears Weeping Rock can be seen below and to the north. Groundwater from Echo Canyon emerges at a spring-line, or fissure between layers of rock, to form the dripping wall. About two-thirds of the way up the grade, a spur trail climbs southward into the cleft of Hidden Canyon (described later).

The main trail turns north and continues to gain altitude among a scattering of ponderosa pines made possible by the relative coolness of these higher elevations. The path soon traverses a slab of slanted stone, with the sheer north face of Cable Moun-tain rising to dizzying heights above the trail.

The path levels off as it enters the cool recesses of Echo Canyon, a hanging chasm carved by runoff. Initially the path clings to the edge of a deep abyss, but the canyon floor soon rises to the level of the trail. Its gradient then eases, and hikers can proceed up its sandy wash. Sheer walls of fluted stone rise on all sides. The path climbs along a shelf as it passes through a narrow section where canyon walls are hardly more than an arm's span apart. The cleft soon opens into a sunny bowl, flanked by rugged peaks to the north and south. After passing through another tight spot, the canyon widens into a valley with sloping walls, and the East Rim Trail branches off to the right.

The main trail now embarks on a challenging ascent, zigzagging its way up the sheer face of stone that rises above. A few pines cling to crevices in the rock, leaning wind-scoured limbs out over Echo Canyon. The path works its way onto a west-facing rib of the mountain, providing welcome shade in the late afternoon. After numerous switchbacks, the trail shoots westward for the final ascent across white cliffs that drop away for a thousand feet below the pathway. Although the trail is quite wide, it hardly seems wide enough to prevent the traveler from being drawn into the yawning abyss.

The path ultimately reaches the top of the Navajo sandstone formation, where it enters a rolling scrubland of piñon and juniper that marks the top of the plateau. Here, the East Mesa Trail climbs away to the right, while the Observation Point route bends southward.

A level trek through deep sand leads to the tip of the promontory and an inspiring view down Zion Canyon. The Great White Throne looms to the south, and to the left the cableworks atop Cable Mountain can be picked out with binoculars. Perhaps the most intriguing feature that can be seen from here is Red Arch Mountain. A great slab of stone broke away from its face in the 1880s, leaving a lofty alcove reminiscent

of a cathedral nave. Views to the north are obscured by a shoulder of chalky sandstone, but some of the reddish pinnacles that guard the Temple of Sinawava can be seen from the western edge of the point.

Key Points

0.0 Weeping Rock trailhead

0.5 Junction with Hidden Canyon Trail. Bear left for Observation Point.

1.0 Trail enters mouth of Echo Canyon.

2.0 Junction with East Rim Trail. Bear left for Observation Point.

3.2 Trail reaches top of grade.

3.6 Junction with East Mesa Trail. Bear left.

4.0 Observation Point

Hidden Canyon Option

The Hidden Canyon route offers a fairly challenging side trip from the Observation Point Trail, featuring a cliff-hanging beginning and a scramble up a trailless wash between towering walls of sandstone at the end. The path begins by zigzagging upward from the trail junction and then skirts westward around a rocky promontory. It soon dips into a narrow draw, where chains have been emplaced to form handrails in precarious spots. The route gets even more hair-raising as it continues its westward traverse above a drop-off of nearly a thousand feet. After a few hundred yards, the path swings southward into the mouth of Hidden Canyon.

Trail maintenance ends here; follow the sandy wash south between the lower cliffs of Cable Mountain (to the left) and the Great White Throne. After about 0.3 mile a small natural arch rises from the canyon floor along the west wall. Just beyond it are the first of the serious obstacles, and some scrambling will be required to get around them. Beyond the first chokepoint erosion has carved a convoluted hollow into the western wall of the canyon. The second impasse leads to a narrowing of the chasm, and soon a vertical cleft bars the way. Passage beyond this point is restricted in an effort to protect the habitat of the Mexican spotted owl.

◀ *Looking down on Red Arch Mountain from Observation Point*

12 Up The Narrows to Orderville Canyon

A one-day out-and-back trip up the lower section of The Narrows

Distance: 6 miles (9.6 km) round-trip
Hiking time: About 3 hours
Best seasons: June–July, September–October
Difficulty: Moderately strenuous*
Water availability: The Virgin River and Order-ville Canyon both carry a permanent flow of water, although the river is quite silty.

Hazards: Flash flood danger
Recommended equipment: Wading staff
Topo maps: Temple of Sinawava; Zion National Park (Trails Illustrated)
Jurisdiction: Zion National Park. See Appendix A for more information.

Finding the trailhead: The trail begins at the Temple of Sinawava parking area at the end of Zion Canyon Road, accessed via the tram. GPS: N37° 17' 1.223"/W112° 56' 48.810"

The Hike

Travelers should expect nearly constant wading on this hike, which follows the North Fork of the Virgin River up through the lower half of the spectacular Narrows of Zion Canyon. Be ready for slippery cobbles in water that may be waist deep and quite cold. Overnight camping is not allowed in this section of the canyon, but no special permit is required to undertake the trek. You will need to check the river flow rates, however, because the Park Service closes the canyon to hikers coming up from the bottom when river flows surpass 150 cubic feet per second. Check for flash flood warnings at park headquarters before starting out; there is little in the way of escape terrain should a cloudburst high in the headwaters send a wall of water down the canyon.

The hike begins on a paved walkway that departs from the Temple of Sinawava parking area. The walkway follows the river, passing through canyon wetlands and grassy bottoms. Watch for the canyon grape, a parasitic vine that grows over taller trees and shrubs to monopolize available sunlight.

At the end of the pathway, the river hike begins. Follow the trails along riv-erside gravel bars and cross the river at shallow spots when sheer walls block progress on land. A trickle of water cas-cades down the east wall of the canyon, marking the elevated mouth of Mys-tery Canyon. The Narrows begin just beyond this point, as immense walls constrict around the watercourse. The wading is virtually constant from this

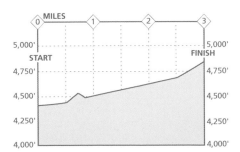

Streaked walls above the Virgin River near the mouth of Orderville Canyon

point onward. The river has undercut the thousand-foot walls of The Narrows, and centuries of erosion have sculpted the walls into fluted and whorled forms. The zebra striping that adorns the cliffs can be attributed to mineral deposits left behind by seeping water.

Orderville Canyon is the first major cleft that joins the canyon from the right. Its lower reaches can be explored without special equipment and offer spectacular slot canyon scenery. Follow it upward through a narrow passageway carved deep into the bedrock. There are several low pour-offs with plunge pools below them—be prepared for waist-deep water and some scrambling. The cleft soon widens into a sunny opening where a vigorous growth of vegetation thrives on water from seeps and springs. One of the springs along the streamcourse has a sulfurous smell, indicating the presence of sulfur salts that were deposited in cracks in the sandstone eons ago.

The canyon soon closes in again, and streaked walls tower ahead. After an overall distance of 0.4 mile from the Virgin River, a 5-foot waterfall blocks further travel. This is the turnaround point; the slippery headwall cannot be negotiated safely without climbing aids.

Up The Narrows to Orderville Canyon

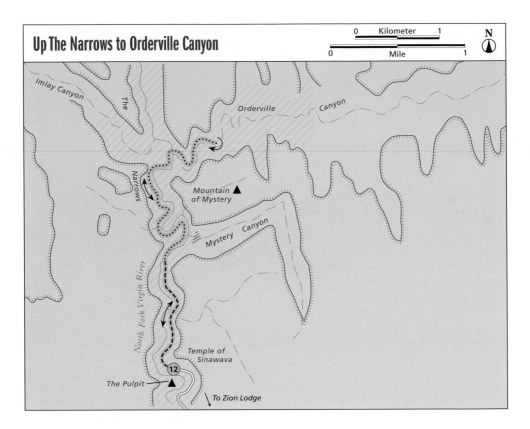

Key Points

0.0   Temple of Sinawava trailhead

1.0   Trail ends. Proceed up rivercourse.

1.4   Mouth of Mystery Canyon

2.6   Mouth of Orderville Canyon. Turn right for more exploration.

3.0   Head of navigation in Orderville Canyon

13 The Narrows of Zion Canyon

A one-way day hike (for the truly hard-core) or backpack down the North Fork of the Virgin River through The Narrows

Distance: 15.4 miles (24.8 km) overall
Hiking time: About 8–10 hours
Best seasons: June–July, September–October
Difficulty: Moderately strenuous*
Water availability: The Virgin River always has water, but it is silty. Big Springs flows permanently; Deep Creek, Goose Creek, Orderville Canyon, and Kolob Creek (summer only) carry clearer water into the canyon. Springs are numerous in the middle section of the Zion Narrows and sparse in the upper and lower sections.
Hazards: Flash flood danger, exposure when water is cold
Recommended equipment: A wading staff is indispensable.
Topo maps: Clear Creek Mountain, Temple of Sinawava; Zion National Park (Trails Illustrated)
Jurisdiction: Zion National Park. See Appendix A for more information.

Finding the trailhead: Drive east from Zion National Park's East Entrance on UT 9 for 2.4 miles to reach a junction with the road to the North Fork and Navajo Lake. This road is impassable when wet or snow-covered. If conditions permit, turn left on this road. The pavement turns to gravel after a few miles; continue northward, crossing the upper gulch of Orderville Canyon and climbing over the high shoulder of a mountain. After 18 miles a bridge spans the Virgin River. Cross the bridge and turn left immediately onto a gravel road (muddy when wet). Follow it for 1 mile to the trailhead, which is just before the road fords the river. The hike ends at the Temple of Sinawava trailhead at the end of Zion Canyon Road, accessed by tram. GPS of start: N37° 23' 2.069"/W112° 50' 20.885"; GPS of finish: N37° 17' 1.223"/W112° 56' 48.810"

The Hike

Possibly the best-known hike in Zion National Park, this wading route follows the Virgin River through the spectacular Narrows of Zion Canyon. Here, fluted walls rise for a thousand feet, crowding the waters into a narrow channel that twists and turns far beneath a thin slot of sky. Although the gradient of the hike is moderate, the near-constant wading over slippery boulders makes the hike a wearying undertaking.

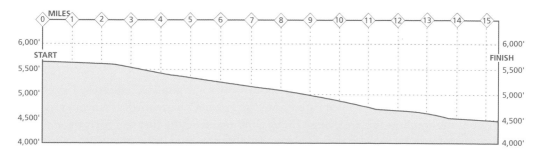

The route can be hiked in a single day by getting an early start, but this is a difficult proposition and should not be attempted by first-timers. Travelers who hike The Narrows between November and June must wear a full wetsuit, because hypothermia is a serious risk at this time of year. A wilderness permit is also required for both day hikers and overnight visitors planning to undertake the full hike down through The Narrows. Get your permit in advance through the online reservation system, as permits for this trip have a tendency to sell out. Bring plenty of warm clothing at all times of year, securely packed to stay dry in case of an unexpected dunking.

A number of special regulations apply to The Narrows hike, established so that this unique wilderness experience can be enjoyed by all who travel through. A maximum daily limit is placed on the numbers of both day hikers and backpackers, and all travelers must carry a wilderness permit. Permits may be obtained no more than twenty-four hours in advance at the main Zion Visitor Center. Camping spots are allotted site-by-site on a first-come, first-served basis. It is illegal to camp anywhere except your allotted site.

Permits for The Narrows hike may be suspended if the weather turns threatening and a flash flood warning is in effect. Hikers who attempt this hike should become thoroughly familiar with the flash flood section (see the Introduction). Much of the canyon has no escape terrain, and flash floods are a routine occurrence here. The Narrows through hike is not permitted from the top down when river flows exceed 120 cubic feet per second.

To begin the hike ford the river and follow the dirt road along the southern edge of the valley. This land is part of the Chamberlain Ranch, and its pastoral landscape is overlooked to the north by gray cliffs of shale. Each traveler should safeguard good landowner-user relations by sticking to the road and leaving all gates as they were found. The first valley ends as wooded foothills close in around the river, but soon a hidden valley of sage meadows opens up ahead. In the middle of this valley stands the original Bulloch cabin, constructed from hand-hewn local timber. The road ends a short distance beyond the cabin, and the route follows riverside trails or the riverbed itself from this point on.

The flow of water is rarely more than knee-deep in the upper reaches of the river, and crossings are frequent as the stream winds between outcrops of Navajo sandstone. This formation is massive, meaning that it lacks visible layering with the associated structural weakness that goes along with stratification. As a result, the Navajo stone forms sheer walls and alcoves, monoliths and arches. The cliffs are intermittent at first, and tall conifers lean out from the riverbanks and cliff tops at crazy angles. There is a lush understory of bigtooth maple in places, and in October this tree erupts into a fiery display of reds and yellows.

The canyon walls soon become continuous, only to be dissected into steep ridges at the point where Simon Gulch enters from the north. Other, nameless canyons join in from the south in this area. Beyond this confluence lie the first real narrows, and the river soon enters a reach dominated by slender monoliths. It is here that the river

Fluted and striated walls near the mouth of Orderville Canyon

pours over a dramatic 12-foot waterfall. To get around this obstacle, follow a path that goes to the left of the river, climbs through a slot in the stone, and then descends to the river below the falls. There are several deep pools in the stretch of canyon that follows, as well as narrow slots where the fluted walls block out all but a fraction of the sky.

The canyon widens considerably at its confluence with Deep Creek. This tributary stream contributes a substantial flow of clear water that more than doubles the volume of the river. Most of the designated camping spots lie within 2 miles downstream of this confluence, and overnight travelers must pay careful attention to landmarks in this area to find the correct campsite.

Below Deep Creek the river turns southward and wide gravel bars line its channel. Crossings can be made through shallow riffles. The current is swifter here than in the upper reaches, and the cobbles are coated with slippery algae. Travelers should proceed slowly and cautiously while wading to avoid a slip that might result in a sprained ankle or twisted knee.

The Narrows of Zion Canyon

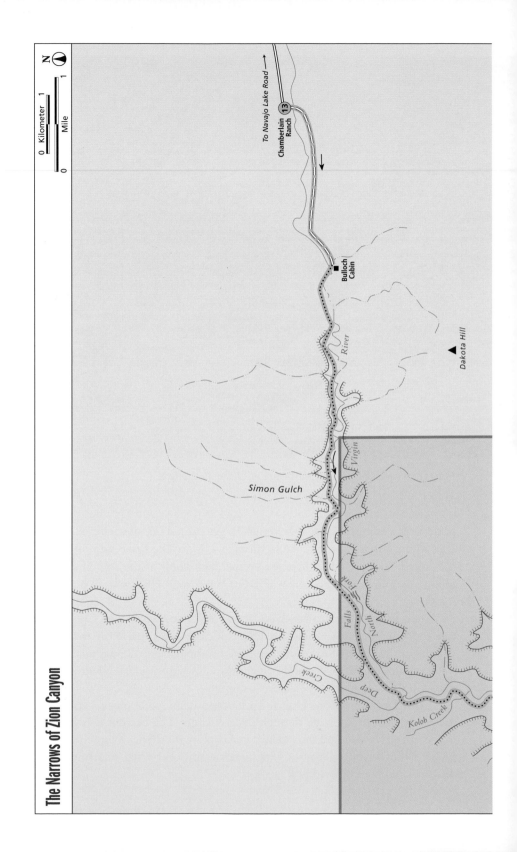

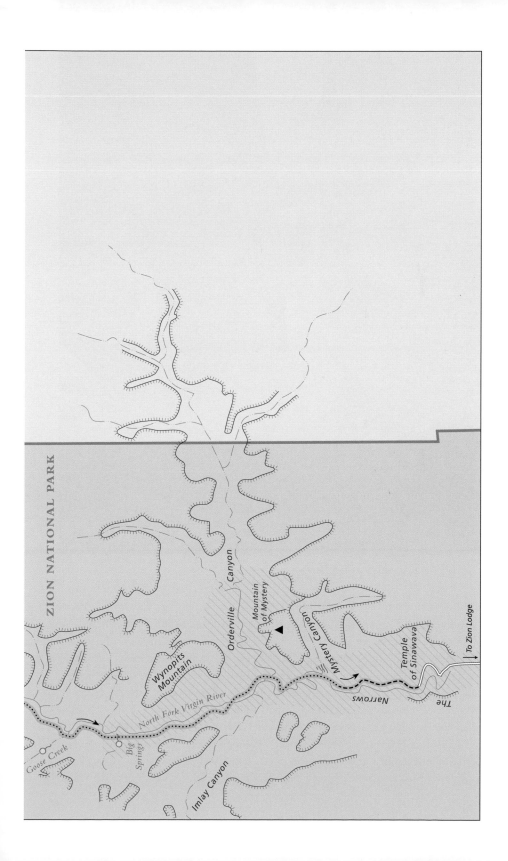

ZION NATIONAL PARK

Goose Creek

Big Springs

North Fork Virgin River

Wynopits Mountain

Imlay Canyon

Orderville Canyon

Mountain of Mystery

Mystery Canyon

Narrows

Temple of Sinawava

The

To Zion Lodge

Waterfall in Ordervillle Canyon

Kolob Creek occupies the next major canyon that joins in from the west. It bears water only during the summer, when water is released from Kolob Reservoir in the headwaters of the drainage for use by irrigators downstream from the park. There are springs between Kolob Creek and The Narrows, but most are overgrown with algae and some emit a fetid smell. The narrow slot of Goose Creek is the next side canyon, and its inconspicuous opening generally bears a trickle of clear water into the river.

Downstream from Goose Creek, the canyon walls sink away into a series of razor-back ridges that are densely forested with conifers. The pools begin to deepen in this area and the wading becomes trickier. Expect waist-deep water in some spots and fast currents in others. Big Springs soon appears on the right wall of the canyon, unleashing a foaming flow of water across a mossy cascade. Travelers who wish to take on water here should approach the springs from above; there are deep and fast-flowing currents immediately beside the water source.

Big Springs marks the upper end of The Narrows, where sheer walls of sandstone rise 1,000 feet above the river. For the next 3 miles, hikers will find it virtually impossible to climb to high ground in the event of a flash flood. There is little vegetation here; periodic floods rampage through The Narrows with amazing force, scouring away any seedlings that might have taken root in the shady depths of the chasm.

Water ouzels are found abundantly throughout The Narrows. These small birds nest in clefts and behind waterfalls, and they dive into the current to fly underwater on stubby wings in their quest for aquatic insects. They are often sighted doing "push-ups" atop riverside boulders.

The river now fills the canyon from wall to wall, making for constant wading over long stretches. The fluted walls rise to staggering heights on both sides of the river, creating a deep gloom in the depths of the canyon. Undercut walls create a tunnel-like effect near the canyon's confluence with Orderville Canyon, a narrow cleft that is well worth a side trip. As the river flows southward from the mouth of Orderville Canyon, the lower walls of the canyon are zebra-striped with minerals leached out of the rocks above by runoff. An abundance of springs and seeps that flow from the canyon walls create numerous hanging gardens of moisture-loving plants, and these in turn create habitat for the Zion snail, which is found only in this isolated corner of Utah.

About 1.1 miles below Orderville Canyon, the walls open out considerably, revealing taller summits surrounding the mouth of Mystery Canyon. This hanging canyon pours forth a ribbon of water that slides down the curved canyon wall. Just beyond it travelers can haul themselves out of the river onto a paved walkway that covers the remaining mile to the Temple of Sinawava trailhead, which is the terminus of the hike.

Key Points

0.0   Trek begins at Chamberlain Ranch ford. Cross river and follow dirt road. Do not hike in the riverbed at this point per the owner's request.

2.5   Bulloch Cabin. Descend to riverbed at the end of the dirt road and follow it downstream.

4.0   First section of The Narrows in upper Zion Canyon

5.5   Simon Gulch enters from the north.

7.3   Waterfall obstacle

8.3   Deep Creek joins from the north.

9.1   Kolob Creek joins from the west.

10.2   Goose Creek joins from the west.

10.9   Big Springs. Camping prohibited below this point. Route enters The Narrows.

12.9   Orderville Canyon enters from the east.

14.0   Mouth of Mystery Canyon

14.4   East bank of river at end of Temple of Sinawava Trail

15.4   Temple of Sinawava trailhead

14 Deep Creek

A multiple-day, out-and-back backpack following a wilderness route down Deep Creek to its confluence with the Virgin River

Distance: 28.4 miles (45.8 km) round-trip

Hiking time: About 7-8 hours each way

Best season: September-October

Difficulty: Moderately strenuous**

Water availability: Fife Creek, Deep Creek, the North Fork of Deep Creek, and Crystal Creek have permanent flows of water.

Hazards: Flash flood danger in Deep Creek Narrows; exposure when water is cold

Recommended equipment: Wading staff

Topo maps: Webster Flat, Cogswell Point, Temple of Sinawava; Kanab and Panguitch (BLM)

Jurisdiction: Bureau of Land Management, Kanab Field Office; Zion National Park. See Appendix A for more information. The route also crosses state and private holdings.

Finding the trailhead: From Cedar City drive east on UT 14 for 15 miles. Turn right on the Webster Flat Road and follow it southward. Stay on the main road, ignoring the side roads. After 4 miles the road leaves Dixie National Forest and enters private land. Continue for another 2.2 miles to reach the culvert over upper Fife Creek. The hike starts from this culvert. GPS: N37° 31' 12.420"/W112° 54' 19.386"

The Hike

This challenging wilderness route follows the rugged valley of Deep Creek into a newly designated wilderness, through montane forest, across arid scrubland, and into a narrow slot canyon as it joins the North Fork of the Virgin River. Most of the land along the route is private, state, or Bureau of Land Management–owned, although the final stretch lies within Zion National Park. Zion National Park is currently not issuing the required permit for camping in the park from Deep Creek. Travelers who wish to take a day trip into Zion from the north must carry a day-use permit and must exit the park the same day.

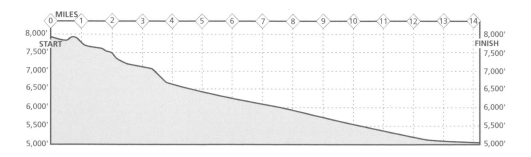

Waterfall on Deep Creek near Big Oak Wash

Private landowners hold much of the land in the upper reaches of the Deep Creek drainage. Hikers must get permission to cross private lands before beginning the trek. Private landowners tolerate hikers as long as they respect private property and travel through quickly. Help maintain good relations with landowners by carrying a map that shows land ownership and camping only on BLM lands.

The hike begins on a livestock path along the left (east) bank of Fife Creek. This is private property; travel through as quickly as possible and avoid damaging fences and other structures along the way. Aspens rise in a loose grove around the waterway, amid a scattering of lava boulders. After a short distance a grassy vale enters from the left (east). Cross the stream here and climb carefully over a buck-and-pole fence made of aspen logs. Follow the right (west) bank of the watercourse for 350 yards, passing several lava outcrops to reach a small dry wash that drains a draw to the west. Turn right to enter the mouth of this draw, then follow a pathway that climbs gently out of the gulch on a southerly heading.

This path leads to an old roadbed that crosses the slopes above the Fife Creek valley. Across the valley the low bands of cliffs belong to the Carmel Formation, made up of marine shales that were laid down when this part of Utah was submerged beneath a shallow sea. The old roadway soon drops into a lush meadow where Big Spring contributes its substantial flow of groundwater to Fife Creek. The roadbed seems to end at the stream bank; follow the west bank downstream for 75 yards to pick up the road as it traverses the slopes above the stream.

The valley floor soon falls away, leaving the roadbed to wander across slopes timbered in a mixed forest of spruce, aspen, and ponderosa pine. About 0.5 mile beyond Big Spring, another roadbed slants down to the stream. Stay with the upper track for 50 yards to reach an opening where pine and manzanita predominate. Here, an old pack trail forks off to the left, descending steadily into the valley. Follow this old trail along the slopes to the west of the stream. A grassy meadow soon presents itself across the valley, overlooked by a rocky brow of shale. The trail drops to the streamside here. A heavily beaten track emerges on the far bank of the stream, but our route follows a narrower trail on the western bank of the creek.

The water now runs across ledges of stone, sliding across rounded faces and tumbling over miniature cascades. The cliffs across the valley resolve themselves into the rock-walled butte of China Point, which guards the confluence of Fife and Deep Creeks. Beyond this confluence the trail tracks the western bank of Deep Creek. The track becomes quite brushy in spots and is often blocked by fallen trees. Deep Creek is a pretty mountain stream in its upper reaches, surrounded by timbered slopes that rise up to the base of tall cliffs. These are the Gray Cliffs of the Carmel Formation, representing the second tier of the geologists' Grand Staircase that leads down into the Grand Canyon. Above this thick layer of marine shale is the freshwater limestone that forms the Pink Cliffs, and below it lies the pale Navajo sandstone, which forms the monoliths of Zion Canyon.

As the valley descends, cool-climate species such as aspen and spruce are steadily replaced by conifers that are more suited to hot weather: Douglas fir and ponderosa pine. The trail ultimately descends from the steep slopes into a cottonwood bottomland as O'Neil Gulch bears the West Fork of Deep Creek into the valley. The old trail ends at the confluence.

The route becomes extremely difficult between O'Neil Gulch and Big Oak Wash, a distance of 1.5 miles. Livestock trails crisscross the elevated bench to the west of Deep Creek through tangled thickets of Gambel oak. The streamcourse itself presents numerous waterfalls, deep pools, and tricky crossings that must be negotiated by travelers who choose to stick to the stream. Both options are arduous; pick your own poison. Both routes converge at the streamcourse after 0.5 mile. From here expect slow going, since tall cutbanks crowd the streamsides and force frequent crossings, and logjams in the streamcourse further complicate the endeavor.

Just above Big Oak Wash, a substantial waterfall provides a challenge to navigation. Hikers will find it necessary to traverse the eroded slopes to the west of the falls to gain passage beyond this bottleneck. Below the mouth of Big Oak Wash, traveling becomes progressively easier as low terraces along the streamsides offer brief escapes from the slippery cobbles of the watercourse. The cliffs soon fall away, to be replaced by arid foothills covered in piñon-juniper scrub. Watch for a narrow band of conglomerate that is exposed along the streamcourse in this area. Conglomerate is a stone that is made up of cobbles or pebbles that have been cemented together in a matrix of sand or mud.

The creek bottoms continue to harbor stands of conifers, and near the mouth of Spring Run Gulch these bottoms expand into extensive pine flats. Before long, lava cliffs bracket the valley, and just beyond their beginning, Crystal Creek flows in from the west. From this point on quicksand will become an ever-present obstacle in the eddies and backwaters of the creek—try to stay on dry ground or on the rocks. Tall cliffs of basalt rise above both sides of the stream. After 1.1 miles a nameless wash flows in from the west.

Navajo sandstone makes its first appearance here. As the stream cuts downward into this impressive formation, the stone presents irregular faces that soon join together to form towering cliffs. Thus the route enters the Deep Creek Narrows, an area admin-

The narrows of Deep Creek

istered by the Bureau of Land Management and under study as a possible Wilderness Area. The great walls are streaked with minerals that were leached out of the formations above by runoff. The cliffs provide a cool and shady environment where bigtooth maple and Douglas fir can thrive. As the canyon winds through countless twists and turns, it becomes difficult to maintain a sense of direction.

After a long jog to the east, a spectacular slot canyon enters from the left, draining a cliff-top flat known as Hog's Heaven. The flat was named for "Hog" Allen, an early pioneer who claimed ownership to much of the land to the east of Deep Creek. According to legend, Hog swore to evict ranchers who came later to stake out legal homesteads, but died before he could carry out his threats. But neighboring ranchers and their families became subject to mysterious and fatal accidents

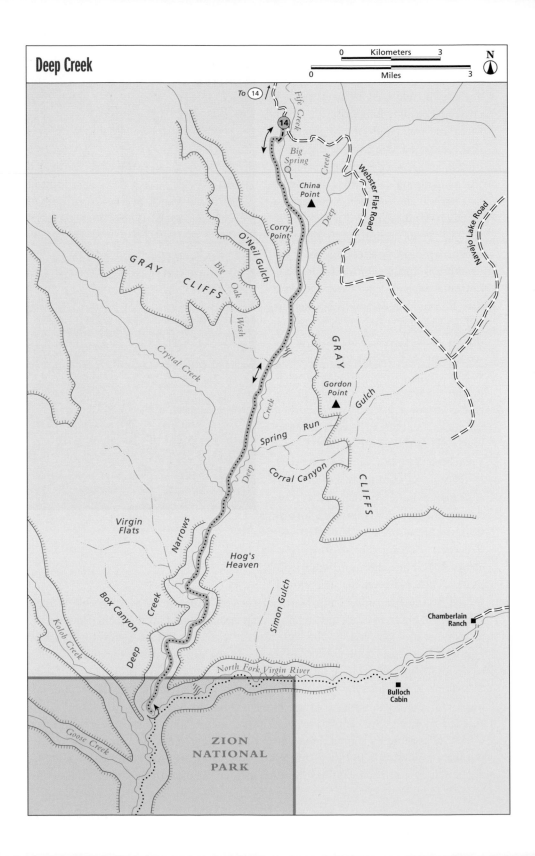

Deep Creek

To (14)

Fife Creek

(14)

Big Spring

Creek

China Point ▲

Deep

Webster Flat Road

Navajo Lake Road

Corry Point

O'Neil Gulch

GRAY CLIFFS

Big Oak Wash

GRAY

Gordon Point ▲

Gulch

Crystal Creek

Creek

Spring Run

Corral Canyon

CLIFFS

Deep

Virgin Flats

Narrows

Hog's Heaven

Simon Gulch

Chamberlain Ranch ■

Box Canyon

Creek

Kolob Creek

Deep

North Fork Virgin River

Bulloch Cabin ■

Goose Creek

ZION NATIONAL PARK

on the anniversary of Hog Allen's death, which encouraged them to abandon the area. It is said that, on certain nights, a mist drifts down the Golden Staircase and settles over Hog Allen's grave. This phenomenon is said to be the spirit of Hog Allen returning to do a dance there.

Below this point traveling becomes progressively more difficult as the pools deepen and become harder to avoid. The canyon walls take on a sloping aspect as Box Canyon enters on the right (west) side of the main gorge. Here, the walls are divided into rough-faced crags by an array of tributary drainages. The walls then close in again for the final stretch to the point where Deep Creek empties into the North Fork of the Virgin River. The milkier waters of the river issue forth from a narrow slot, creating some confusion as to which stream is the tributary and which is the main flow. The Narrows of Zion Canyon lie downstream from this point, but the National Park Service was not issuing permits to hike The Narrows via Deep Creek at the time this book was written.

Key Points

0.0	Fife Creek culvert
0.5	Route ascends into draw to the west.
0.7	Route strikes old road. Follow it southward.
1.1	Big Spring. Bear south along streambank to reacquire road.
1.7	Old pack trail descends to creek. Follow it downward.
2.7	Confluence of Fife and Deep Creeks. Trail follows Deep Creek downstream.
4.1	Trail ends at O'Neil Gulch. Choose a route down the valley.
5.5	Waterfall obstacle
5.6	Big Oak Wash enters from the west.
7.5	Spring Run Gulch/Corral Canyon wash enters from the east.
8.9	Crystal Creek enters from the west.
10.0	Route enters Deep Creek Narrows.
13.2	Box Canyon enters from west.
13.7	Zion National Park boundary. No camping past this point without special permit.
14.2	Deep Creek flows into North Fork of the Virgin River.

The Desert Lowlands

The southwestern corner of Zion National Park is typified by low deserts dominated by cacti, spiny succulents, and widely spaced desert shrubs. It is a land of forbidding buttes and eroded "painted desert" badlands. This is perhaps the most primeval corner of the park, and trails (where they exist) tend to be rugged and may require good route-finding skills. The area is transformed into a muddy morass in winter and early spring, and it is far too hot for hiking during the summer months. The best season to visit this desert landscape is autumn, when temperatures cool off and the ground offers dry and solid footing. Permits for overnight expeditions are available at the main Zion Visitor Center near Springdale.

Coalpits Wash with springtime flows near the confluence with Scoggins Wash (hike 20).

15 Eagle Crags

An out-and-back climb to the foot of Eagle Crags in the Vermilion Cliffs

Distance: 6.2 miles (9.6 km) round-trip
Hiking time: About 3 hours
Best seasons: March–May, September–November
Difficulty: Moderately strenuous
Water availability: None
Hazards: Unstable footing on steep, rocky slopes

Topo maps: Springdale West, Smithsonian Butte; Zion National Park (Trails Illustrated)
Jurisdiction: Bureau of Land Management, St. George Field Office. See Appendix A for more information.

Finding the trailhead: From the South Entrance of Zion National Park, drive 4.7 miles west on UT 9 to Rockville. Head south (left) on Grafton Road and go 0.3 mile to Bridge Road, an unimproved road. Bridge Road has an uneven surface and traverses up steep slopes with few places to turn around. A high-clearance vehicle is recommended from this point on. Several private residences are located at the top of the hill. When the road splits into three branches, continue up the middle road. After 1.4 miles look for a trailhead sign and pullout area on the right. GPS: N37° 8' 51.66" / W113° 1' 51.79"

The Hike

This is a moderately strenuous hike into the Mount Canaan Wilderness with both gradual and steep changes in elevation. The trail surface is uneven and rocky in most areas, with the exception of some areas east and south of the crags, which are predominantly sand. The trail itself travels across land managed by the Bureau of Land Management to reach the foot of Eagle Crags, a series of knifelike pinnacles rising from a lone butte. It then climbs a series of switchbacks to provide closer views of the towering spires.

From the trailhead follow the path to the right of the trailhead sign, and head down a slope to the south. The trail is predominantly sandy, rocky, and uneven and is used heavily by horse parties. If you encounter horses on the trail, step aside and yield

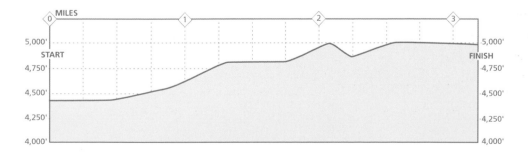

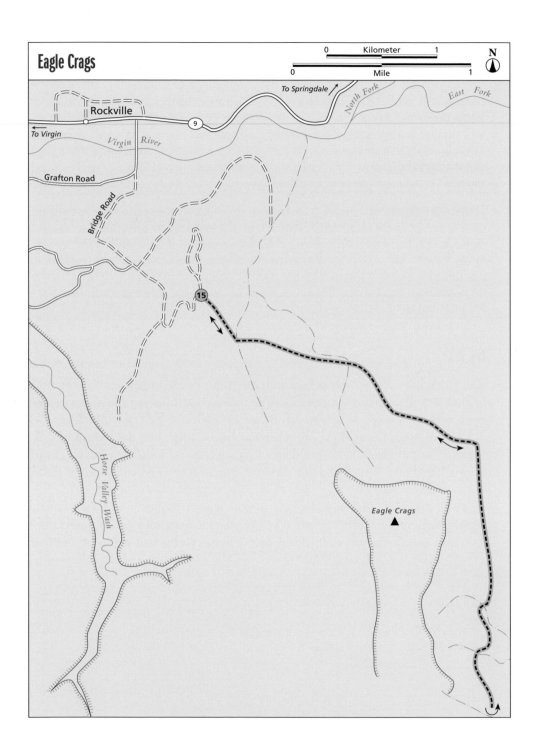

Eagle Crags

Kilometer
0 ──────────── 1

Mile
0 ──────────── 1

N

To Springdale

North Fork

East Fork

Rockville

9

To Virgin

Virgin River

Grafton Road

Bridge Road

15

Horse Valley Wash

Eagle Crags
▲

the right-of-way. Early on the trail, hikers can see the Eagle Crags to the south and Shunesburg Mountain to the east.

The trail continues downhill until it crosses a draw and ascends the opposite foothill on a southeasterly heading. During this ascent visitors will encounter a hiker gate through a barbed-wire fence. Pass through the gate and continue to climb southeast across the foothills of the Crags. Along the way are eastward views of the Vermilion Cliffs and South Mountain.

After eventually turning down into a draw and traversing another wash, the path turns east and parallels the wash as it makes its way around the base of the foothill to the right (south). The trail then approaches a confluence and turns south, staying on the west side and paralleling the contributing wash. The trail crosses the wash and continues southeast.

Views of Eagle Crags are sometimes hidden by the foothills as the trail winds around to the northeast side of the formation. The trail soon emerges onto an open slope, however, and begins to ascend below the east side of the crags. This slope offers uninterrupted views of Shunesburg Mountain, the Vermilion Cliffs, and South Creek.

At the top of the slope, the trail turns right and heads up to the crags via a series of switchbacks. This is a moderate climb over an uneven, rocky path. At the foot of the crags, the trail straightens out and briefly levels off. The quite narrow path then begins to climb across a steep slope—watch your footing. At the end of this slope, the trail passes a large, flat, overhanging rock from which junipers are growing. After more climbing, hikers reach the crest of the foothill and the eastern end of the crag formations.

Looking up at the spires, travelers will see the reason for the name Eagle Crags. Enjoy the fine views across the valley to the east before you head back along the same route from this great turnaround spot.

Hikers can follow the upward path a short distance to its very end as it wraps around to the south side of the crags. Staying in the upland areas, the route passes over two draws. The path across the draws is narrow and uneven with loose rocks and steep slopes. Use careful footing along this stretch. Beyond the draws the path gradually loses elevation. As it heads down toward the head of South Creek, the trail abruptly ends in a series of small runoff washes. Another path leads down a very steep slope into a large draw, but it ends abruptly on the other side.

Key Points

0.0   BLM trailhead sign

3.1   Trail ends below Eagle Crags.

16 Water Canyon

A leisurely hike to the narrows of Water Canyon or a vigorous day trip to the top of Canaan Mountain

Distance: 1 mile (1.8 km) or 1.7 miles (3 km) one way
Hiking time: About 0.75 hour–2 hours
Best seasons: March–May, September–November
Difficulty: Moderate to the Water Canyon narrows; strenuous to the top of Canaan Mountain
Water availability: Water Canyon bears a permanent stream.

Hazards: Unstable footing on steep, rocky slopes and wet slickrock
Topo map: Hildale (trail not shown)
Jurisdiction: Bureau of Land Management, St. George Field Office. See Appendix A for more information.

Finding the trailhead: Follow UT 59 east from Hurricane (or west from Fredonia, Arizona) to the east end of the town of Hildale. Turn east on Utah Avenue, which runs straight and then turns north (and becomes Maxwell Parkway) as it follows Short Canyon upward. After 3 miles turn right on Water Canyon Road, a gravel road suitable for passenger cars. Follow it 2.1 miles to its end at a stock watering pond. The trail begins at the upper end of the pond. GPS: N37° 2' 7.947" / W112° 57' 10.855"

The Hike

This route begins as a well-defined trail to a slot canyon and then becomes a steep and somewhat primitive route to the top of Canaan Mountain. From the top it is possible to navigate at will across the top of the mesa in many directions, but don't expect any trails to guide you. Water is scarce on the mesa top, so bring a plentiful supply with you for extended bushwhacking on top. If you have strong backcountry navigation skills, it is possible to travel up Water Canyon, travel cross-country atop Canaan Mountain, and descend Squirrel Canyon for a loop trip. Even though Squirrel Canyon is the easier climb, Water Canyon is the recommended first leg because the upper end of this trail is exceedingly hard to locate when approached from above.

The hike begins along a broad and sandy path that follows the west bank of the Water Canyon watercourse. Many spur paths run down to the water, offering reflections of the sheer cliffs on the opposite side of the canyon. Follow the higher trail to continue up-canyon. After 0.3 mile the trail undertakes its first stiff climb. At the top scan the big red wall across the canyon to view a natural arch at the upper edge of the canyon wall. From this point steep ups and downs lead along the base of the cliffs.

Soon the path winds through oak scrub to reach the narrows of Water Canyon, where the walls close in to form a rounded tunnel reminiscent of The Subway in

The Narrows of Water Canyon ▶

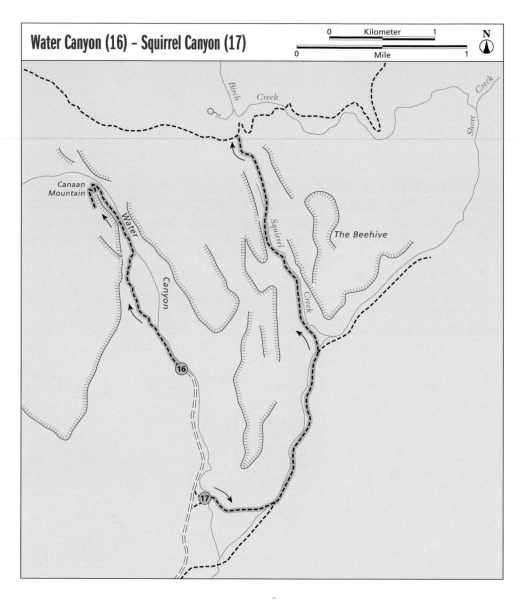

Zion National Park. Scramble up beside a little trickle of waterfall, being careful of your footing on the algae-covered slickrock. The canyon dead-ends in the alcove beyond, which is dominated by a solitary pillar of stone. From this point on, the hike follows a primitive footpath with steep grades and sheer drop-offs.

To continue, dogleg back to the south to locate the scramble path that follows the ledges up the west wall of the canyon. Soon this path splits; the right-hand path descends to a silent inner sanctum where a sandy beach is hemmed in by vertical walls, while the left branch of the trail begins the strenuous climb out of the canyon. This path ascends unrelentingly across precarious ledges and sandy slopes.

The use of handholds and footholds and elementary scrambling techniques is occasionally necessary. Emerging into a rockscape of deeply textured, cross-bedded sandstone, the route alternates between dogged climbs and level traverses. The beehive formations on the far side of the chasm are reminiscent of Zion Canyon. After a level stretch through groves of ponderosa pine and silver fir, the trail begins a series of breath-stealing switchbacks, leading up through the manzanita toward the canyon rim. The path ultimately runs south into a rocky cove at the base of a sharp prow of sandstone. Here the trail disintegrates, but it is possible to follow the myriad avenues up the slickrock to reach the level top of Canaan Mountain. From the top it is possible to bushwhack to countless cliff-top overlooks with views in all directions; just make sure that you can find your way back to the top of the trail for the return trip.

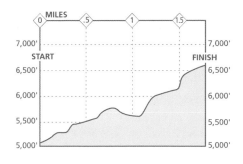

Key Points

0.0 Water Canyon trailhead

1.0 Water Canyon narrows. Route becomes primitive and steep.

1.7 Route ends atop Canaan Mountain.

17 Squirrel Canyon

A day hike up a broad canyon to the top of Canaan Mountain, ending at the junction with the Broad Hollow Trail

---

See map on page 80.
Distance: 3 miles (4.8 km) one way
Hiking time: About 6 hours
Best seasons: March–May, September–November
Difficulty: Moderately strenuous

Water availability: Short Canyon and Squirrel Canyon typically carry water.
Topo map: Hildale
Jurisdiction: Bureau of Land Management, St. George Field Office. See Appendix A for more information.

Finding the trailhead: Follow UT 59 east from Hurricane (or west from Fredonia, Arizona) to the east end of the town of Hildale. Turn east on Utah Avenue, which runs straight and then turns north (and becomes Maxwell Parkway) as it follows Short Canyon upward. After 3 miles turn right on Water Canyon Road, a gravel road suitable for passenger cars. Follow it for 0.9 mile, then turn right onto a short spur leading to a parking area near the mouth of Water Canyon. The trail departs from the northeast side of the parking area. GPS: N37° 1' 29.061" / W112° 57' 7.836"

The Hike

This trail provides an easier but longer journey through the Canaan Mountain Wilderness Study Area to the top of Canaan Mountain, with a massive dome of slickrock known as The Beehive as the main attraction. The hike begins on a heavily beaten all-terrain vehicle trail that descends to cross the wash of Water Canyon. After mounting the bluff beyond, the route follows a road and a fence line through piñon–juniper scrub before descending to cross the watercourse of Short Canyon. It then wanders up the bottomlands of this broad canyon, alternating between groves of cottonwood and sandy shrub fields. The conical butte that is visible ahead is The Beehive.

After 2.2 miles the trail reaches the confluence of Squirrel Canyon and Short Canyon. Turn left as the route climbs into an impressive cottonwood grove on a high shelf above the watercourse. As the path ascends Squirrel Canyon, stout bands of cliffs rise on both sides and a lone tower of stone looms ahead, splitting the canyon into two branches. The trail climbs to the west of this battlement, ascending the left-hand gulch, choked with Gambel oak, birch, and bracken. After a steady ascent the path crosses the streamcourse and undertakes a vigorous ascent of the rock buttress that divides the canyon. A steep slog leads to the crest of this wall, leading to grandstand views of The Beehive's massif of reddish slickrock.

Slickrock in upper Squirrel Canyon ▶

The trail continues upward, following the spine of the ridge through a landscape of orange slickrock dotted with ponderosa pines. Weathered stone stretches in all directions as the route climbs the final pitch to the top of the divide between Squirrel and Birch Canyons. From here you can look out across red rock domes, battlements, and pine-studded swells stretching in all directions. From this point a well-worn trail runs west toward the top of Canaan Mountain and east toward Broad Hollow.

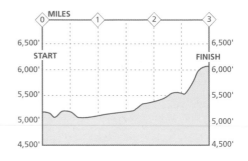

Key Points

0.0 Squirrel Canyon trailhead

0.1 Trail crosses Water Canyon stream.

0.5 Trail crosses Short Canyon watercourse. Turn left on far bank.

2.2 Junction with Squirrel Canyon Trail. Turn left and cross Short Canyon wash as the route enters Squirrel Canyon.

2.6 Trail crests rocky wall; overlook of The Beehive.

3.0 Trail ends at junction with the Broad Hollow Trail.

18 Chinle Trail

A traverse through the low desert of southwestern Zion, ending at Coalpits Wash

Distance: 8.1 miles (13 km) one way
Hiking time: About 4 hours
Best season: June–February
Difficulty: Moderate*
Water availability: Coalpits Wash; check with the Zion Visitor Center for seasonal water availability.

Hazards: Extremely hot and dry during summer
Topo maps: Springdale West; Zion National Park (Trails Illustrated)
Jurisdiction: Zion National Park. See Appendix A for more information.

Finding the trailhead: From the South Entrance of Zion National Park, drive 3.5 miles west on UT 9 to Anasazi Way. A sign on the right marks the trailhead parking area. GPS: N37° 9' 40.91"/W113° 1' 8.94"

The Hike

From the parking area on Anasazi Way, follow the trail to the park boundary. Follow the path northwest as it smooths out into a wide, sandy trail. It's easy hiking here, through pleasant, open scrubland. This portion of the trail offers clear and consistent views of Mount Kinesava and the Three Marys ahead to the north. A backward glance reveals the magnificent spires known as the Eagle Crags.

The trail continues its level trek until it reaches a bench that overlooks Huber Wash. The path then gradually descends a hundred feet or so to traverse a small wash below the southwestern face of Mount Kinesava. Beyond the wash it immediately begins a gradual 150-foot climb onto the Petrified Forest Bench. This bench marks the top of the Chinle Formation, a Triassic shale that contains shards of petrified wood. (It is illegal to collect or disturb samples of petrified wood; leave them for others to enjoy.) Once at the top of the bench, the trail crosses Huber Wash.

From Huber Wash to Scoggins Wash, the landscape changes only slightly. A more diverse vegetation now includes juniper, piñon pine, and sagebrush. This plant community is typical of desert uplands and requires more rainfall than the low desert scrub that characterized the early portions of the trail. Cougar Mountain now looms on the northwest horizon. Eastward views encompass the Towers of the Virgin, featuring the West Temple and the Sundial. Once the trail reaches

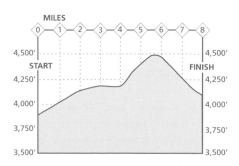

The Towers of the Virgin as seen from the Chinle Trail above Scoggins Wash

the northern part of the bench, hikers can take in westward views of Scoggins Wash. The trail briefly parallels the cliffs overlooking Scoggins Wash before it continues northeast. It then makes a gradual descent into the wash.

The path traverses Scoggins Wash and climbs westward onto a mesa. The trail continues westward through a small saddle, heading toward three knolls. At the foot of the knolls, it turns southwest and follows a rocky wash downward. The path follows this wash for about 0.2 mile before leaving the streamcourse and passing through another small saddle. The ascent toward the saddle is deeply rutted from runoff. The path then traverses a meadow before meeting the Old Scoggins Stock Trail, which drops 150 feet down a cliff to reach Scoggins Wash.

Beyond the stock trail the Chinle Trail continues west and soon runs between two knolls. As the foothills to the right open up, the trail turns north. At the top of the grade, the trail enters the perimeter of the Kolob Fire, which eliminated the junipers and piñon pines and opened up the views. Coalpits Wash lies below a cliff line to the left (west). There is a designated campsite before it begins its descent here. As the trail drops, Cougar Mountain, Smith Mesa, and Lambs Knoll can be seen ahead to the north–northwest. On its final descent the trail approaches and parallels the wash, finally reaching the bottom just above a pretty waterfall that lies upstream from Coalpits Spring.

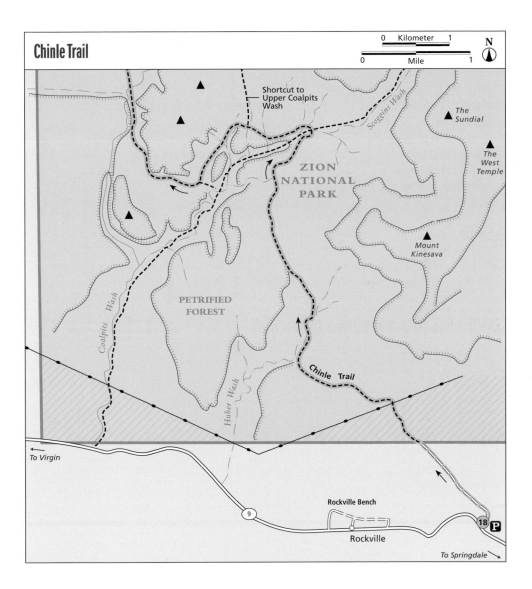

Key Points

0.0 Parking area on UT 9

1.4 Park boundary and Chinle trailhead

3.3 Trail crosses Huber Wash.

5.3 Trail crosses Scoggins Wash.

6.6 Junction with the Old Scoggins Stock Trail. Stay right.

8.1 Coalpits Wash

A shortcut route from the Chinle Trail to Upper Coalpits Wash

Distance: 1.2 miles (2 km) one way
Hiking time: About 0.5 hour
Best season: September–May
Difficulty: Moderate*
Water Availability: None
Hazards: Extremely hot and dry during summer months

Topo maps: Virgin, Springdale West; Zion National Park (Trails Illustrated)
Jurisdiction: Zion National Park (NPS)
GPS of start point: N37° 12' 31.381"/W113° 3' 23.055"

The Hike

This route departs from the Chinle Trail and traverses a saddle to Upper Coalpits Wash. From Scoggins Wash follow the Chinle Trail to the second large wash on the

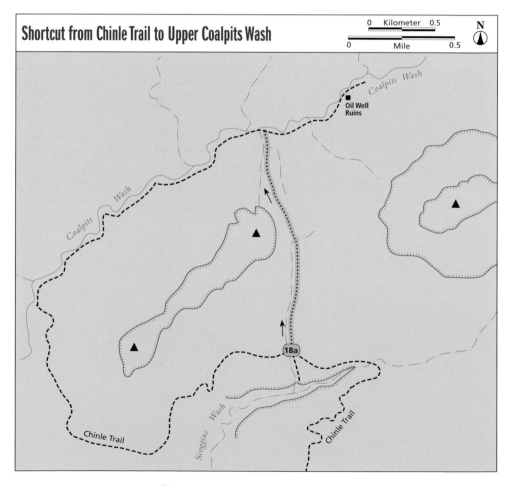

Shortcut from Chinle Trail to Upper Coalpits Wash

right (north). Follow this wash north-ward to a point where it turns north-east toward a large butte that juts out from the Towers of the Virgin. Leave the wash here and head north over-land through the saddle between two prominent knolls. Beyond this saddle are many unmapped washes. Bear west to intersect a wash just north of the western knoll. Follow its banks or the streamcourse itself on a northward bearing toward Cougar Mountain. Just before reaching Coalpits Wash, the mouth of the tributary wash is congested with large boulders. Drop down into the wash and scamper over the boulders to get down to Coalpits Wash.

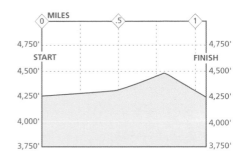

Key Points

0.0 Chinle Trail

1.2 Coalpits Wash

19 Huber Wash

A route following Huber Wash through painted desert terrain in the southwestern corner of Zion National Park to Chinle Trail

Distance: 2.4 miles (3.9 km) one way
Hiking time: About 1.25 hours
Best season: September–May
Difficulty: Moderate
Water availability: Check with the main Zion Visitor Center for seasonal water availability.

Hazards: Extremely hot and dry during summer
Topo maps: Springdale West; Zion National Park (Trails Illustrated)
Jurisdiction: Zion National Park. See Appendix A for more information.

Finding the trailhead: From the South Entrance of Zion National Park, drive 6 miles west on UT 9 to a pullout area on the right (north) side of the road. If driving east on UT 9 from the town of Virgin, look for the pullout area about 100 yards east of the Huber Wash road sign. The route begins at the gate and the gravel road. GPS: N37° 9' 52.168" / W113° 3' 47.521"

The Hike

This route takes the hiker up Huber Wash through some of the delicate desert terrain in Zion's southwest corner. The Chinle and Moenkopi geologic formations in this section of the park were laid down during the Triassic Period. Examine the overlying Chinle Formation for shards of petrified wood. Bear in mind that disturbing these natural treasures is against the law; observe and enjoy them, but leave them intact so that others may have the same experience.

To begin the hike pass through the gate that is visible from the pullout parking area. Cattle graze in this area, so please close all gates as you pass through. Follow the utility road north past the Utah Power & Light Company transformer station. The gravel road soon changes to a dirt track and splits. Follow the left fork west down into the wash. Once in the wash, turn north and pass through the Zion National Park boundary hikers' gate, which is to the right (east) of the wash.

The desert scrub terrain here is dominated by yucca and juniper. Trees are sparse, and between them are patches of fragile cryptobiotic soil; watch your step. The wash occupies a wide, low-lying area with several possible routes. To protect delicate soils and plants, constrain your hiking to the area within the washbed and below the high water mark wherever possible. This entire area, especially the washes, may be extremely muddy after heavy rains.

At the beginning of the route, views include the Rockville Bench to the

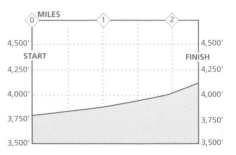

View of Mount Kinesava from Huber Wash

southeast, the Petrified Forest Bench to the north, and Mount Kinesava to the northeast. As hikers meander north along the wash, Mount Kinesava becomes more prominent.

At the route's halfway point, the wash forks. The main channel of Huber Wash enters from the right (northeast). Follow this channel as the Rockville and Petrified Forest Benches begin to narrow the wash into a canyon.

Option: Hikers who wish to follow the same route back to their vehicle should end their trek at a dry waterfall with a petrified logjam on the high shelf to the right of the wash. The National Park Service is extremely concerned about protecting Zion's geologic resources, so please leave the petrified wood undisturbed.

Hikers who are prepared to hike out along the Chinle Trail can bypass the dryfall obstacle. Backtrack approximately 100 feet and climb over boulders onto the shelf located on the left (west) side of the canyon. Seek out a narrow chimney through which you can climb onto the mesa above. Hikers will need to shed their packs to complete this maneuver; day packs can be passed overhead with no problem. Backpacks, however, are trickier and may require a 20-foot length of rope to pull them onto the mesa.

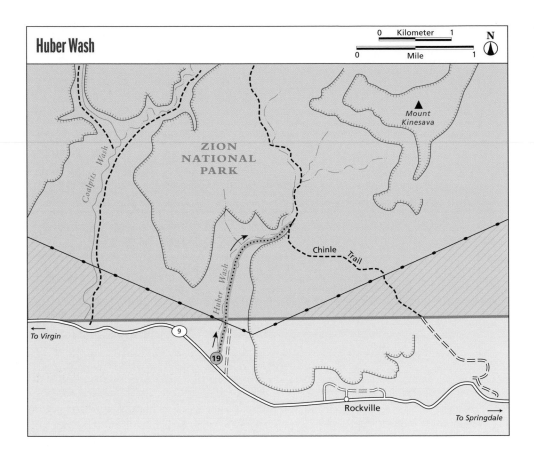

Once through the chimney, work your way northeast toward the foothills of Mount Kinesava. You will soon reach the Chinle Trail, a 3-foot-wide path along the banks of a narrow wash.

Key Points

0.0 Parking area
0.4 Park boundary and hiker gate
2.4 Junction with Chinle Trail

20 Coalpits Wash

A route through Zion's southwest section, ending in Upper Coalpits Wash

Distance: 7 miles (11.3 km) one way
Hiking time: About 3.5 hours
Best season: September–May
Difficulty: Moderate**
Water availability: Check with the main Zion Visitor Center to see if seasonal water is available in Upper Coalpits Wash.

Hazards: Extremely hot and dry
Topo maps: Springdale West; Zion National Park (Trails Illustrated)
Jurisdiction: Zion National Park. See Appendix A for more information.

Finding the trailhead: From the Zion Visitor Center, drive 7.3 miles west on UT 9 to a dirt pullout on the north side of the road. Coalpits Wash and a road sign identifying it are located to the west. Park your car and walk north along the dirt road to the hikers' gate at the park boundary. GPS: N 37°10' 14.10"/W113° 4' 52.62"

The Hike

This route takes the hiker through some of the delicate painted–desert terrain located in the southwest section of Zion National Park. This portion of the park was formed during the Triassic Period, 200 to 230 million years ago. During that time the region was a low-lying plain covered by shallow seas. Early in the Triassic Period, marine and mud deposits consisting of gypsum, limestone, shale, and siltstone were laid down. Today these form the Moenkopi Formation, characterized by the pastel bands of orange and white that form the painted desert. A fire burned through this area in 2006, eliminating much of the piñon-juniper scrub across 17,632 acres and favoring the growth of grasses.

Above the Moenkopi Formation lies the Chinle Formation, comprising both conglomerate and petrified forest deposits. The conglomerate part of the formation, known as the Shinarump Member, consists of rock particles cemented together by sand. It forms a caprock above the Moenkopi Formation and can be seen at the tops of the buttes and mesas. According to Paiute legend, the wolf god Shinav kept his magical weapons (now petrified wood) hidden in this rock formation. The petrified forest part of the Chinle Formation contains trees and river logjams that were covered by thick deposits of volcanic ash and mud and ultimately fossilized.

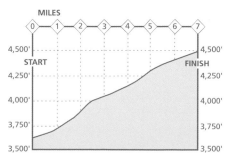

From the hikers' gate a well-worn path leads north along the eastern side of the wash. Ancient cottonwood trees adorn the bottomlands just north of the park boundary. As the path emerges into a scrub forest of piñon pine and juniper, the pastel bands of the Moenkopi Formation can be seen in cliffs to the west. Farther upstream, the brown basalt from lava flows that originated from Crater Hill eruptions can be seen to the west of the wash. The path can be followed easily along the east side of Coalpits Wash up to its confluence with Scoggins Wash.

The portion of Coalpits Wash between Scoggins Wash and the Chinle Trail is bordered by narrow benches and congested with boulders, with small waterfalls during the wettest parts of the year. In the lower reaches hikers will find a fairly consistent path along the west bank of the wash. However, as you continue upstream, the benches along the stream become narrow and somewhat brushy. This makes it necessary to drop into the wash from time to time. The abundance of large boulders along the watercourse also makes it necessary for hikers to pick their way around and over rocks along this stretch.

About 100 feet before the junction with the Chinle Trail, a portion of the washbed passes under a small rock alcove. A hanging garden adorns this alcove, which is very pretty when water is flowing in the stream. About 75 feet above the alcove, the walls of the wash open up into a small waterfall area surrounded by cottonwood trees and views of Cougar Mountain to the north. This serene spot makes a good place to stop and take a siesta, and a spring in the watercourse offers water throughout most of the year.

From here the Crater Hill shortcut drops into Coalpits Wash. Continuing just a few steps upstream along the slickrock, travelers will find a trail and a small signpost noting the junction of the Chinle Trail on the right (east) bank of Coalpits Wash. Farther up Coalpits Wash from the Chinle Trail to Jennings Wash, travelers will follow a well-worn path on the right (east) bank of the streamcourse. This portion of the route is characterized by burned hillsides guarding pleasant meadows, with remaining cottonwoods providing some shade along the banks of the wash. Although the path sometimes disappears in the streambed, it appears again as it cuts across meanderings via streamside benches. Scout for any of the many good campsites along this portion of Coalpits Wash. Scenic views along this stretch encompass the Towers of the Virgin, the Altar of Sacrifice, The Bishopric, and Cougar Mountain.

After the wash passes the southeast corner of Cougar Mountain, hikers can begin looking for oil well ruins along the right (south) bank of Coalpits Wash. The ruins are a fragile historical treasure; do not disturb them or camp nearby.

Jennings Wash lies about 0.1 mile upstream from the oil well ruins. Beyond this point the path fades and then reappears again as it climbs in and out of the wash. Farther upstream, the path disappears entirely and the terrain becomes more difficult

◀ *Coalpits Wash*

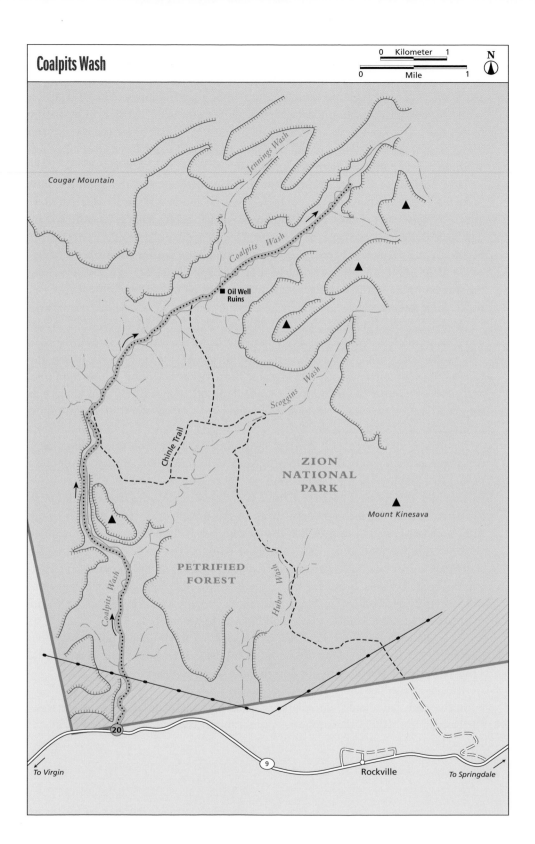

Coalpits Wash

0 Kilometer 1
0 Mile 1

N

Cougar Mountain

Jennings Wash

Coalpits Wash

■ Oil Well
Ruins

Scoggins Wash

Chinle Trail

ZION
NATIONAL
PARK

Mount Kinesava

PETRIFIED
FOREST

Huber Wash

Coalpits Wash

20

9

To Virgin   Rockville   To Springdale

to hike as cliffs close in around the wash. The streambed constricts as the benches bordering it become narrow and brushy.

Two tributary washes soon enter from the south, and between them is a picturesque series of short waterfalls. Climb onto the rock shelf to the right (south) to bypass the falls. Before pouring over the falls, the water flows through a small alcove where vegetation grows from the stratified rock overhanging the stream. From this point on hikers must scurry over and around boulders to reach the end of the route.

Just beyond the falls the cliff walls constrict to form a narrow canyon. The route follows the watercourse. Travelers will soon encounter a second waterfall, with sheer cliffs encroaching upon the falls on every side. The route ends here; bypassing this obstacle requires technical climbing and is not recommended.

Key Points

0.0 Hikers' gate

1.8 Confluence with Scoggins Wash. Bear left.

3.4 Coalpits Spring. Junction with the Chinle Trail. Stay in the wash.

5.0 Junction with shortcut route to Upper Coalpits

5.5 Oil well ruins

5.6 Confluence with Jennings Wash. Bear right.

7.0 End of route

21 Crater Hill to Upper Coalpits Wash

A short, hot hike from Crater Hill to Coalpits Spring

Distance: 2.1 miles (3.4 km) one way
Hiking time: About 1 hour
Best season: September–May
Difficulty: Moderate**
Water availability: Check with the Zion Visitor Center for seasonal availability of water in Upper Coalpits Wash.

Hazards: Extremely hot and dry during summer
Topo maps: Springdale West; Zion National Park (Trails Illustrated)
Jurisdiction: Zion National Park. See Appendix A for more information.

Finding the trailhead: From the main Zion Visitor Center, drive 13.6 miles west on UT 9. Turn right onto an unimproved road (four-wheel-drive vehicle recommended). Follow the road 1.7 miles to a fork. Take the left fork and continue 2.8 miles to a parking area and hikers' gate at the park boundary. GPS: N37° 13' 10.933" / W113° 6' 30.751"

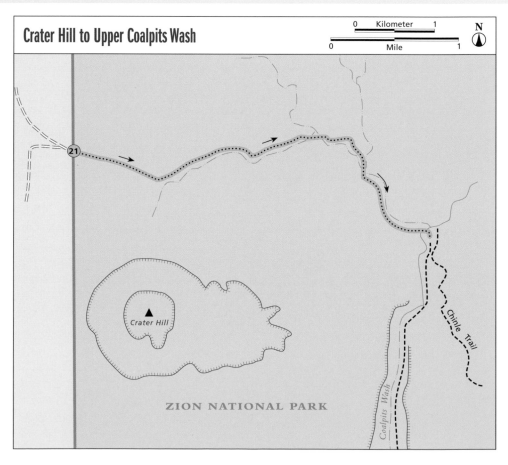

Crater Hill to Upper Coalpits Wash

The Hike

From the parking area this path heads southeast between a small knoll to the north and Crater Hill to the south. Follow the trail on a southeast bearing through open scrubland to reach the wash, northeast of Crater Hill.

Once at the wash, follow its banks. Wherever possible, drop down into the wash to minimize impact upon the delicate desert terrain. The streamcourse consists of sand, cobblestones, and pebbles. Because of the sand and red clay soil, this area becomes a muddy gumbo after heavy rains.

About 0.2 mile before Coalpits Wash, hikers will encounter a 15-foot drop down large boulders. Scramble down the rocks or climb higher to get around the obstacle. Hikers who climb down will find that the wash bed gets pretty brushy on the final stretch before Coalpits Wash. If boulders and bushwhacking don't appeal to you, climb up to the right and find a route along a gradual slope down to the wash. At the bottom of this grade is Coalpits Spring, a 4-foot waterfall with cottonwoods and junipers lining its banks.

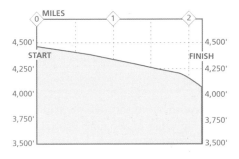

Key Points

0.0 Hikers' gate at park boundary

2.1 Upper Coalpits Wash

22 Scoggins Wash

A route up Scoggins Wash through low desert terrain

Distance: 5.3 miles (8.5 km) one way
Hiking time: About 2.5 hours
Best season: September–May
Difficulty: Moderate**
Water availability: None

Hazards: Extremely hot and dry during summer
Topo maps: Springdale West USGS; Zion National Park (Trails Illustrated)
Jurisdiction: Zion National Park. See Appendix A for more information.

Finding the trailhead: From the Zion Visitor Center, drive 7.3 miles west on UT 9 to a dirt pull-out on the north side of the road. Coalpits Wash and a road sign designating such are located to the west. Park your car and walk north along the dirt road to the hikers' gate at the park boundary. GPS: N37° 10' 14.10"/W113° 4' 52.62"

The Hike

This route travels through the painted desert of southwestern Zion National Park to the headwaters of Scoggins Wash. The trek begins at the southern park boundary and travels north up Coalpits and Scoggins Washes. Along the route hikers are rewarded with close views of Mount Kinesava, the Towers of the Virgin, and Cougar Mountain.

The first leg of the route follows Coalpits Wash upstream to its confluence with Scoggins Wash. From the hikers' gate a well-worn path travels through a pleasant cottonwood grove. The path soon emerges into scrub forest with banded cliffs of the Moenkopi Formation to the west. Follow the path along the east side of the wash to the confluence of the streamcourses. A large butte overlooks the confluence from the north, while the walls of the Chinle Bench encroach upon the east side of Scoggins Wash. Cougar Mountain rises in the distance to the north.

From the confluence the route runs northeast along the east side of Scoggins Wash. From here the route winds along the benches and dips down into the bed of the wash. Hikers may be able to pick up an intermittent pathway that follows Scoggins Wash.

About 1.1 miles up Scoggins Wash is the intersection with the Old Scoggins Stock Trail. The trail is marked by a small sign on the left (west) bank of the wash. Beyond this point hikers must travel mostly along the uneven rocky bottom of the wash and may find it necessary to scurry over boulders from time to time as they approach the headwaters of the drainage. In addition to boulders, you will encounter a dry waterfall. Bypass this by climbing up the left bank of the wash.

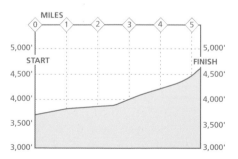

Scoggins Wash near the junction with the Chinle Trail

At this point the washbed gradually rises to meet the top of the mesa to the right (east). This is an indication that you are approaching the junction with the Chinle Trail. Once the cliffs on the left give way, views open up to reveal the Altar of Sacrifice, the West Temple, and Mount Kinesava to the northeast, and Cougar Mountain to the northwest. From here a contributing wash branches off to the left, while Scoggins Wash continues northeast. The Chinle Trail intersects Scoggins Wash just beyond this confluence.

Beyond the Chinle Trail another wash branches off to the right. Your route continues northeast up Scoggins Wash toward the Altar of Sacrifice. The wash bottom now holds cobblestones and sticky red clay. Vegetation in this area is consistent with the rest of the desert terrain: sagebrush, desert shrubs, and juniper. A few cattails grow along the watercourse.

The wash soon forks, with one branch heading southeast toward Mount Kinesava and the other heading northeast toward the Altar of Sacrifice. Follow the left fork toward the Altar of Sacrifice. Towering cliff walls rise on either side of the wash along this portion of the route; eastward views include the Sundial and the West Temple.

Eventually hikers will encounter two large boulders blocking the washbed. Bypass the boulders by climbing high onto the left bank. Beyond them the wash is rockier with considerably more boulders and gravel. About 0.3 mile northeast of the boulders, travelers encounter another bottleneck choked with large boulders. The slopes on either side are steep and unstable with loose rock and clay. Our route description ends here; travel beyond this point is not recommended.

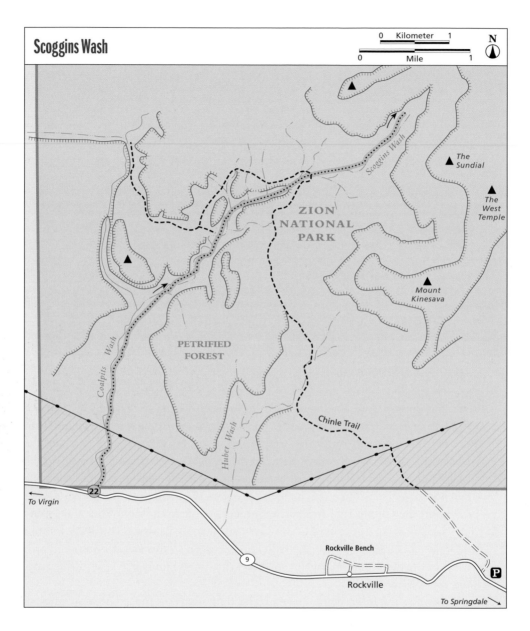

Scoggins Wash

0 Kilometer 1
0 Mile 1
N

ZION
NATIONAL
PARK

The Sundial

The West Temple

Mount Kinesava

PETRIFIED FOREST

Coalpits Wash

Huber Wash

Scoggins Wash

Chinle Trail

22

To Virgin

Rockville Bench

9

Rockville

P

To Springdale

Key Points

0.0 Hikers' gate

1.8 Confluence of Scoggins and Coalpits Washes. Bear right into Scoggins Wash.

2.9 Old Scoggins Stock Trail descends into the wash.

3.9 Chinle Trail crosses Scoggins Wash.

5.3 End of route

The Kolob Terrace

This broad region encompasses the high plateau to the west of Zion Canyon. Hiking routes are more primitive, and day-hiking opportunities are rather limited. The nearest town is Virgin, Utah, which offers limited services; Springdale is a better bet for finding hiking essentials. A primitive auto campground with six sites can be found atop Lava Point, and there is also a seasonally staffed fire lookout here. However, backpacking permits are not issued at Lava Point and must be obtained at the main Zion Visitor Center at the mouth of Zion Canyon. Snows typically close Kolob Terrace trails and routes between November and April.

The Cliffs of Mount Majestic tower above Behunin Canyon (hike 28).

23 Right Fork

A long, out-and-back day hike or short backpack up the canyon of the Right Fork to Barrier Falls

Distance: 11.8 miles (19 km) round-trip
Hiking time: About 6 hours
Best seasons: May–June, September–October
Difficulty: Moderately strenuous**
Water availability: The Right Fork carries a permanent flow of water.

Hazards: Flash flood danger in upper reaches
Recommended equipment: Wading staff
Topo maps: The Guardian Angels; Zion National Park (Trails Illustrated)
Jurisdiction: Zion National Park. See Appendix A for more information.

Finding the trailhead: From the town of Virgin, take the paved Kolob Reservoir Road for 6.5 miles to reach the park boundary. The trailhead is a small and nondescript parking area 0.4 mile beyond the park boundary. GPS: N37° 16' 15.36" / W113° 6' 11.98"

The Hike

This route offers a primitive backcountry experience in a rugged landscape of stark buttes and steep-walled canyons. The high points of the trip are the many picturesque waterfalls near the end of the hike. Walking is fairly easy in the lower reaches of the drainage, but it becomes quite challenging above Double Falls. Beyond this point expect lots of scrambling over piles of rock that have fallen from the sheer walls of the canyon. The hike ends at Barrier Falls, which has a slippery headwall that cannot be negotiated without mountaineering gear. A few hardy souls have been known to rappel down the upper reaches of the canyon from above, a feat that requires plenty of rope and a high level of climbing expertise.

From the trailhead follow a well-beaten path to the rim of the lava cliffs. The piñon-juniper scrub of the uplands is sprinkled with a diverse array of cacti, including the prickly pear, cholla, and hedgehog cactus. From the top of the cliffs, a steep and slippery path drops across unstable rock debris to reach the canyon floor. Make a mental note of the exact spot that this faint track reaches the wash—since it is poorly marked, it may be difficult to find on the return trip.

The route then follows North Creek upward, passing a whorled band of slickrock on its way to the confluence of the two forks of the stream, Left and Right. The pale summit of South Guardian Angel rises ahead, crowning a massif of reddish sandstone guarded by sheer cliffs.

Follow the Right Fork upward from the confluence as it passes between low walls of red sandstone. This first canyon opens into a broad valley surrounded by

Waterfall and rocky buttes near Trail Canyon ▶

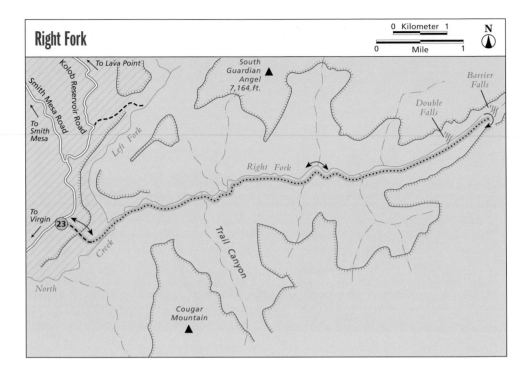

Right Fork

0 Kilometer 1

N

0 Mile 1

To Lava Point
Kolob Reservoir Road
Smith Mesa Road
To Smith Mesa
Left Fork
To Virgin
23
Creek
North
South Guardian Angel 7,164 ft.
Right Fork
Trail Canyon
Cougar Mountain
Double Falls
Barrier Falls

forbidding buttes. The dry wash of Trail Canyon enters from the south in the midst of this valley, and there are old corrals above its confluence with the Right Fork. Sandy trails cross the valley floor, bearing hikers through loose stands of cottonwood and past scattered yuccas.

After the valley constricts again, a side canyon enters from the left. Here the gravelly streambed is interrupted by low ledges of stone that create broad waterfalls on a miniature scale. The rugged buttes that surround the canyon rear their ragged summits to dizzying heights above the watercourse.

Following the stream upward, travelers soon reach a point where two streams of similar size converge at a confusing confluence. The left-hand drainage bears the main stem of the Right Fork, and hikers should follow it upward between low walls that form a partial roof above the water. A deep pool soon bars the way, and travelers must wade atop submerged ledges through knee-deep water to get through.

Above this point the stream flows across bare slickrock, with numerous ledges that form tiny stairstep cascades. Massive and unbroken walls of Navajo sandstone soar high above both sides of the canyon. Immense boulders have crashed down from the heights to litter the streamcourse; watch for one that has been fractured to allow passage through its center.

The walking is fairly easy from this point all the way to a double cascade known locally as Double Falls. Here, the water pours over two fascinating overhangs, and hikers may walk along the ledge behind the lower falls without getting wet. The path around this obstacle climbs the slope to the right (south) of the falls, a steep traverse through dense brush. Traveling becomes difficult beyond this slope because the streamcourse is choked with rockfalls throughout its remaining length. The next major obstacle is a chockstone falls, and the route again climbs the slopes to the right to avoid it.

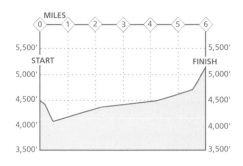

Travelers must negotiate several more picturesque cascades that pour skeins of glittering water into deep emerald pools. A north-facing cascade known as Barrier Falls marks the end of the hike, tucked into a natural amphitheater between towering cliffs. Hikers cannot progress safely beyond this point without climbing aids.

Key Points

0.0   Right Fork trailhead. A good trail runs eastward.

0.3   Edge of lava cliffs and start of steep descent

0.5   Floor of North Creek valley. Follow the creek upstream.

1.1   Confluence of Left and Right Forks of North Creek. Turn east up the Right Fork.

2.2   Trail Canyon enters large basin from the south.

4.3   Major confluence of canyons. Turn left to stay with the Right Fork.

5.5   Double Falls

5.9   Barrier Falls

24 Wildcat Canyon and Connector Trails

A high-country day hike or backpack from the Hop Valley trailhead to Lava Point

Distance: 8.7 miles (14 km) one way
Hiking time: About 4.5 hours
Best season: May–October
Difficulty: Moderate*

Water availability: A seep east of Pocket Mesa is intermittent; a spring in the lava talus of Wildcat Canyon is reliable.
Topo map: Zion National Park (Trails Illustrated)
Jurisdiction: Zion National Park. See Appendix A for more information.

Finding the trailhead: From the town of Virgin, follow Kolob Reservoir Road north for 13 miles and park at the Hop Valley trailhead. The trail passes the Wildcat Canyon trailhead near its midpoint and winds up at the Lava Point trailhead. GPS of start: N37° 20' 24.08" / W113° 6' 47.49"; GPS of finish: N37° 22' 49.97" / W113° 1' 20.61"

The Hike

This trail runs across the high country between the Hop Valley trailhead and Lava Point, linking the Hop Valley and West Rim Trails and providing access to several primitive canyon routes. The Northgate Peaks make a worthwhile side trip.

From the Hop Valley trailhead, hike north a dozen yards to reach a marked junction, then turn east as the Connector Trail follows an old roadbed up a shallow grade. As the trail crosses Kolob Reservoir Road, look north for views of the solitary needle of Red Butte, the massive walls of Gregory Butte and Timber Top Mountain in the distance, and some unusual rock formations capping the low ridge to the north. The two sparsely wooded hills that bracket the trail here are Spendlove Knoll (to the south) and Firepit Knoll (to the north). These are extinct cinder cones that hark back to the time when lava flows poured forth from cracks in the earth and turned this region into a smoking volcanic wasteland.

The trail crosses the road (watch for cairns on the far side) and enters the upper end of the Lee Valley. Here, isolated groves of Gambel oak sprinkle vast meadows of

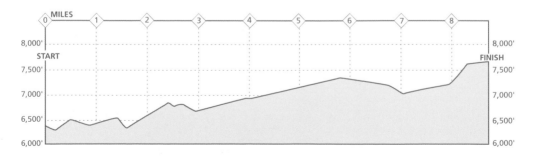

Jobs Head

grass and sagebrush. Views open up immediately to the east and south: Pine Valley Peak rises straight ahead, with the taller Northgate Peaks to the right of it. The top of North Guardian Angel protrudes above a ragged ridge of reddish stone, while the white sail of South Guardian Angel rises off the end of the red ridge. Looking down the Lee Valley, hikers can see the distant summits of the Altar of Sacrifice and West Temple presenting their blocky profiles. The jagged peak just to the right of them is Mount Kinesava.

The trail crosses a dirt road and wanders across the flats, following cedar posts where the path is faint. The red cliffs of Jobs Head soon appear to the north, rising from wooded slopes. To the east of them, an enormous alcove has been carved into a rounded hive of Navajo sandstone; cupped within the alcove is a pine-clad hillock.

The trail crosses several minor draws before reaching Pine Spring Wash. The bed of this major waterway is usually dry, revealing white cobbles of Navajo sandstone jumbled together with black boulders of volcanic basalt. The path begins to climb after crossing the wash, and it soon rounds a low ridge of wind-hewn hoodoos. It then makes its way up an incline of slickrock; hikers should navigate by the cairns in this area. Atop the grade the trail levels out and traverses the hillside to reach a saddle behind Pine Valley Peak. A clear view of North Guardian Angel now presents itself.

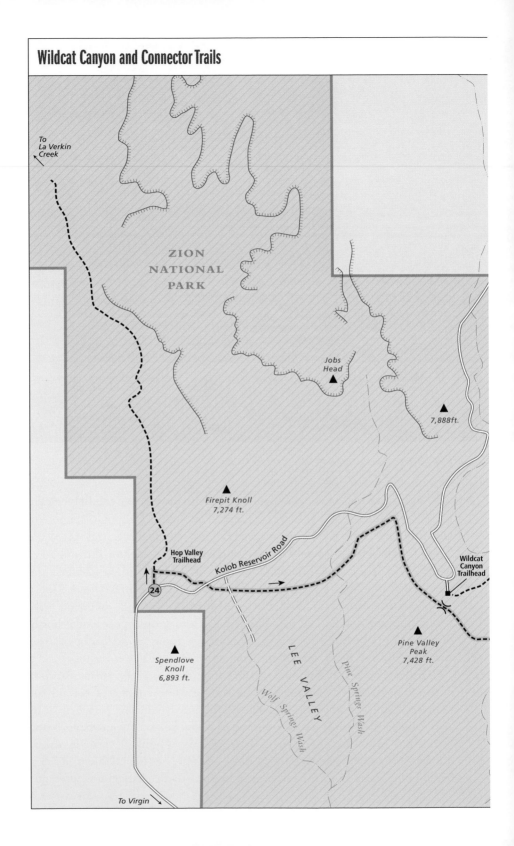

Wildcat Canyon and Connector Trails

To La Verkin Creek

ZION NATIONAL PARK

Jobs Head ▲

▲ 7,888 ft.

▲ Firepit Knoll
7,274 ft.

Hop Valley Trailhead

Kolob Reservoir Road

Wildcat Canyon Trailhead

24

▲ Spendlove Knoll
6,893 ft.

LEE VALLEY

Pine Springs Wash

Wolf Springs Wash

▲ Pine Valley Peak
7,428 ft.

To Virgin

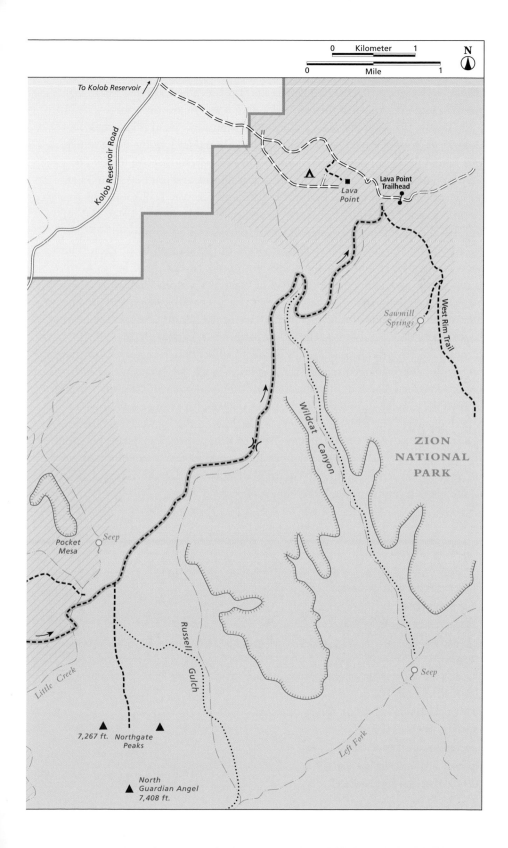

0   Kilometer   1

0   Mile   1

N

To Kolob Reservoir

Kolob Reservoir Road

Lava Point Trailhead

Lava Point

Sawmill Springs

West Rim Trail

Wildcat Canyon

ZION NATIONAL PARK

Pocket Mesa

Seep

Seep

Russell Gulch

Little Creek

Left Fork

7,267 ft.   Northgate Peaks

North Guardian Angel 7,408 ft.

True to its name, Pine Valley is filled with shady groves of ponderosa pine, interspersed with grassy swales. Near the Northgate Peaks Trail junction, the white cliffs of Pocket Mesa can be seen to the north. There is a pothole seep beneath the eastern wall of this mesa. To reach it turn left at the first trail junction and follow this path to a small, sandy wash. Follow the wash upstream and take the right fork when it branches. This branch follows the foot of Pocket Mesa on its eastern side and leads to the water source.

Hikers bound for Lava Point should continue straight ahead through the two trail junctions (the northward trail accesses the Wildcat trailhead, and just beyond it a spur runs southward to the Northgate Peaks). The Wildcat Canyon Trail soon embarks upon a gentle ascent through the forest. There are no views until the chalky cliffs of Russell Gulch appear through the trees. The trail follows this gulch upward.

Soon a break in the forest allows distant views of the monoliths of Zion. The gulch then curls eastward into a shallow, meadowy vale, and the trail bends north through the woods and enters the headwaters of Wildcat Canyon. Gambel oak, bigtooth maple, and quaking aspen clothe the upper reaches of the canyon and provide spectacular displays of color in mid-October. Views of the White Cliffs stretch away to the south, and a dark band of lava cliffs looms above the canyon's head.

The trail descends steadily as it rounds the head of Wildcat Canyon and on the way down passes a well-marked spring that gurgles through the lava talus beneath a thicket of bracken fern. The trail then drops across the main wash and steadily climbs the far wall of the canyon, finally rounding a point that offers parting views down the length of the drainage. The path then follows a side draw to the top of Horse Pasture Plateau. Just before meeting the West Rim Trail, the route passes an old grain drill left over from the pioneer days. Hikers can get good views of the Lava Point lookout from this spot. Upon reaching the West Rim Trail, turn left for the final 0.1-mile climb to the hike's terminus at the Lava Point trailhead.

Key Points

0.0	Hop Valley trailhead
0.1	Turn right on Connector Trail, which splits away to right at marked junction.
0.6	Trail crosses Kolob Reservoir Road.
1.6	Pine Spring Wash
2.8	Saddle behind Pine Valley Peak
4.0	Junction with Wildcat Canyon Trail and spur trail from Wildcat Canyon trailhead. Keep going straight ahead.
4.1	Junction with spur trail to Northgate Peaks. Continue straight ahead.
4.8	Trail reaches Russell Gulch.
6.0	Trail crosses divide into Wildcat Canyon watershed.
6.8	Spring in lava talus slope
7.2	Trail crosses the floor of Wildcat Canyon.
8.6	Junction with West Rim Trail. Turn left.
8.7	Hike ends at Lava Point trailhead.

25 Northgate Peaks

A short day hike to an overlook between the Northgate Peaks

Distance: 2.2 miles (3.5 km) one way
Hiking time: About 1 hour
Best season: May–October
Difficulty: Easy

Water availability: A seep east of Pocket Mesa is intermittent.
Topo map: Zion National Park (Trails Illustrated)
Jurisdiction: Zion National Park. See Appendix A for more information.

Finding the trailhead: From the town of Virgin, follow the paved Kolob Reservoir Road northward. The road crosses the boundary of Zion National Park three times on its way to the Wildcat Canyon trailhead at mile 16. The hike begins here. GPS: N37° 20' 28.16"/W113° 4' 31.69"

North Guardian Angel from the Northgate Peaks overlook

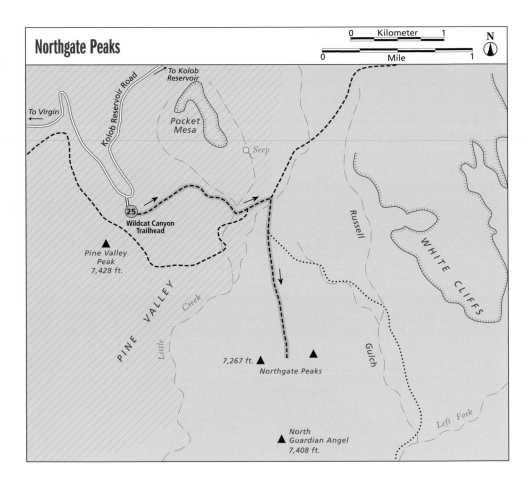

0   Kilometer   1

0   Mile   1

N

To Kolob
Reservoir

Kolob Reservoir Road

To Virgin

Pocket
Mesa

Seep

Russell

WHITE

CLIFFS

25

Wildcat Canyon
Trailhead

Pine Valley
Peak
7,428 ft.

PINE VALLEY

Creek

Little

7,267 ft.

Northgate Peaks

Gulch

Left Fork

North
Guardian Angel
7,408 ft.

The Hike

This trail offers an easy day trip with fine scenery, but it receives relatively little use because of its location in a remote corner of the park. The trek begins in the shadow of Pine Valley Peak, a lone pinnacle of bone-white Navajo sandstone. The path heads eastward across open sage meadows; soon a sprinkling of pines rises to either side. Upon approaching the compact mass of Pocket Mesa, the path veers southward and the pines coalesce into a gladed woodland.

In the midst of the savannah, the trail reaches a junction with the Wildcat Canyon and Connector Trails; turn left here. After an eastward jog of 0.1 mile, you'll see a signpost marking the

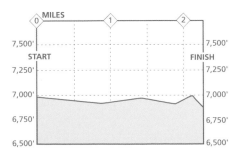

spot where the Northgate Peaks Trail breaks away to the south. Turn right and follow the path to the top of a rise, where a well-beaten spur splits to the left en route to an overlook of the white cliffs of Russell Gulch and onward into the canyon of the Left Fork. The main trail continues straight ahead, following the crest of a promontory that is cloaked in copses of pine and grassy meadows. This path runs out onto a lava outcrop presenting a spectacular view of the Northgate Peaks and North Guardian Angel.

Key Points

0.0 Wildcat Canyon trailhead
0.9 Junction with Wildcat Canyon and Connector Trails. Turn left.
1.0 Junction with Northgate Peaks Trail. Turn right (south).
2.2 Northgate Peaks overlook

26 Left Fork

A day hike following a wilderness self-rappel route down the Left Fork canyon and ending at Left Fork trailhead

---

Distance: 8.1 miles (13 km) overall
Hiking time: About 8 hours
Best seasons: May–July, September–October
Difficulty: Strenuous** (through hike); moderately strenuous* (lower reaches only)
Water availability: The Left Fork carries a permanent flow of water below the swimming obstacle; there is a reliable spring at the mouth of The Subway.

Hazards: Flash flood danger above The Subway
Recommended equipment: Wading staff; 50 feet of rope or tubular webbing is required to self-rappel over obstacles.
Topo maps: The Guardian Angels; Zion National Park (Trails Illustrated)
Jurisdiction: Zion National Park. See Appendix A for more information.

Finding the trailhead: The trek begins at the Wildcat Canyon trailhead. To get there follow Kolob Reservoir Road north from the town of Virgin for 8.1 miles. The trailhead is large and well marked. The hike ends at the Left Fork trailhead. GPS of start: N37° 20' 27.82"/W113° 4' 33.36; GPS of finish: N37° 16' 59.885"/W113° 5' 42.118"

The Hike

Following one of the most popular routes in Zion National Park, this hike penetrates the spectacular canyon of the Left Fork. The area receives so many visitors that the National Park Service has implemented a permit system for day hikers, much like the system that is currently in place for The Narrows. Visitors should use the online reservation system to secure permits for this very popular area. Features of the trip include The Subway, with its spectacular overhanging walls, and dinosaur tracks from the Jurassic Period along the Left Fork's lower reaches. Through hikers will need to bring rope to rappel down boulders, overhangs, and waterfalls that bar the way. The through hike takes a long day to complete, but day hikers may approach the route from below and penetrate as far upstream as The Subway (a distance of 3.4 miles) before obstacles make the canyon impassable.

Hiking down the slickrock along Russell Gulch

Begin the trek by following the Northgate Peaks routing: From the Wildcat Canyon trailhead, follow the trail to the first junction. Turn left onto the Wildcat Canyon Trail at the foot of Pocket Mesa, then take a quick right onto the Northgate Peaks spur. After a few yards on this trail, the pines open into a sage meadow. A well-beaten track veers away to the left. This track is the beginning of the Left Fork route, and it runs out onto slickrock above a small, wooded draw.

Contour southward on the slickrock, staying above the trees to reach a rather bare knoll. From here follow the sloping rock to the bottom of the draw. Looking down the draw, hikers can now see down into the sloping defile of Russell Gulch, with massive cliffs of Navajo sandstone rising beyond it. To the south Greatheart Mesa dominates the landscape.

Follow the slickrock along the southwest side of the draw, passing through another patch of pines and descending across more slickrock. A squat hoodoo soon rises above the watercourse. Cross the draw here and climb behind the hoodoo, then angle northeast across the sloping stone to reach the bottom of Russell Gulch.

Follow the main wash of Russell Gulch downstream. Gentle slopes of slickrock soon present themselves above the eastern side of the streamcourse. Angle upward across this shallow slope of rock to reach a saddle in the pinkish stone. The saddle is flanked to the right (east) by a rocky butte that is studded with numerous pines growing from a cleft in its face.

After passing through the saddle, the route descends through a great bowl of naked stone, where the cross-bedded sandstone forms great sweeping curves. At the bottom of the bowl, a beaten and sandy track leads toward a pine-clad butte marked "5750" on the topographic map. Hikers must negotiate a small ravine before climbing onto a level bench below the western face of this knob.

The path now leads through scattered ponderosa pines and copses of Gambel oak, finally reaching a lofty point that overlooks the confluence of Russell Gulch and the Left Fork. Both are deep gorges at this point, and the descent looks daunting from here. Follow a crude path that drops onto the Left Fork side and then winds around into the mouth of Russell Gulch, descending a steep couloir. The descent is extremely steep over sand and loose rocks—be careful. Avoid dislodging boulders onto fellow hikers, and use handholds to steady your descent. The path ultimately angles northward along the base of the cliffs, finally bottoming out below an over-hanging pour-off on the floor of Russell Gulch.

Walk to the mouth of the canyon and turn right to begin descending the Left Fork. The walking is easy at first, and stagnant pools are bypassed readily during dry weather. Great walls rise on both sides of the canyon, and a lush growth of box elder, bigtooth maple, and Douglas fir lines the watercourse.

After a few hundred yards, the first obstacle presents itself: The canyon is blocked by a rockfall of epic proportions. After negotiating a maze of fallen boulders, hikers will be presented with a 20-foot drop-off. You have two options for gaining passage around this obstacle. Hikers with climbing experience may attempt to chimney down the crevice to the right of the boulder, then drop into the sand below it. The other option is to self-rappel over its rounded face with the aid of a rope.

Below the rockfall lies a section of slickrock where the water has carved deep pot-holes. Most can be avoided entirely, but hikers face some shallow wading in this area. The canyon soon narrows into a corridor, heralding the second major obstacle of the hike. Here, two deep and frigid pools block the way. There is no way around them and the water is always cold: Be prepared to swim through the bone-numbing water. The first pool is a 30-foot swim; the second is 10 feet of swimming and a wade across a shallow but slippery underwater ledge. Hikers who time their trip to reach this spot in early afternoon may get the benefit of a few rays of sunshine to help them dry off and warm up.

A short distance below the swimming obstacle, springs emerge from the canyon floor and provide a constant flow of water down the streamcourse. Great rounded overhangs line the lower walls of the canyon at this point. Stay in the watercourse to minimize your impact.

As the trek continues downstream, expect waist-deep wading on the way to an obstacle known locally as Keyhole Falls. Here, soaring walls rise 500 feet as the can-yon narrows to a thin slit. The waterfall itself is a 6-foot pour-off over a vertical face that leads into a thigh-deep pool. Loop a rope through the convenient hole in the stone above and to the left (south) of the falls. It is a slippery descent, and travelers should approach it with extreme caution.

The Subway

Below the falls is an intricate gallery of whorled and fluted stone, with delicate holes and fretwork where the swirling waters have sculpted the bedrock. A fault in the stone has been deepened by the water into a frigid channel, and the route clings to a narrow ledge above this submerged rift.

As the canyon doglegs west, the gallery opens into the upper end of a curved tunnel known as The Subway, one of the truly outstanding natural features of Zion National Park. Here, rounded overhangs almost block out the sky, giving a subterranean feel to this water-carved passageway in the rock. At several spots travelers must venture onto roofed ledges to avoid impassable drop-offs. At one point it is necessary to self-rappel down from the ledges, using a bolt-and-chain setup on the left (south) wall of the canyon that has been emplaced for this purpose. This is the final obstacle requiring the use of a rope.

Below this point hikers can walk past aquamarine pools set into the stone of the canyon floor to reach the mouth of The Subway. A substantial spring gushes forth from the north side of the canyon.

The next segment of the trek passes picturesque cascades, which are overlooked by beveled walls streaked with iron and manganese compounds. As the canyon continues westward, the cascades become progressively smaller. The creek ultimately passes a pocket of sagebrush where a few gnarled cottonwoods grow. A steep ravine joins the

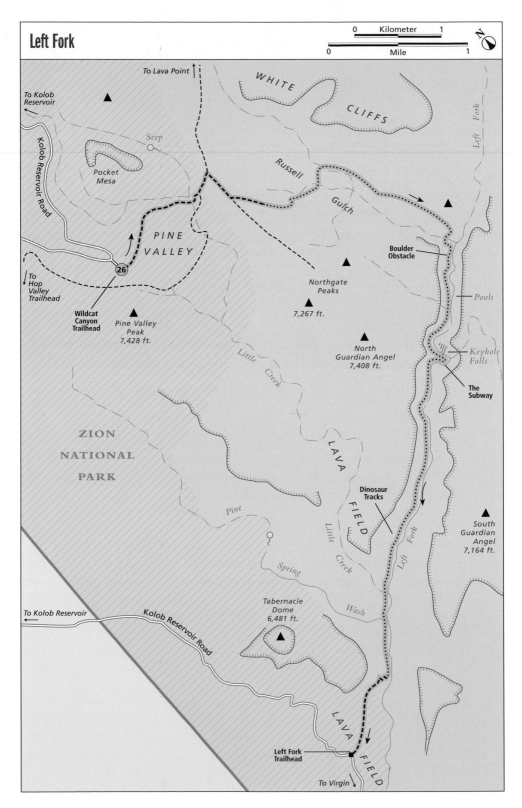

Left Fork

0 — Kilometer — 1

0 — Mile — 1

N

To Lava Point

WHITE CLIFFS

Left Fork

To Kolob Reservoir

Kolob Reservoir Road

Seep

Pocket Mesa

Russell

Gulch

Boulder Obstacle

PINE VALLEY

26

To Hop Valley Trailhead

Wildcat Canyon Trailhead

Pine Valley Peak 7,428 ft.

Northgate Peaks

7,267 ft.

Pools

North Guardian Angel 7,408 ft.

Keyhole Falls

The Subway

ZION

NATIONAL

PARK

Little Creek

LAVA

FIELD

Dinosaur Tracks

Little Creek

South Guardian Angel 7,164 ft.

Pine

Left Fork

Spring

Wash

To Kolob Reservoir

Kolob Reservoir Road

Tabernacle Dome 6,481 ft.

LAVA

FIELD

Left Fork Trailhead

To Virgin

canyon from the south near this point. Just beyond it several tilted slabs of pale gray mudstone are covered in dinosaur tracks. This stone is a fossilized lakebed from the Kayenta Formation, bearing tracks laid down by dinosaurs during the early Jurassic Period. According to experts at Dinosaur National Monument and the Smithsonian Institution, the tracks probably belonged to a bipedal carnivore of the genus Eubrontes.

At the dinosaur tracks look for a finger of lava cliffs above the north side of the canyon. After passing below these cliffs, the route crosses the mouth of the narrow ravine that bears Little Creek, which is often dry. Old cattle trails ascend to the Lee Valley from here; these are sometimes mistaken for the exit route. Stay in the canyon bottoms past the permanent flow of Pine Spring Wash. The eastern palisades of Tabernacle Dome rise above the west bank of Pine Spring Wash, and these cliffs have been eroded into twisted hoodoos and rocky crags. While passing below these cliffs of sedimentary stone, take notice of the tongue of lava that rises beyond them. The exit route follows the contact zone between these two bedrock types.

The route leaves the streamside at two well-beaten campsites and soon climbs across piñon-juniper slopes between the two rock formations. After ascending steeply to the base of the sandstone, the track traverses the cleft at the edge of the lava and climbs to the top of the lava cliffs. After some small-scale ups and downs, the path levels out on arid scrubland at the top of the plateau. There are fine parting views of the ragged cliffs to the south, as well as to the bald, red summit of Tabernacle Dome. The path ultimately crosses a bouldery wash and arrives at the Left Fork trailhead on Kolob Reservoir Road.

Key Points

- **0.0** Wildcat Canyon trailhead
- **0.9** Junction with Wildcat Canyon Trail. Turn left.
- **1.0** Junction with Northgate Peaks spur trail. Turn right.
- **1.3** Left Fork route splits away to the left and descends toward Russell Gulch.
- **2.4** Route reaches floor of Russell Gulch and then climbs onto slickrock to the east.
- **2.8** Route crests slickrock saddle.
- **3.6** Final descent into canyon at confluence of Russell Gulch and the Left Fork. Follow Left Fork downstream as the obstacle course begins.
- **4.5** Keyhole Falls; upper end of The Subway
- **4.7** Lower end of The Subway; end of difficult obstacles
- **6.4** Dinosaur tracks
- **6.6** Little Creek joins from the north.
- **6.9** Pine Springs Wash joins from the north.
- **7.2** Exit route leaves the wash and climbs away to the north.
- **7.5** Primitive trail reaches top of lava cliffs.
- **8.0** Trail crosses Grapevine Wash.
- **8.1** Hike ends at Left Fork trailhead.

27 Wildcat Canyon

A long day trip following a wilderness route down Wildcat Canyon

Distance: 4.7 miles (7.6 km) one way
Hiking time: About 2.5 hours
Best seasons: May–June, September–October
Difficulty: Moderately strenuous**
Water availability: Water appears in Wildcat Canyon at the foot of the lava talus slope; a seep near the head of the Left Fork is brackish and intermittent.
Topo maps: Kolob Reservoir, The Guardian Angels; Zion National Park (Trails Illustrated)
Jurisdiction: Zion National Park. See Appendix A for more information.

Finding the trailhead: The route begins at the Lava Point trailhead. From the town of Virgin, take the paved Kolob Reservoir Road northward. After a time the road climbs to the top of the Kolob Terrace and enters Zion National Park. It soon leaves the park for a while and then reenters it just before reaching the Hop Valley trailhead. Continue on the main road to a spur road that leads southward to Lava Point after an overall distance of 21 miles. Turn right on this road and follow it for 1 mile to a split in the road. In dry weather you can turn left and follow the rough dirt road another 1.3 miles to the Lava Point trailhead. In wet weather bear right at the junction and proceed to the Lava Point Campground, from which a connecting trail descends to the trailhead. GPS: N37° 22' 53.72" / W113° 1' 22.70"

The Hike

This route makes a challenging day trip across a stark and forbidding landscape dominated by the bone-white cliffs of the Navajo Formation. The hike is hot and dry during summer, with little water available along the way. Travelers are advised to carry more water than is really necessary. Climbers can use this route to access the upper reaches of the Right Fork canyon via a low pass to the west of Greatheart Mesa.

From the Lava Point trailhead, follow the West Rim Trail for 0.1 mile to its junction with the Wildcat Canyon Trail. Turn right onto this side trail, which drops from the top of the Horse Pasture Plateau into the sloping country that bears the headwaters of Wildcat Canyon. A long grade leads down to the canyon floor, where hikers following the Wildcat Canyon route should leave the trail and follow the wash downward through a thick tangle of aspens and brambles. This woodland offers brilliant displays of fall foliage in early October.

Expect slow going early in the trek, since the canyon floor is choked with fallen trees and lava boulders that have been washed down from surrounding slopes. The first outcrops of the alabaster-white Navajo sandstone soon appear on the left, and an extensive talus slope of broken lava pours down the opposite slope of the valley. Water flows freely beneath the lava boulders and sometimes surfaces in the streamcourse in this area.

Aspen gives way to Gambel oak and ponderosa pine as the streamcourse steepens its downward gradient. A box canyon with sheer walls soon joins the main canyon

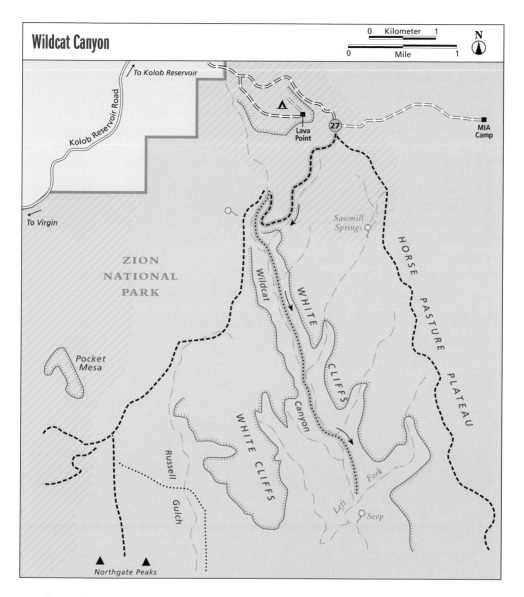

0   Kilometer   1

0   Mile   1

N

To Kolob Reservoir

Kolob Reservoir Road

To Virgin

Lava
Point

27

MIA
Camp

Sawmill
Springs

ZION
NATIONAL
PARK

Wildcat

WHITE

HORSE PASTURE PLATEAU

CLIFFS

Pocket
Mesa

WHITE CLIFFS

Canyon

Russell Gulch

Left Fork

Seep

Northgate Peaks

from the left (east). Traveling is considerably easier below this juncture. Bleached walls of sandstone now flank both sides of Wildcat Canyon, but these walls are often obscured by pines that cover the lower slopes. A second canyon enters from the east, and below it the runoff has carved a narrow gorge that is choked with impenetrable thickets of seep willow. For easiest traveling, climb across the slickrock to the right (west) to reach the sandy slopes above.

The cliffs on the western side of the canyon ultimately peter out, and the mouth of the third eastern canyon marks the spot where the route descends to cross the main wash. The route then climbs across the slopes to the east of the wash, passing through several minor saddles. Hikers can then descend to the headwaters of the Left

Fork, which offers a wilderness playground of slickrock knolls and potholed washes. South Guardian Angel is visible to the west, and Greatheart Mesa towers above a maze of slickrock country that stretches away to the south. Stagnant water may be found in the potholes of the Left Fork above its confluence with the wash of Wildcat Canyon; a more reliable seep lies just up the first southern tributary canyon below this confluence.

Key Points

- **0.0** Lava Point trailhead
- **0.1** Marked trail junction. Turn right onto Wildcat Canyon Trail.
- **1.5** Trail reaches the floor of Wildcat Canyon. Leave the trail and proceed down the streamcourse.
- **2.1** First side canyon enters from the east.
- **3.3** Route climbs onto slopes west of the wash.
- **4.0** Route descends to cross wash and then climbs onto the east slope.
- **4.7** Hike ends at confluence of Wildcat Canyon and the Left Fork.

28 West Rim

A long day hike or backpack along the top of the Horse Pasture Plateau from Lava Point to the floor of Zion Canyon

Distance: 14.2 miles (22.9 km) one way
Hiking time: About 7 hours
Best season: May–October
Difficulty: Moderately strenuous north to south; strenuous south to north
Water availability: Sawmill Spring, Potato Hollow Spring, and West Rim Spring are reliable.

Hazards: Some cliff exposure below West Rim Spring
Topo maps: Kolob Reservoir, The Guardian Angels, Temple of Sinawava; Zion National Park (Trails Illustrated)
Jurisdiction: Zion National Park. See Appendix A for more information.

Finding the trailhead: The route begins at the Lava Point trailhead. The West Rim Trail emerges at the Grotto trailhead, at mile 3.2 on Zion Canyon Road. GPS of start: N37° 22' 45.766"/W113° 1' 20.353"; GPS of finish: N37° 15' 28.592"/W112° 56' 58.601"

The Hike

This route is the most popular backpacking trail in Zion National Park, featuring easy access to remote country with striking vistas throughout the hike. Reservations for wilderness campsites are often completely booked, so book your campsite in advance. The trail follows the top of the Horse Pasture Plateau, often skirting close to the rims to reveal views of the canyons and monoliths to the west. Be especially careful to minimize your impact along this route so that future hikers can enjoy the ambience of untouched wilderness found here. Three springs provide a dependable supply of water along the way; remember to treat it before drinking. Camping is prohibited within 0.25 mile of these springs. An extensive wildfire burned the top of the Horse Pasture Plateau during the summer of 1996; the landscape now shows some recovery.

The trail begins by descending onto the level surface of the Horse Pasture Plateau, which extends like a long, level finger toward the heart of Zion Canyon.

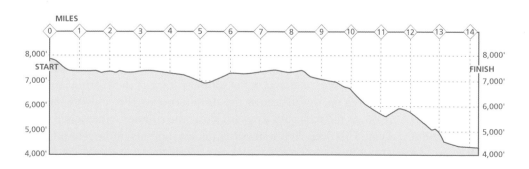

The path quickly passes a junction with the Wildcat Canyon Trail and makes its way to the eastern edge of the uplands. In the distance the land rises in great swells interrupted by sheer faces of gray shale and rosy limestone. After a mile of traveling, hikers will pass a short spur path that descends into the draw to the west to reach Sawmill Springs.

The main trail sticks to the top of the plateau, where numerous charred stumps and snags attest to frequent lightning strikes in the high country. The white cliffs that surround Goose Creek soon become visible below and to the east, but the dramatic views really begin as the trail glides up to a high overlook that faces west. From here hikers can look straight down the canyon of the Left Fork for a stunning view of South Guardian Angel. The fang-shaped crag to the right of it is North Guardian Angel, which reveals itself more fully as the trail continues southward.

The path soon drops from the crest of the plateau onto a narrow finger ridge to the east. This leads down into a gully that bears travelers down into the grassy meadows of Potato Hollow. Copses of trees limit views in this area as the trail follows this narrow valley to a spring that feeds an old stock tank. Many old aspens that once surrounded the spring have died off, but their offspring are thriving in the understory and will soon repopulate the area.

From here the trail turns south, climbing steadily to regain the ridgetops. It skirts the head of Sleepy Hollow and then climbs the final pitch to reach a junction with the Telephone Canyon Trail. A fire caused by lightning in 1980 opened up the forest in this area, allowing westward views of Greatheart Mesa.

The main trail continues its steady ascent along the spine of the ridge through a sparse growth of piñon pine, manzanita, and juniper. Early views take in the smooth white cliffs that line the headwaters of the Right Fork of North Creek. South Guardian Angel lifts its white sail above a maze of red rock farther west, and the even swell of the Pine Valley Range rises on the western horizon.

The trees fall away as the trail reaches the summit of the plateau, and astounding views stretch westward, changing in aspect as the path makes its way south. In the foreground the white upper layers of Navajo sandstone have been dissected into great monoliths by runoff and then sculpted by the wind into graceful domes and beehives. Looking down the Right Fork, you'll see how the iron-rich lower layers of the Navajo Formation have been deeply mortised as erosion works its craft along vertical fissures in the reddish stone. The Inclined Temple dominates the southern quadrant of the scene, rising above the barren wilderness of the Phantom Valley.

As the trail mounts a second high knoll, it enters a stand of tall ponderosa pines that herald a southeastward swing through the trees. The path seeks a shallow draw wooded in Gambel oak, following it down to the southern edge of the Horse Pasture Plateau. Here views stretch southward across the deeply incised rifts and towering pillars of Heaps Canyon. As the path runs eastward along the rimrock, views open up down Behunin Canyon. This deep cleft frames the distant summits of the Mountain of the Sun and the Twin Brothers. One can look out across the level tops of Mount

Looking westward at Inclined Temple and Ivins Mountain

Majestic and Cathedral Mountain, which are covered with a dense mat of manzanita that gives the appearance of a well-manicured lawn.

The trail then rounds the southern tip of the plateau and zigzags down from the caprock to the rim of the Navajo Formation, where it rejoins the Telephone Canyon Trail. A short spur descends northward to reach West Rim Spring, where a slow flow of water seeps from the ground to feed a pool choked with algae. The area around the spring was burned when an illegal campfire went out of control in 1992; it is now against park regulations to camp within 0.25 mile of the water source. Unusual trees such as the Arizona cypress, with its neatly corrugated bark, and the quaking aspen, with its ivory-colored hide, can be found around the spring.

The main trail now begins its descent, traversing a sheer wall of sandstone. Look northward for an unobstructed view of the mouth of Mystery Canyon, which is flanked by tall pillars that rise above The Narrows. The path soon works its way into the upper end of Behunin Canyon and then drops into the saddle at its head. From here it drops into the northern gulch and enters a lush woodland of spruce

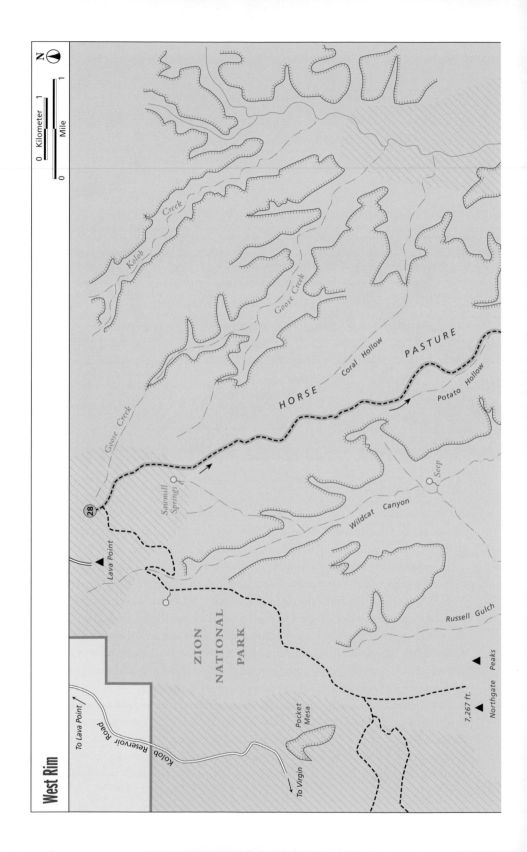

West Rim

ZION NATIONAL PARK

To Lava Point

Kolob Reservoir Road

To Virgin

Pocket Mesa

Lava Point

28

Sawmill Springs

Goose Creek

Goose Creek

Kolob Creek

HORSE

Coral Hollow

PASTURE

Potato Hollow

Seep

Wildcat Canyon

Russell Gulch

Northgate Peaks

7,267 ft.

0   Kilometer   1

0   Mile   1

N

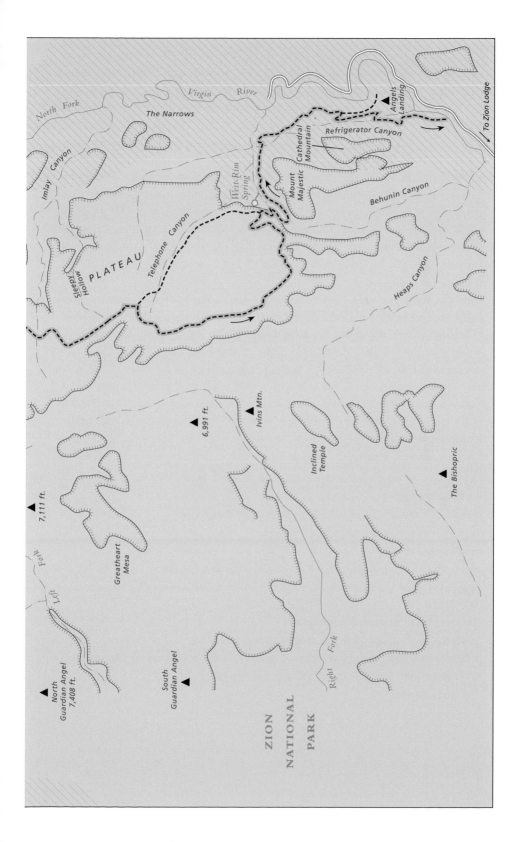

Virgin River

North Fork

The Narrows

Imlay Canyon

Sleepy Hollow

PLATEAU

Telephone Canyon

West-Rim Spring

Mount Majestic

Cathedral Mountain

Refrigerator Canyon

Angels Landing

To Zion Lodge

Behunin Canyon

Heaps Canyon

7,111 ft.

6,991 ft.

Ivins Mtn.

Inclined Temple

The Bishopric

Left Fork

Greatheart Mesa

North Guardian Angel 7,408 ft.

South Guardian Angel

Right Fork

ZION NATIONAL PARK

and Douglas fir underlain by bigtooth maple and Gambel oak. These trees are rarely found at such low elevations in this part of Utah. The presence of this plant community can be explained by the fact that the northern aspect of the gulch provides plenty of shade—the plants experience less evaporation here than they would in surrounding areas.

The trail continues a steady descent as it swings around the base of Mount Majestic's northern bulwark. It bottoms out at a bridge over a side canyon and then begins a steady climb. To the north the valley floor is carved from windblown rock and a sparse collection of pines grows from chinks in the mounds of stone. As the path nears the top of the grade, it brings a fine view north to the Mountain of Mystery. A sandy pitch leads over the top, and the north buttress of Cathedral Mountain rears its wind-scoured cliffs to the south. To the east the Great White Throne and Red Arch Mountain rise prominently along the far wall of Zion Canyon, while Angels Landing juts from the near wall.

Finding the route becomes a bit tricky as the trail follows a series of cairns over naked bedrock. The route roughly follows the ridgetop as it descends to the base of Angels Landing, where it reaches a trail junction at Scout Overlook. Turn right to reach the trailhead as the path drops into the head of Refrigerator Canyon. A series of narrow switchbacks called Walter's Wiggles bears travelers to the floor of the narrow cleft, where the grade levels off. Firs and maples grow in the cool depths of the canyon. At the mouth of the cleft, the path drops rather sharply to the floor of Zion Canyon. It then follows the Virgin River southward to reach a bridge that leads to the Grotto trailhead, which marks the end of the hike.

Key Points

0.0 Lava Point trailhead

0.1 Junction with Wildcat Canyon Trail. Keep going straight ahead.

1.0 Spur trail descends westward to Sawmill Springs.

5.2 Potato Hollow Spring

6.8 Junction with Telephone Canyon cutoff trail. Bear right for West Rim Trail.

9.8 Telephone Canyon Trail rejoins West Rim Trail at West Rim Spring. Turn right for descent into Zion Canyon.

10.3 Trail reaches saddle above Behunin Canyon.

11.2 Footbridge over nameless draw; no camping south of this point

12.4 Junction with Angels Landing Trail at Scout Overlook. Turn right to continue the descent.

14.1 Junction with West Bank Trail. Cross footbridge over Virgin River.

14.2 The Grotto trailhead

29 Hop Valley

A backpack from Kolob Reservoir Road through the Hop Valley to La Verkin Creek

Distance: 6.7 miles (10.8 km) one way
Hiking time: About 3.5 hours
Best seasons: March–May, September–November
Difficulty: Moderate* south to north; moderately strenuous* north to south
Water availability: Water in the Hop Valley flows permanently but is contaminated by

livestock; La Verkin Creek flows permanently; Beatty Spring is reliable.
Recommended equipment: Gaiters
Topo map: Zion National Park (Trails Illustrated)
Jurisdiction: Zion National Park. See Appendix A for more information.

Finding the trailhead: From the town of Virgin, follow Kolob Reservoir Road north for 13 miles, crossing the Zion National Park boundary three times, to reach the well-marked Hop Valley trailhead. GPS: N37° 20' 24.08"/W113° 6' 47.49"

The Hike

This trail begins in the sage flat atop the Kolob Terrace and then descends through the narrow dale of the Hop Valley before dropping to the banks of La Verkin Creek. The trail is hot and dusty in the summer, with lots of deep sand along the upper portions of the route that will make gaiters a welcome complement to your footwear. The trail crosses a large parcel of private land encompassing most of the Hop Valley. This valley is grazed by cattle each year, and water that flows through it may be contaminated by cattle droppings. A better source of drinking water (although it still must be purified) is Beatty Spring, which lies a few hundred yards west of the trail's junction with the La Verkin Creek Trail.

The path begins by heading northeast across rolling sage flats interspersed with widely scattered copses of Gambel oak. Although the route is level here, deep sand makes the hiking rather toilsome in places. When the trail gets faint, follow the fence posts that have been planted along the route. The lone pinnacle of Red Butte rises

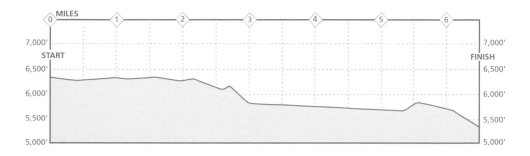

Sheer walls above the lower end of the Hop Valley

to the west, while an escarpment of reddish cliffs rises above the eastern edge of the flats. Atop the escarpment a thin layer of black basalt originated as a lava flow less than fifteen million years ago. The rounded summit at the south end of the rise is Firepit Knoll, an old cinder cone. Ahead, the red mesas above La Verkin Creek crowd the horizon.

After 1.5 miles the trail enters a private inholding where cattle graze throughout the snow-free season. Close the gate to make sure that livestock don't escape into the park, and follow the jeep trail eastward toward the cliff escarpment. It soon drops into a hollow and crosses a watercourse. (The old road has been washed out here, requiring a short detour.) Just beyond this point the track splits. Stay with the right-hand track, which follows the spine of a finger ridge as it descends to the head of the Hop Valley. It makes a steady descent across loose gravel, and cliffs to the east tower above the track. Erosion has dissected the walls into banded pillars that look like the ramparts of a Byzantine palace. A low wall rises to the west as well, hemming in the narrow bottomlands.

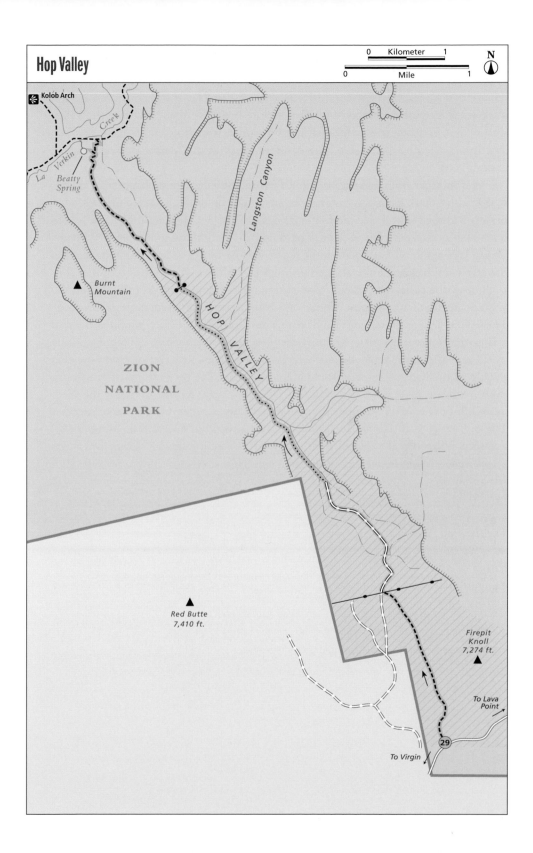

Hop Valley

0   Kilometer   1

0   Mile   1

N

Kolob Arch

La Verkin Creek

Beatty Spring

Langston Canyon

Burnt Mountain

HOP VALLEY

ZION

NATIONAL

PARK

Red Butte
7,410 ft.

Firepit
Knoll
7,274 ft.

To Lava
Point

29

To Virgin

As the jeep trail reaches the valley floor, it peters out. Follow one of the many livestock trails that track the watercourse down the valley. Seeps and springs contribute a slow trickle of water to form a small creek; it is contaminated by the livestock and must be properly purified before use. The grassy floor of the valley spreads out between sheer cliff walls, and a nameless canyon enters from the east. The broad opening of the side canyon offers views of the remote high country of Langston Mountain.

After another mile a blocky monolith marks the entrance to Langston Canyon, which also enters from the east bearing a trickle of water. Half a mile below its mouth, a barbed-wire fence marks the far edge of the private inholding. Climb onto the bench to the east of the wash to find the hikers' gate through the fence. By comparing vegetation on both sides of the fence, visitors will get a striking impression of the effects of livestock on streamside plant communities.

The trail leads across a sandy, pine-covered bench and then drops back into the wash. It emerges at a signpost on the west bank, several hundred yards downstream. The water disappears into the sand in this area and flows underground to form a spring that emerges near La Verkin Creek. Meanwhile the trail climbs vigorously over the shoulder of a hill and then drops over a stairstep series of sandy benches thickly clothed with Gambel oak and ponderosa pine. The path ultimately reaches an overlook point high above the floor of La Verkin Creek. Across the valley the sheer monolith of Gregory Butte appears quite narrow when viewed from this perspective. The bulkier cliffs of Timber Top Mountain rise beyond it. The trail then undertakes a workmanlike descent toward the canyon floor, meeting the La Verkin and Willis Creek Trails about 100 feet above the streamcourse.

Key Points

- **0.0** Hop Valley trailhead
- **0.1** Wildcat Canyon Trail splits away to the right. Keep going straight.
- **1.5** Trail enters private inholding. Pass through gate and follow jeep track to the right (east).
- **3.0** Jeep track ends on the floor of the Hop Valley. Follow the streamcourse downward.
- **4.4** Langston Canyon enters from the east.
- **5.0** Trail leaves private inholding through hikers' gate on east bank.
- **5.2** Final streamcourse crossing and climb onto the slopes to the west
- **6.7** Junction with La Verkin Creek and Willis Creek Trails

The Finger Canyons of the Kolob

The short but striking Kolob Finger Canyons lie within the northwestern corner of Zion National Park. Soaring faces of Navajo sandstone rise to jagged points above the finger canyons, tinted in hues of orange and salmon. Trails in this area are predominantly short ones, although the canyon of La Verkin Creek penetrates deep into the Kolob Terrace and offers access to more remote backcountry. Easy access from I-15 makes this part of Zion National Park very popular, especially on weekends. Strict regulations govern backcountry camping here—camping is not allowed in the finger canyons of Taylor Creek, and camping along La Verkin Creek is restricted to a few designated sites that must be individually reserved. Staff at the visitor center at the beginning of the Kolob Canyons Road issue wilderness permits. There are no auto campgrounds in this area, and the nearby town of New Harmony offers only limited services.

Cliffs above La Verkin Creek (hike 30)

30 La Verkin Creek

A short backpack up La Verkin Creek and an optional spur trail to Kolob Arch

Distance: 6.9 miles (11.1 km) one way
Hiking time: About 3.5 hours
Best season: March–November
Difficulty: Moderate west to east; moderately strenuous east to west

Water availability: La Verkin Creek flows permanently; Beatty Spring is reliable.
Topo maps: Kolob Arch; Zion National Park (Trails Illustrated)
Jurisdiction: Zion National Park. See Appendix A for more information.

Finding the trailhead: Follow I-15 northward and exit at the Kolob Canyons turnoff. Follow the road past the visitor center for 3.5 miles to the Lee Pass trailhead. GPS: N37° 27' 2.154" / W113° 11' 24.445"

The Hike

This is the only trail suitable for backpacking in the Kolob Canyons area, and it provides access to Willis Creek and the Hop Valley for more extended journeys. The trail is immensely popular and is often crowded on weekends. A special permit system is in effect for camping along La Verkin Creek, and designated campsites will be assigned by the ranger who issues your wilderness permit. Permits can be obtained at the Kolob Canyons Visitor Center. An optional short side trip from La Verkin Creek leads to Kolob Arch, one of the few freestanding arches in Zion National Park.

The trail begins in the arid foothills, soon descending a finger ridge into the Timber Creek valley. A scrub forest of piñon pine and juniper allows frequent views of the towers that guard the western rim of the Kolob Terrace. Beatty Point and Nagunt Mesa rear their jagged pinnacles skyward to the east, while to the south the broad profile of Timber Top Mountain ends at the sharp spire of Shuntavi Butte. At the bottom of the grade, the trail strikes the wash of Timber Creek and follows it through riparian meadows studded with old cottonwoods and box elders. Excellent views of the spires appear to the east, and numerous side canyons wind westward from the pinnacles, inviting further exploration.

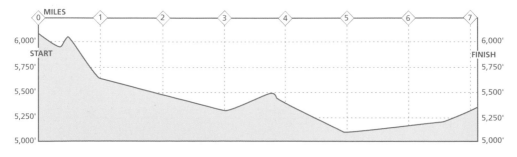

Kolob Arch

The path ultimately rounds the foot of Shuntavi Butte and ascends through arid scrubland to a low saddle. Here, new views open up to the east and south. Beyond the valley of La Verkin Creek, stone pillars rise like broken teeth from the upper slopes of Neagle Ridge. Behind this ridge are the massive walls of Burnt Mountain, while Red Butte sends its lone pinnacle toward the heavens to the south. The trail now begins a substantial descent to reach the floor of the La Verkin Creek valley. "La Verkin" is a corruption of the Spanish *La Virgen,* a mistaken reference to the Virgin River. The trail bottoms out near the remains of an old corral built by Mormon pioneers. A short side trip follows the stream downward to a series of waterfalls, where the creek pours over successive sills of resistant bedrock.

The trail now follows the north bank of La Verkin Creek into the mountains, as peaks rise on both sides of the valley. The great south wall of Gregory Butte rears its rugged countenance to the north, while across the valley a massive, streaked overhang connects Burnt Mountain with Neagle Ridge. Expect lots of sandy traveling as the path traverses grassy meadows studded with water-loving hardwoods. Ponderosa pine becomes prevalent as the trail approaches a junction with the Kolob

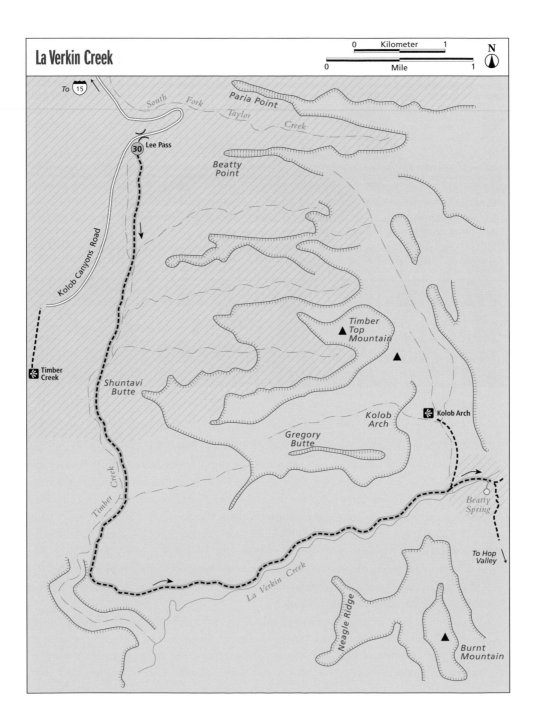

La Verkin Creek

0   Kilometer   1

0   Mile   1

N

To (15)

South   Fork

Taylor   Creek

Paria Point

(30) Lee Pass

Beatty
Point

Kolob Canyons Road

Timber Top
Mountain

Timber
Creek

Shuntavi
Butte

Kolob
Arch

Kolob Arch

Gregory
Butte

Timber Creek

Beatty
Spring

To Hop
Valley

La Verkin Creek

Neagle Ridge

Burnt
Mountain

Arch spur trail. There is a vigorous climb to cross a spring-fed rill just before this well-marked junction.

Beyond the junction the La Verkin Creek Trail continues eastward and soon fords the main creek. On the far bank Beatty Spring pours forth a reliable flow of clear water from the midst of the rocks. The trail then climbs a short pitch to a junction with the Hop Valley Trail; beyond this point the route becomes the Willis Creek Trail.

Key Points

0.0 Lee Pass trailhead

0.9 Floor of Timber Creek valley

3.8 Trail crosses low saddle to La Verkin Creek drainage.

4.9 Trail reaches La Verkin Creek just above waterfalls.

6.6 Junction with spur trail to Kolob Arch (*Option,* see below: 0.5 mile, moderate). Continue straight ahead for Hop Valley and Willis Creek Trails.

6.7 Trail crosses La Verkin Creek at Beatty Spring.

6.9 Junction with Hop Valley and Willis Creek Trails.

Kolob Arch Option

This short trail follows a side canyon northward from La Verkin Creek to a viewpoint below Kolob Arch. Although the route follows the streambed, there are many steep ups and downs with some tricky footing over broken rock. The path reaches the viewpoint after 0.5 mile, and a sign serves notice that the National Park Service does not recommend travel beyond this point. Hikers who climb higher for a better view of Kolob Arch should take pains to avoid damaging vegetation and hastening erosion. Kolob Arch graces the eastern buttress of Gregory Butte. This freestanding arc of stone measures more than 330 feet in width and is among the largest natural arches in the world.

31 Willis Creek

An extended trip from La Verkin Creek up the Willis Creek canyon with an option to Beartrap Falls

Distance: 4.5 miles (7.2 km) one way
Hiking time: About 2.5 hours
Best season: March–November
Difficulty: Moderate*
Water availability: La Verkin Creek, Willis Creek, and Beartrap Canyon have permanent flows of water.

Hazards: Flash flood danger
Topo maps: Kolob Arch, Kolob Reservoir; Zion National Park (Trails Illustrated)
Jurisdiction: Zion National Park. See Appendix A for more information.

Finding the trailhead: Hike 6.7 miles up the La Verkin Creek Trail or 6.7 miles down the Hop Valley Trail to reach the Willis Creek route beginning at a signpost. GPS: N37° 25' 0.45" / W113° 8' 46.90"

The Hike

This trail ascends the upper reaches of La Verkin Creek and then passes through the narrow canyon of Willis Creek to reach the park boundary. A traditional access route runs from there to Kolob Reservoir through wooded country, but public access to this route has been closed by the Spilsbury family, which owns some of the land that it crosses. Access to this route occasionally is granted to travelers who obtain written permission from these landowners. For most hikers the Willis Creek Trail offers an interesting side trip from the La Verkin Creek valley, featuring slot canyons that capture all the grandeur of The Narrows without the treacherous wading. There are a number of fords across La Verkin Creek, but all of these are shallow, with a current hardly sufficient to pose a problem.

From the junction below Hop Valley, the trail follows the canyon of La Verkin Creek eastward. A short descent leads to the spot where a spring pours forth the waters of the Hop Valley amid a jumble of enormous boulders. This north-facing slope is forested by a rich variety of hardwoods; the southern exposure just across the valley supports only juniper and desert scrub. To the east are fine views of Gregory Butte. The path soon descends and makes the first of many stream crossings as a sheer wall of stone rises skyward to the south. It creates enough shade to permit hardwoods to grow on both sides of the valley from this point on.

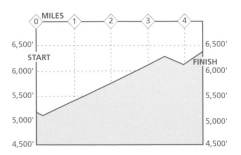

Castellated walls above La Verkin Creek

After 1.3 miles Herbs Point crowds the streamcourse from the north, heralding the beginning of a spectacular section of narrows. This stretch of canyon with thousand-foot vertical walls is reminiscent of The Narrows, without the treacherous river fords. Safe camping spots, which are plentiful to the west, become scarce beyond this point.

Beartrap Canyon is the first major cleft that enters from the south. (**Option:** A side trip of 0.3 mile, featuring easy walking between confined walls, leads to Beartrap Falls. Here, amid a hanging garden of bright green foliage, a graceful arc of water shoots out over a 12-foot drop-off into a quiet pool.)

The main trail continues up La Verkin Creek and, after a nameless canyon enters from the north, reaches elevated benches where backpackers can camp safely. A short distance beyond this point, a massive ziggurat of stone rises above the confluence of La Verkin and Willis Creeks. The trail turns east up Willis Creek, which is the smaller of the two. It rises and falls as it sticks to the slopes above a watercourse that is generally dry. The trail settles into a gradual ascent as it enters a woodland of bigtooth maple, topped by full-grown Douglas fir. An enormous wall of stone rises sheer on the north side of the canyon, planed straight as if it was sculpted by an architect.

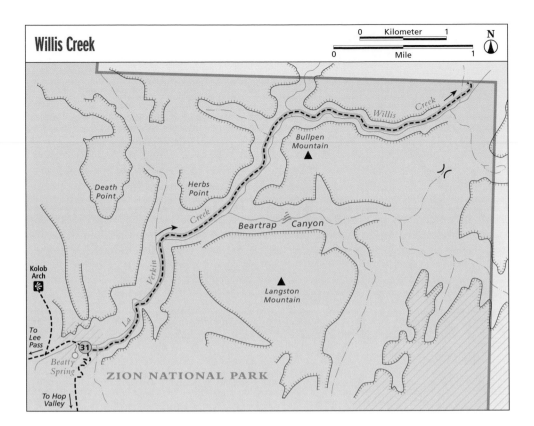

Willis Creek

Rising to the south is a cliff that is contorted into fascinating irregularities, with knobs, overhangs, and alcoves streaked with desert varnish.

Somewhere in the middle reaches of the canyon, free-flowing water appears in the streamcourse. It accompanies the visitor for the remainder of the hike. The walls sink down as the creek approaches its headwaters, where an assortment of washes and draws converge in a sunny, pine-clad basin. The trail passes straight through the basin and then makes a vigorous ascent to an arid hilltop that overlooks the surrounding country. A gate marks the boundary of Zion National Park, and special written permission is required to proceed farther across lands of the Spilsbury Ranch.

Key Points

0.0 Junction with Hop Valley and La Verkin Creek Trails. Follow the trail eastward along La Verkin Creek.

1.9 Beartrap Canyon enters from the east (*Option:* 0.3 mile to falls, easy).

2.7 Confluence of La Verkin and Willis Creeks. Follow primitive trail up Willis Creek.

4.3 Canyon opens into a wide basin.

4.5 Public access ends as trail crosses onto private lands.

32 Middle Fork of Taylor Creek

A trail along the Middle Fork of Taylor Creek, ending at Double Arch Alcove

Distance: 2.5 miles (4 km) one way
Hiking time: About 1 hour
Best season: March–November
Difficulty: Easy
Water availability: Reliable

Topo maps: Kolob Arch; Zion National Park
(Trails Illustrated)
Jurisdiction: Zion National Park. See Appendix
A for more information.

Finding the trailhead: Follow I-15 to the Kolob Canyons Visitor Center. From the visitor center drive 2 miles east along the park road to a parking area on the left (north) side of the road. Look for the trailhead sign on the east side of the parking lot. GPS: N37° 27' 44.56"/W113° 11' 50.65"

The Hike

This easy trail takes hikers up the canyon of the Middle Fork of Taylor Creek to two historic homestead cabins and Double Arch Alcove. An alcove is a "blind" arch formed in a rock face through which there are no gaps for daylight to pass. In addition to Double Arch Alcove, hikers are rewarded with spectacular views of Tucupit Point and Paria Point as they approach the canyon. The creek bed is fairly narrow, so be prepared to get wet at numerous stream crossings.

The trail begins from a sign at the east end of the parking lot. The path immediately descends a set of wooden steps down to the creek bed. The vegetation bordering the creek consists of manzanita, sagebrush, juniper, ponderosa pine, and piñon pine. From the bottom of the staircase, the path turns right and heads upstream toward the mouth of the canyon, with views of Horse Ranch Mountain off to the left (northeast). Portions of the trail are sandy and may offer difficult traveling after rains.

The path is easy to follow as it crisscrosses the watercourse several times. Beyond the sixth crossing hikers may confuse the path with other social trails in the area. The main trail departs from the north bank of the stream, crosses a small island and then picks up again on the south bank. As streamside benches begin to narrow, travel along the trail becomes a bit more difficult. The trail climbs up and out of the stream bottoms several times.

After a mile the trail reaches the confluence of the North and Middle Forks. Look for a trail sign and the Larson homestead cabin in this area. Gustav

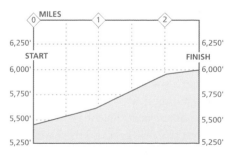

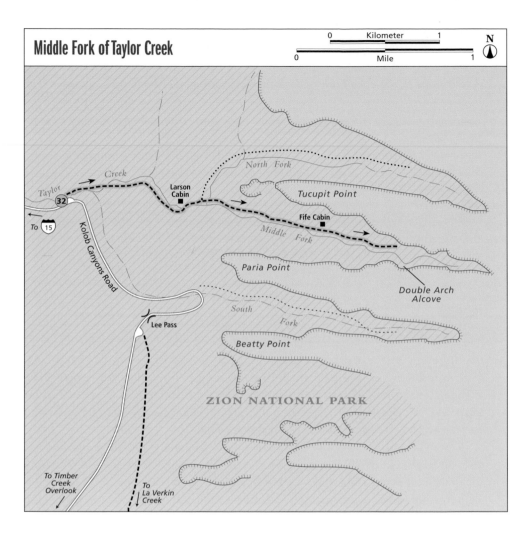

Kilometer

Mile

N

North Fork

Creek

Taylor

32

To 15

Kolob Canyons Road

Larson
Cabin

Tucupit Point

Fife Cabin

Middle   Fork

Paria Point

Double Arch
Alcove

South

Fork

Lee Pass

Beatty Point

ZION NATIONAL PARK

To Timber
Creek
Overlook

To
La Verkin
Creek

Larson built the cabin in 1930 from white fir logs hauled in by wagon from Cedar City. He spent summers here from 1930 to 1933, homesteading the Kolob area and raising pigs.

Beyond the cabin the trail crosses the North Fork and ascends into the canyon between Tucupit and Paria Points. Once inside the canyon, the trail stays low along the creek bed. A second homestead cabin can be found about three-quarters of the way up the canyon on a bench above the north bank of the creek. Arthur Fife built this cabin from white fir logs in 1930. Fife was a teacher at Southern Utah State College, now Southern Utah University. When not teaching, he spent his time at the cabin raising goats.

As hikers near the end of the trail, the path climbs onto the south bench to bypass a fallen tree lying in the creek bed. The trail ends at Double Arch Alcove, with its spectacular streaked overhang that encloses a shady pocket.

Easy traveling along the trail beside Taylor Creek

Key Points

0.0 Trailhead

1.0 Confluence of North and Middle Forks of Taylor Creek

2.5 Trail ends at Double Arch Alcove.

33 North Fork of Taylor Creek

An unmaintained path that takes the hiker up the North Fork of Taylor Creek

Distance: 2.4 miles (3.9 km) one way
Hiking time: About 1.5 hours
Best season: March–November
Difficulty: Moderate*
Water availability: Seasonal

Topo maps: Kolob Arch; Zion National Park
(Trails Illustrated)
Jurisdiction: Zion National Park. See Appendix
A for more information.

Finding the trailhead: Follow I-15 to the Kolob Canyons Visitor Center, then drive 2 miles east along the park road to a parking area on the left (north) side of the road. Look for the Middle Fork of Taylor Creek trailhead sign on the east side of the parking lot. Follow the trail until it reaches the North Fork, where this hike branches off to the north and east. GPS: N37° 27' 44.56" / W113° 11' 50.65"

The Hike

This route follows an unofficial path up the North Fork of Taylor Creek into the canyon between Horse Ranch Mountain and Tucupit Point. To reach the North Fork, follow the Middle Fork Trail from its start at the east end of the parking lot. The path immediately descends a set of wooden steps down to the creek bed. From the bottom of the staircase, the path turns right and heads upstream toward the mouth of the canyon. Portions of the trail are sandy and may offer difficult traveling after rains. The path is easy to follow as it crisscrosses the watercourse several times. Beyond the sixth crossing hikers may confuse the path with other social trails in the area. The main trail departs from the north bank of the stream, crosses a small island, then picks up again on the south bank. As streamside benches begin to narrow, travel along the trail becomes a bit more difficult. The trail climbs up and out of the stream bottoms several times.

After a mile the trail reaches the confluence of the North and Middle Forks. A well-worn path leaves the confluence and follows the North Fork upstream around the north side of Tucupit Point.

As the track departs from the Middle Fork Trail, views of Horse Ranch Mountain reveal themselves to the northeast. The sheer orange walls of Tucupit Point soon form a wall to the south of the creek, and the path turns eastward, heading upstream into the canyon. The

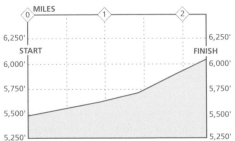

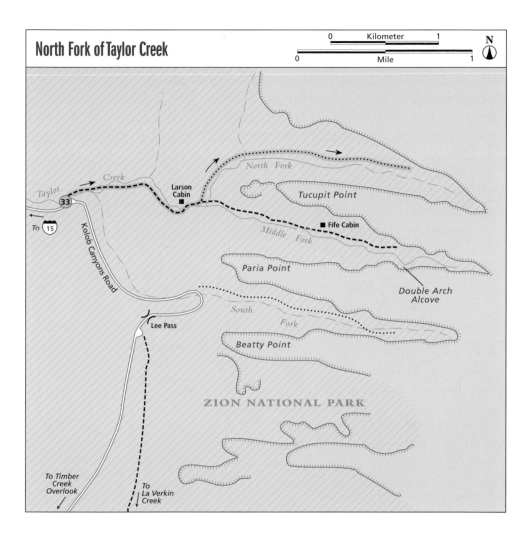

North Fork creek bed is narrow and densely vegetated here. The path avoids most of the heavy brush by staying out of the creek bed and traversing the benches above the stream. The path is often obscured by pine needles, sagebrush, and horsetails along this stretch. The dominant woody plants include piñon pine, ponderosa pine, Douglas fir, and manzanita.

About halfway up the canyon, the vegetation opens up and the path disappears onto a slope strewn with boulders, lava rock, and Gambel oak. Angle your way downslope over the boulders and through the brush until you reach the creek bed. From here the streamcourse is less brushy and is easier to follow. Side paths leave the streamcourse to shortcut the various meanderings of the creek.

As the route progresses upstream, hikers must scurry over large boulders strewn about the streambed and/or bypass them by climbing up the steep banks. At the end of the route, a 20-foot obstacle blocks passage along the creek bed where sheer walls form the south bank of the creek. This obstacle may be bypassed by backtracking and climbing onto the left (north) bench. However, we do not recommend it. To do so involves scurrying over sloping rocks that overhang the creek bed by about 20 feet. Peppered with loose stones and vegetation, these rocks provide unreliable traction and pose a serious safety hazard.

Key Points

0.0 Middle Fork trailhead

1.0 North Fork confluence

2.4 End of route

34 South Fork of Taylor Creek

A route into the canyon between Paria Point and Beatty Point

Distance: 1 mile (1.6 km) one way
Hiking time: About 0.5 hour
Best season: March–November
Difficulty: Moderate*
Water availability: None

Topo maps: Kolob Arch; Zion National Park
(Trails Illustrated)
Jurisdiction: Zion National Park. See Appendix
A for more information.

Finding the trailhead: Drive north on I-15 to the Kolob Canyons Visitor Center. From the visitor center drive 3.1 miles east on the park road to a parking lot on the right. From the parking area walk east about 50 feet to the outside curve (east side) of the turn in the road. An unmarked path slopes down toward the canyon. GPS: N37° 27' 18.94"/W113° 11' 8.42"

The Hike

This route follows an unofficial trail up the South Fork of Taylor Creek. It was created by a former park ranger who frequented this canyon because of its rock-climbing potential. The trail takes hikers through a beautiful forest within the sheer canyon walls, growing on soil from rock slides and sedimentation.

From the trailhead follow the path as it traverses diagonally down the slope above the north bank of the creek. Once inside the canyon mouth, solution holes and arch formations present themselves on the walls of Beatty Point to the right (south). Vegetation along the creek consists of ponderosa pine, sagebrush, cattails, and ancient cottonwoods. During the first half of the hike, the trail remains on the north side of the creek.

Early on, the trail leads up into the head of a small side wash where hikers can explore an alcove formation. Continuing on, the trail climbs past a second and then a third wash as it goes through stands of Douglas fir, white fir, maple, and Gambel oak. Several alcoves and arch formations can be seen along the canyon walls above the trail. The trail ultimately climbs up the north slope away from the creek and bypasses a rock slide that has blocked the creek bed.

Once it negotiates this obstacle, the path winds through a forest of maple, fir, and Gambel oak in the depths of the canyon. Views of the canyon walls overhead are blocked by the dense forest canopy. The trees also obscure all views

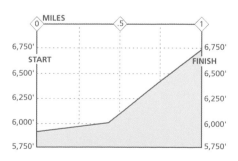

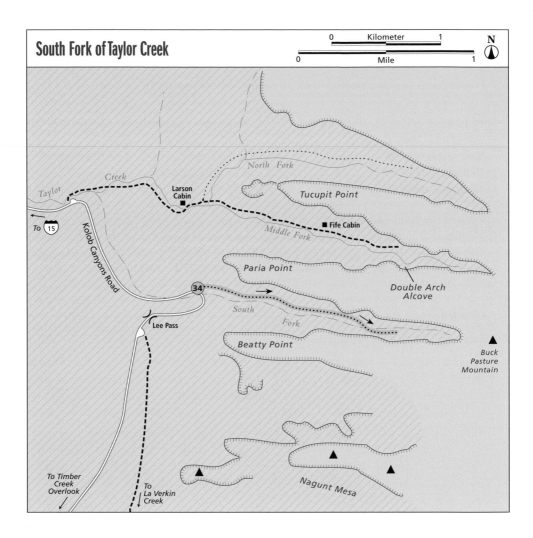

South Fork of Taylor Creek

of the watercourse. Eventually the greenery opens up to reveal the narrowing canyon walls. The path drops into the streambed and follows it up the canyon's south side.

At the end of the route, a 20-foot rockfall blocks the canyon. The boulders can be bypassed with some scrambling, but more boulders block passage beyond.

Key Points

0.0   Kolob Canyons Road
1.0   End of route

35 Camp Creek

A long, out-and-back day trip along a wilderness route up Camp Creek

Distance: 7.6 miles (12.4 km) round-trip
Hiking time: About 5 hours
Best season: March–November
Difficulty: Moderate*
Water availability: Camp Creek flows permanently below its narrows and at its headwaters.

Hazards: Flash flood danger in upper reaches of Camp Creek
Topo map: Zion National Park (Trails Illustrated)
Jurisdiction: Zion National Park. See Appendix A for more information. The land near the trailhead is owned privately.

Finding the trailhead: Follow I-15 northward from the Kolob Canyons Visitor Center and turn off at exit 42 (the New Harmony exit). Turn right, staying to the east of the highway on the paved frontage road, which swings northward toward Kanarraville. Follow this road for 1.7 miles to CR 1925 South. Public access to the original trailhead has been cut off by the landowners; park along the frontage road and walk up CR 1925 South to Wipishani Lane. Turn left on Wipishani and continue to bear left to reach the pull-around at the base of the hills. The hike begins through the Zion National Park gate. GPS: N37° 30' 11.359" / W113° 11' 47.278"

The Hike

This little-known canyon in the northwestern corner of the park is one of Zion's forgotten treasures. It penetrates the far northwestern corner of the park, offering access to a spectacular hidden canyon. Private landowners have been trying to close off public access to the trailhead that leads to the Camp Creek drainage; consult with park rangers for the latest details on hiking the Camp Creek route.

To begin the hike, pass through the gate and make your way up the steep, informal trail that leads northwest up the ridgeline. You will intersect the Camp Creek Trail just above a water storage tank on the national park boundary; the constructed trail begins at a hikers' gate directly behind the tank.

This old cattle-drive trail is no longer maintained by the park, and it is badly rutted as it crests the hilltop and descends into the Camp Creek valley. The broad band

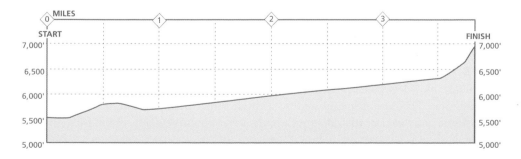

of limestone exposed below the trail belongs to the Kaibab Formation, which also makes up the Hurricane Cliffs and the top layer of the Grand Canyon. This rock layer has sufficiently resisted erosion to form a sheer waterfall where the creek cuts through it. The falls cannot be viewed easily from above.

The trail disappears as it reaches the banks of the watercourse. Hikers may pick up snatches of it along the stream banks but will find it equally easy to hike up the streambed itself. The chocolate-colored hills flanking the valley belong to the Moenkopi Formation. These hills are robed in the characteristic piñon-juniper scrub of the desert uplands, while the valley floor is home to a rich and diverse riparian community that features hardwoods and grasses.

A thin band of grayish boulders along the streambed announces the Shinarump conglomerate, a layer of cobbles and mud that solidified into stone more than 200 million years ago. The Paiute Indians who once ranged this area believed that the petrified wood found in this rock was the hidden magical weaponry of their wolf god, Shinav. This layer gives way in turn to a broader band of loose, purplish rock known as the Chinle Formation. In some areas this layer also contains fossilized wood.

Pines appear in the valley as the route follows the wash into the cooler uplands, where rainfall is more frequent. The deep maroon color of the surrounding hills in this area denotes the Moenave and Kayenta Formations. Two dry washes soon enter the valley, one from each side, and sculpted walls of Navajo sandstone rise ahead. This formation, which is the youngest and topmost layer of the sedimentary sequence visible along the route, forms the impressive canyon that bears the headwaters of Camp Creek.

Progress soon becomes more difficult as the streamside vegetation becomes a dense tangle of brush (watch out for thorns!). The flowing water disappears here, and through most of the upper canyon it flows beneath the surface gravels of the wash.

The wash soon passes between great pillars of stone that form a natural portal at the mouth of the canyon. Great towers and sheaves of rock stand on end, sculpted into fascinating shapes by wind and water.

Following the wash eastward, you will pass walls that rise higher and soon present immense cliffs streaked with desert varnish. White fir and bigtooth maple thrive in the cool inner recesses of the canyon, creating a pocket of montane forest in the midst of the arid lands. An enormous alcove with an arching roof on the north wall of the canyon marks the spot where the streamcourse negotiates a series of slickrock potholes. To continue the trek scramble onto the bare rock to the left (watching for loose slabs) and climb over a shoulder of the hill. Return to the streamcourse after safely bypassing the obstacle.

Beyond this point the gradient increases markedly, and the wash is choked with boulders, blowdowns, and logjams. The canyon walls are pocked with solution holes in this area. These holes are created by seepwater that trickles through pores in the sandstone and dissolves the calcium carbonate that binds the grains of sand together.

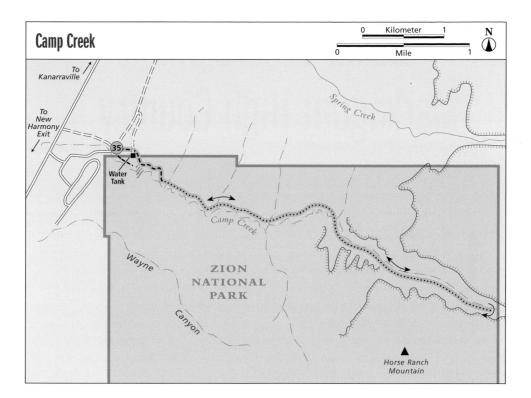

Watch for a narrow ravine to the right—it ends at a spectacular pour-off across a rounded face that rises above a slanted slot through the bedrock. Above this point the flowing water appears again in the main canyon, occupying a narrow, increasingly steep gully. The next obstacle is a series of steep slickrock pour-offs. It is possible (but not recommended) to climb higher using the extremely steep paths that bypass the potholes, first on the right and later on the left. From the top of these paths, hikers can reach the spot where the drainage ends at a box canyon. At this point only 20 feet of vertical sandstone separate the traveler from the top of the plateau. However, this final pitch cannot be scaled without mountaineering aids.

Key Points

0.0 Trailhead. Climb along ridgeline, following way trails.

0.2 Water tank on Zion National Park boundary. Trail departs behind tank.

0.6 Floor of Camp Creek valley

2.3 Entrance to Camp Creek Narrows

3.8 Hike ends at head of box canyon.

Cedar Breaks and Markagunt High Country

T he Markagunt Plateau is one of the loftiest uplands in western Utah. Indeed, a rich forest of subalpine fir and spruce graces the rolling surface of the plateau, interspersed with broad, grassy meadows where elk and mule deer come to graze. Bristlecone pines cling to the windy precipices on the rims of the plateau, surviving extremes of cold and drought.

The plateau bedrock is freshwater limestone of the Claron Formation, which weathers into the same colorful spires as those found in Bryce Canyon National Park. More recently, volcanic activity has created vast, jumbled fields of lava, frozen in time. Brian Head, the highest point on the plateau, is of volcanic origin as well. Its slopes have become a popular destination for downhill skiers.

Because of the plateau's high elevation, hiking opportunities are limited to the summer months. The deep snowdrifts of winter often linger until June, and autumn snows force road closures as early as October. Cool summer temperatures atop the Markagunt

Meadows and aspen groves near Lundell Spring (hike 40)

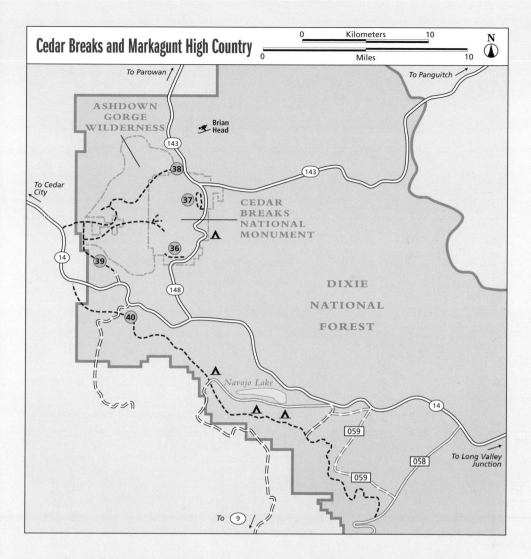

| 0 | Kilometers | 10 |

| 0 | Miles | 10 |

N

To Parowan

To Panguitch

ASHDOWN
GORGE
WILDERNESS

Brian
Head

143

38

143

37

To Cedar
City

CEDAR
BREAKS
NATIONAL
MONUMENT

36

14

39

148

DIXIE

NATIONAL

FOREST

40

Navajo Lake

14

059

058

To Long Valley
Junction

059

To 9

make it a haven from the scorching heat found at lower elevations. In winter the area receives enough snow for cross-country skiing. Access to the Markagunt Plateau is via UT 14, which runs between Cedar City and Long Valley Junction. The highway is plowed free of snow during the wintertime but only during daylight hours.

The jewel in the crown of the Markagunt Plateau is Cedar Breaks National Monument. This small preserve encompasses a broad amphitheater filled with cliffs banded in orange and red, castellated with craggy spires and natural arches that rival Bryce Canyon in splendor. Several short day-hiking trails exist within the monument, but backcountry camping is not allowed. The surrounding forestlands are managed by Dixie National Forest, which offers fine opportunities for longer backpacking trips. The new Virgin River Rim Trail and the Ashdown Gorge route both offer wild country of national park caliber, without the attendant crowds.

36 Spectra Point-Ramparts Trail

A short, out-and-back day hike along the rim of the Cedar Breaks

Distance: 3 miles (5.0 km) round-trip
Hiking time: About 1.5 to 2 hours
Best season: June–September
Difficulty: Moderately strenuous due to elevation gain and loss

Water availability: The small stream to the west of Spectra Point flows permanently.
Hazards: Cliff exposure, lightning
Topo map: Cedar Breaks National Monument
Jurisdiction: Cedar Breaks National Monument. See Appendix A for more information.

Finding the trailhead: From Cedar City drive east on UT 14 for 17.9 miles, then turn north on UT 148. Follow this road for 3 miles to reach the Cedar Breaks Visitor Center. The Ramparts Trail departs from the west end of the visitor center parking lot. GPS: N37° 36' 42.86" / W112° 50' 15.55"

The Hike

This trail follows the south rim of the Cedar Breaks amphitheater, revealing sweeping vistas of the ragged walls and eroded pinnacles that fill the basin. From the parking lot the path ascends for a short distance to the cliff tops above Jericho Canyon. Here it skirts among wind-scoured stands of Englemann spruce and subalpine fir. Some of these trees have been tortured by windblown snow to such an extent that they have taken on the dwarfed krummholz growth form. This low, matlike growth results when windblown crystals of ice prune off the buds that protrude above the snowdrifts.

Views are spectacular from the outset of the hike, featuring multicolored spires and fins of weathered limestone. The bands of red, orange, and even lavender are derived from the oxidation of iron and manganese, which were deposited when the rock-forming sediments here were laid down at the bottom of an enormous freshwater lake. As the trail winds in and out of the trees, hikers get southward views of the meadowy top of the Markagunt Plateau.

After a mile a spur path runs out to the end of Spectra Point. This long finger of chalky limestone extends northward into the heart of the Cedar Breaks amphitheater. It is one of the finest vantage points for viewing the area's hoodoos and walls, especially during morning and evening, when slanting light illuminates the stone. Prominent features of the badlands include Bristlecone and Chessmen Ridges, which rise from the center of the amphitheater, castellated with tortured pinnacles of all descriptions.

Growing from the arid soils of Spectra Point are hardy specimens of bristlecone pine, twisted by winter gales and splintered by summer lightning storms. The oldest

◀ *View across Slip Canyon from The Rampart*

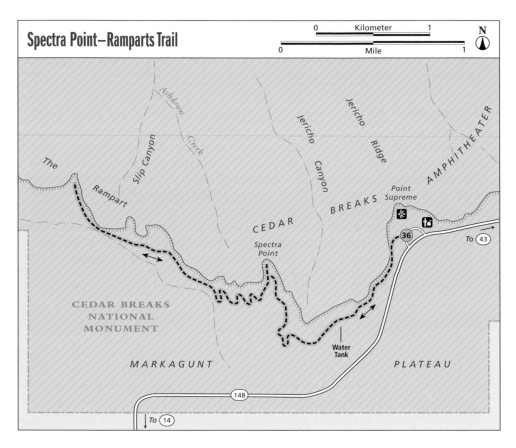

Spectra Point–Ramparts Trail

specimen on the point is more than 1,600 years old; the longest-lived bristlecone, located in California, has survived for more than 4,500 years.

The main trail departs westward from Spectra Point, zigzagging downward into a wooded glen occupied by a crystal-clear rivulet. Spruce, fir, and limber pine tower overhead, shading luxuriant swards of grasses and wildflowers that include lupine, aster, bluebells, and larkspur. The trail descends at a steady clip, making occasional forays to the rims for views of the badlands that stretch away below.

The trail ends at a high overlook of The Rampart, which bears a scattered growth of bristlecone pine. From this point views stretch from the forested floor of the basin all the way to the banded cliffs that rise 2,000 feet all around it.

Key Points

0.0 Trail leaves parking lot.

0.8 Spectra Point

1.5 Trail peters out atop The Rampart.

37 Alpine Pond

A short loop trail through wooded country atop the Markagunt Plateau

Distance: 2.1 miles (3.4 km) round-trip
Hiking time: About 1 hour
Best season: June–September
Difficulty: Moderate

Water availability: Alpine Pond always has water but is ecologically fragile; take water only from the outlet stream below the pond.
Topo map: Cedar Breaks National Monument
Jurisdiction: Cedar Breaks National Monument. See Appendix A for more information.

Finding the trailhead: The trail departs from the Chessmen Overlook, 1.7 miles beyond the Cedar Breaks Visitor Center on UT 148. The trail can also be accessed from the Alpine Pond trailhead, 1 mile farther north. GPS: N37° 37' 53.113"/W112° 49' 53.020"

The Hike

This trail forms a loop through the subalpine forest above the east rim of the Cedar Breaks amphitheater. It is a self-guiding nature walk, with pamphlets provided at either trailhead. We describe the trek as a 2.1-mile loop from the Chessmen Overlook, but hikers can also approach the loop from the Alpine Pond trailhead at its north end or choose between several shorter point-to-point hikes.

From the overlook follow the Lower Trail downward through a forest of stately spruce and fir. A handful of bristlecone pines grow along the rim of the amphitheater, and gaps in the trees allow glimpses of the northern half of the Cedar Breaks. Less rugged than the southern reaches, the cliffs and spires that appear here are sprinkled with a sparse growth of conifers. The trail follows the rim for almost a mile and then enters a wooded dale that bears the headwaters of Rattle Creek.

The path climbs to the source of the waters, a tiny spring-fed lake known as Alpine Pond. This crystal-clear pool is cupped within a miniature basin surrounded by elegant spires of spruce and fir. It is a favorite watering hole for local wildlife, and it

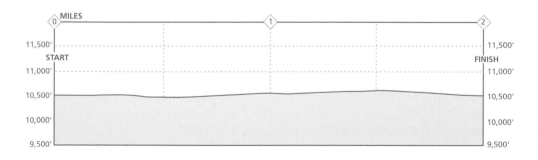

Hiker on the way to Alpine Pond SHUTTERSTOCK

nourishes a vibrant growth of aquatic plants. A connecting path zigzags upward from the foot of the pond to reach the Upper Trail, bisecting the loop and offering shorter hike options for travelers who find themselves pressed for time.

The main trail follows the western shore of the pond and then ascends gradually through a series of pocket meadows. It soon reaches a quarrylike slope of broken rock. Unlike the sedimentary stone that forms the Cedar Breaks amphitheater, this stone is a much younger volcanic rock. Laid down as a thick bed of volcanic ash, it was transformed under great heat and pressure into a resistant stone known as welded tuff. Over the centuries water has worked its way into fissures in the tuff and then frozen and expanded, wedging boulders away from the parent rock. The resulting apron of rock debris is known as a talus slope. The loose boulders make an ideal nesting habitat for a variety of rodents. Look for badger-size yellow-bellied marmots, smaller pikas or "rock rabbits," and diminutive Uinta chipmunks.

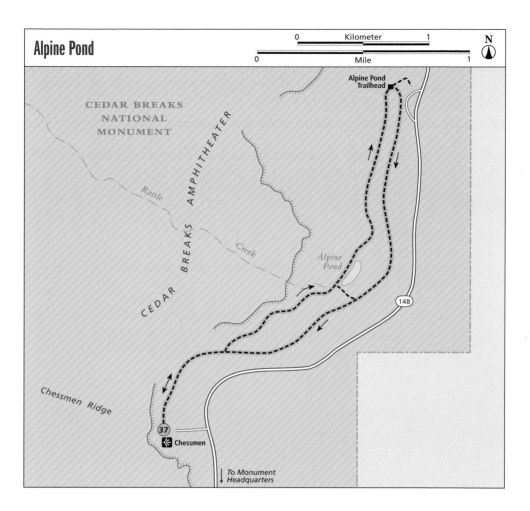

CEDAR BREAKS
NATIONAL
MONUMENT

AMPHITHEATER

Rattle

Creek

CEDAR BREAKS

Alpine
Pond

Alpine Pond
Trailhead

148

Chessmen Ridge

37

Chessmen

To Monument
Headquarters

0   Kilometer   1

0   Mile   1

N

The path soon climbs toward the Alpine Pond trailhead; turn south on the Upper Trail to complete the loop. The trail wends its way through a mature spruce-fir woodland. This forest is an important foraging area for the red squirrel, which harvests cones throughout the summer and hoards them in underground caches for use during the winter months. Some caches are inevitably forgotten, and in favorable conditions the seeds within these lost cones can sprout and help renew the forest.

Numerous snags rise among the living trees in this area, the victims of frequent lightning storms that rage across the high Markagunt Plateau. To local wildlife these trees become even more valuable after they die: They support populations of insects that are a valuable food source and may also become homes for cavity-nesting mammals and birds. Two of the more prevalent cavity-nesting birds found in this area are the flicker and the mountain bluebird.

The trees give way to grassy glades, and sun-loving aspens thrive along the edges of the meadows. Conifers grow in clumps in this area, with skirts of their tiny offspring surrounding them on every side. Many of these "seedlings" are actually clones of the parent trees, thrown off when lower boughs took root in the soil and grew into independent trees.

After passing the cutoff trail that descends to Alpine Pond, the Upper Trail continues southward along the edge of the vast meadows that are so characteristic of the crest of the Markagunt Plateau. These meadows offer brilliant displays of wildflowers throughout the summer, highlighted by paintbrush and fleabane. Herds of deer sometimes graze here during autumn. The path ultimately finds its way back to the Chessmen Overlook, after an overall distance of 2.1 miles.

Key Points

- **0.0** Chessmen Overlook trailhead
- **0.2** Trail splits. Follow Lower Trail, to the left.
- **0.6** Alpine Pond. Junction with cutoff to Upper Trail. Follow Lower Trail around the western shore of the pond.
- **1.1** Junction with short spur to Alpine Pond trailhead. Turn right onto Upper Trail to complete the loop.
- **1.5** Cutoff trail descends to Alpine Pond. Bear left.
- **2.1** Trail ends at Chessmen Overlook.

38 Rattlesnake Creek–Ashdown Gorge

A long day hike or short overnight trip down a primitive route from the Markagunt Plateau to the lowlands, followed by a wade through Ashdown Gorge

Distance: 9.5 miles (15.3 km) one way
Hiking time: About 5 hours
Best season: June–September
Difficulty: Moderate* east to west; strenuous* west to east
Water availability: Rattlesnake and Ashdown Creeks have permanent flows of water.

Hazards: Flash flood danger in Ashdown Gorge
Recommended equipment: Wading staff
Topo maps: Brian Head; Flanigan Arch
Jurisdiction: Dixie National Forest. See Appendix A for more information.

Finding the trailhead: From Cedar City drive east on UT14 for 17.9 miles, then turn north on UT148. Follow this road for 7.5 miles, passing through Cedar Breaks National Monument. The road changes to UT143. The trailhead is just beyond the monument's north boundary on the west side of the road. The Ashdown Gorge route emerges at a hidden parking area on the banks of Crow Creek. The parking area is accessed by a narrow gravel road (difficult to see) that drops down to the creek from mile 7.6, just below a long row of concrete barriers. GPS of start: N37° 39' 43.031"/W112° 50' 18.166"; GPS of finish: N37° 38' 31.539"/W112° 57' 8.487"

The Hike

This rugged route makes a long descent along the edge of the Cedar Breaks amphitheater and then follows a wading route down Ashdown Creek through its spectacular gorge. Both the Rattlesnake Creek Trail and the Ashdown Gorge Wilderness Area are administered by the Dixie National Forest, and details on the latest route conditions can be obtained at the ranger station in Cedar City. Ashdown Gorge is highly susceptible to flash flooding, so if wet weather threatens, travelers should exit via the Long Hollow Road. For a longer trip travelers can ascend Ashdown Creek into the canyons of the Cedar Breaks.

The trek begins by following an old jeep track westward along the boundary fence of Cedar Breaks National Monument. Upon entering a stand of Englemann

spruce and subalpine fir, this two-rut track veers away from the boundary. Turn left here onto a well-beaten path that continues to follow the fence. As the fence ends, a spur path leads southward to an overlook of the Cedar Breaks. Orange Ridge and Adams Barrier raise colorful pinnacles above the rugged defile of Adams Canyon, a major finger drainage of the Cedar Breaks amphitheater.

The main trail loses altitude as it drops through a pocket meadow. A second spur path soon departs for the edge of the breaks, revealing an even better view of Orange Ridge. The Rattlesnake Creek Trail then embarks upon a steep descent down a series of switchbacks that carry the traveler through an aspen-dominated woodland. Watch for rock cairns and blazes on the tree trunks as the path crosses another pocket meadow and then continues its descent through the trees.

The path soon runs out onto steep, grassy slopes that face southwest. The chalky crest of Snow Ridge across the deep ravine at the foot of the slope, and the deep cleft of Ashdown Gorge, can be glimpsed beyond the tip of the ridge. To the northwest Navajo Ridge presents an escarpment of orange cliffs that rise above the headwaters of Rattlesnake Creek. The trail zigzags down the meadowy slope and into the ravine, where it crosses north-facing slopes that support a dense growth of spruce and fir. Upon reaching the toe of Snow Ridge, the path emerges onto the long, grassy expanse of Stud Flat. Cairns mark the way, and the opening in the trees showcases the cliffs of Navajo Ridge.

After crossing Stud Flat the trail drops into the steep-walled valley of Rattlesnake Creek. Dense groves of conifers shade the descent to the watercourse, which carries a fairly reliable flow of water. Shortly after reaching the creek bottoms, the trail reaches a confluence with the dry wash of Tri Story Canyon. Here the trail crosses Rattlesnake Creek and follows its north bank downward through open timber. Some of the ponderosa pines in this area have attained old-growth proportions.

After following the creek for 1.6 miles, the path reaches a marked junction with the High Mountain Trail. There is a good camping spot at this junction. Turn left and cross the creek where a blocky sill of bedrock has created a small waterfall.

The path now climbs high around the finger ridge that separates the valleys of Rattlesnake and Ashdown Creeks. Fine views crop up along the way, looking up into the amphitheater of the Cedar Breaks. The path descends along the north rim of Ashdown Gorge to reach the valley floor above its upper end. Just before reaching Ashdown Creek, the trail enters a small parcel of private land. Pass through quickly without leaving a trace of your passage, and do not camp here.

For a side trip hikers may proceed upstream past an old sawmill to reach the floor of the Cedar Breaks amphitheater after a distance of about 4 miles. If Ashdown Creek is high or stormy weather is imminent, hikers should leave via the Long Hollow exit route, which climbs high over the south ridge and deposits hikers at Crystal Spring.

◄ *Formations at the mouth of Rattlesnake Creek*

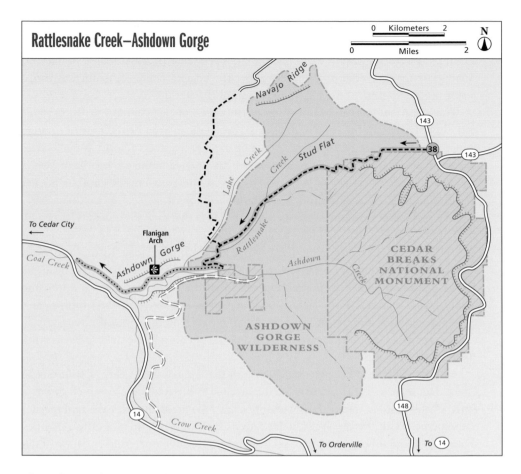

If weather and water conditions are favorable, travelers can wade down the shallow streambed through the spectacular canyon scenery of Ashdown Gorge.

As low walls of Navajo sandstone rise on both sides of Ashdown Creek, the route carries hikers into national forest and past a good camping spot at a bend in the gorge. In the upper reaches of the canyon, the flow of the water has carved out deep overhangs that form a roof over the streambed. Stately firs provide a colorful counterpoint to the buff-colored walls of the canyon. The streaks of gray adorning the walls are from chemicals leached out of leaf litter by rainfall and then deposited by seeping runoff.

The walls soar higher as the stream cuts downward, and soon cliffs rise hundreds of feet above the water. After 0.9 mile of canyon trekking, hikers will reach the spot where Rattlesnake Creek pours in a flow of clear water from the north. This major confluence is guarded by a fascinating array of stone obelisks.

Downstream from the confluence the walls soar higher still and the canyon floor widens markedly. About 0.8 mile below Rattlesnake Creek, a cluster of great pinnacles soars above the north wall of the canyon. Flanigan Arch is nestled among them, a delicate causeway of stone that joins two of the outcrops. After a few more twists of the streamcourse, hikers arrive at the mouth of Ashdown Gorge. Ashdown Creek joins the waters of Crow Creek here, and the highway can be seen ahead. Continue downstream, following the banks of the deepened creek. Watch for a highway maintenance pad along the south bank of the stream; it is the easiest place to climb out of the creek and gain access to the roadway.

Key Points

0.0 Upper trailhead

0.6 Short spur departs left for Adams Canyon overlook.

0.8 Short spur path to second overlook

2.3 Trail runs out onto Stud Flat.

2.9 Trail reaches end of Stud Flat and begins descent to Rattlesnake Creek.

3.6 Floor of Rattlesnake Creek valley

3.9 Tri Story Canyon joins from the northeast. Trail fords Rattlesnake Creek.

5.2 Junction with Alpine Trail. Turn left and ford Rattlesnake Creek at waterfall.

6.0 Crest of divide between Rattlesnake and Ashdown Creeks

6.5 Ashdown Creek. Follow the creek downstream.

6.6 Route enters Ashdown Gorge.

7.5 Confluence of Rattlesnake and Ashdown Creeks

8.3 Flanigan Arch

9.0 Mouth of Ashdown Gorge. Crow Creek flows in from the southeast. Continue downstream.

9.5 Hike ends at a parking area on west bank of stream.

39 Cedar Breaks Bottoms

A backpack route that begins at Crystal Spring in Dixie National Forest and ends in Cedar Breaks National Monument with several trail options

Distance: 8.9 miles (14.3 km) one way
Hiking time: About 5-6 hours
Best season: June-November
Difficulty: Moderately strenuous
Water availability: Ashdown Creek has a permanent flow of water.

Hazards: Uneven, rocky surfaces
Topo maps: Webster Flat; Flanigan Arch; Brian Head; Navajo Lake
Jurisdiction: Dixie National Forest; Cedar Breaks National Monument. See Appendix A for more information.

Finding the trailhead: From Cedar City drive east on UT14 past the Cedar Canyon Campground and up a series of switchbacks to FR 301. This is an unimproved road, which can be identified by a Forest Service gate on the north side of UT 14. Follow FR 301 north 0.9 mile to the trailhead sign at Crystal Spring. GPS: N37° 36' 28.41"/W112° 53' 50.02"

The Hike

The portion of the hike that falls within the national monument is a Research Natural Area and is closed to camping. This area escaped the heavy grazing pressure that damaged most other plant communities on the Markagunt, and it contains relict species that are found nowhere else in the area. Please tread lightly here. The trail begins in a mixed stand of fir and aspen that quickly opens up into a small meadow within the first 0.5 mile. It then enters a forested area and descends about 400 feet along a moderately steep grade. The trailbed consists of loose soil and makes for easy traveling. At the bottom of the slope, the path levels off somewhat and traverses an open grove of aspens. A trail sign announces a junction with the Blowhard Mountain Trail in the center of the gladed bottom, which is known as Potato Hollow.

Note: The old Potato Hollow Trail provides the most direct access to Ashdown Creek and the Cedar Breaks Bottoms but traverses a private property within the Ashdown Gorge Wilderness. Out of respect for the private landowners, use the Blowhard Mountain Trail through Long Hollow as an alternate route to Ashdown Creek. The route still requires crossing private property via an unimproved road. Travel respectfully and stay on the road through this stretch of land.

From the Potato Hollow Trail sign, follow the Blowhard Mountain Trail as it traverses westward into Long Hollow. It tracks the right bank of the Long Hollow streamcourse, where white fir trees soon crowd the trail. Long Hollow is grazed by sheep during summer months; consequently, many side trails branch off the main footpath. Stay on course by following the well-worn path paralleling the Long Hollow draw.

Looking across Cedar Breaks from above

The path continues its gradual descent along the right bank until it briefly climbs down into the wash and begins a short climb back up the right side. A Forest Service gate is located at the top of the ascent. Close the gate behind you and quickly begin a gradual descent as the trail continues to follow Long Hollow leftward. From this point, the route is all downhill, making a gradual 1,000-foot descent to Ashdown Creek.

Beyond the gate a pleasant combination of aspens and conifers shades the descent, with an added bonus of juniper on the upper slopes. Unfortunately, the wilderness experience in the Long Hollow draw is somewhat diminished by the presence of a dilapidated Forest Service boundary fence that parallels the left side of the trail. Continue down a moderate slope of loose soil and pebbles into the draw and cross to the left bank.

The trail briefly moves west away from the draw through another aspen meadow. As the path returns to the draw, piñon pine and Gambel oak join the aspen and fir. An old split-rail fence on the left side of the trail marks the final descent to an unimproved dirt road and the next phase of this trek.

Cedar Breaks Bottoms

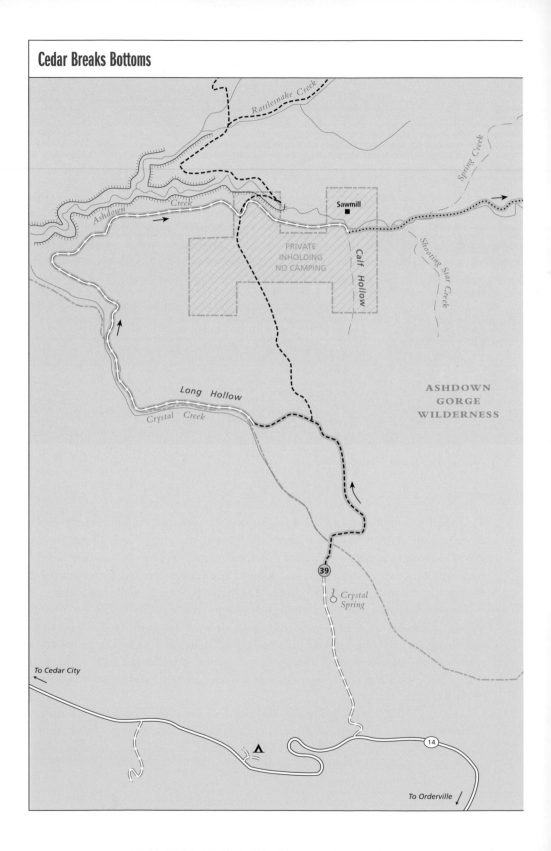

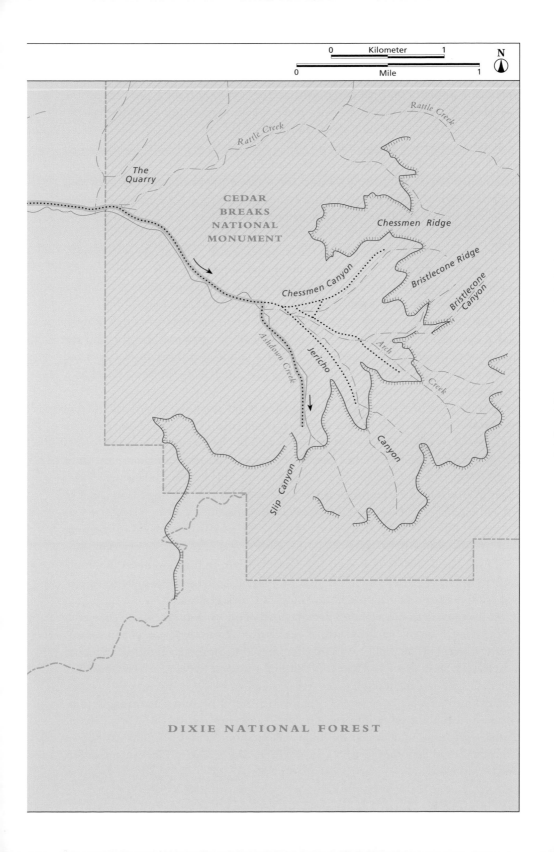

0   Kilometer   1

0   Mile   1

N

The
Quarry

Rattle Creek

Rattle Creek

CEDAR
BREAKS
NATIONAL
MONUMENT

Chessmen Ridge

Chessmen Canyon

Bristlecone Ridge

Bristlecone
Canyon

Ashdown Creek

Jericho

Arch

Creek

Slip Canyon

Canyon

DIXIE NATIONAL FOREST

Follow the unimproved road northward as it climbs above the cliffs that form Ash-down Gorge. This portion of the route is long and tedious. However, hikers should note that portions of the road traverse private property—stay on the path. Follow the road about 3 miles down to Ashdown Creek, where the road ends across from an old sawmill located on private land on the north bank.

Ashdown Creek is a braided stream with a wide, rocky bed. The concentration of pink limestone here lends the creek bed a pastel hue, and the banks are densely veg-etated with conifers, junipers, and shrubs. Turn eastward, following the stream upward toward its source. The creek bed holds loose rocks of varying size. The benches along the banks, brushy in places with large amounts of deadwood, are broken by steep slopes from 4 to 8 feet high.

The Cedar Breaks National Monument boundary lies approximately 1.5 miles upstream. Camping is not permitted within the monument, though ample campsites can be found on a bench on the north bank of the creek approximately 1.3 miles upstream from the road. This bench is fairly open and offers easy hiking.

Continue upstream, staying on the bench. A large outcropping of rock known as the Quarry is located about 0.2 mile beyond the monument boundary, on the north side of the creek. The Quarry overlooks the confluence of Ashdown Creek and Rattle Creek, which flows down from Adams Canyon. Follow Ashdown Creek as it bends around to the southwest.

Travelers can take advantage of unimpeded travel along the left (north) side of Ashdown Creek from the Rattle Creek confluence to Crescent Hollow. As you approach the hollow, which is on the south side of the creek, the bench becomes overgrown with vegetation. The creek banks become steeper and higher here. Since staying on the bench involves lots of bushwhacking and climbing, hikers may find it easier to drop into the watercourse at this point and find a route along the stream. The red and pink cliffs of Chessmen Ridge soon loom ahead.

More pink cliffs come into view as Ashdown Creek makes a bend to the right (south). Bristlecone pines grow along the north bank near the creek's confluence with Arch Creek. Follow Ashdown Creek to the south to find another wall of pink cliffs above the east bank of the stream. The walls of the canyon continue to narrow and grow steeper as you approach the Ashdown Creek headwaters.

Just before reaching the pink cliffs at the head of the canyon, hikers will encounter a large rockfall on the left (east) side of the canyon. A narrow waterfall and stream-course enters from the right (west) side. To proceed beyond this obstacle, climb onto a small rock shelf above it. Here you will find towering canyon walls where small waterfalls spill over the top following wet weather.

Finding the route over boulders and steep slopes becomes increasingly diffi-cult from this point on. A look up into Slip Canyon reveals that it is heavily con-gested with large boulders. At this point hikers should backtrack down Ashdown Creek and head up either Jericho Canyon, Arch Creek, and/or Chessmen Canyon, described below.

Key Points

0.0   Trailhead at Crystal Spring

1.2   Junction with Blowhard Mountain Trail to Long Hollow. Bear left for Long Hollow.

2.5   End of Blowhard Mountain Trail, beginning of jeep trail/unimproved road.

5.5   Jeep trail/unimproved road ends at Ashdown Creek.

7.0   Cedar Breaks National Monument boundary

7.2   The Quarry

8.2   Arch Creek joins Ashdown Creek.

8.9   Head of navigation on Ashdown Creek

Chessmen Canyon Option

Hikers can take a side journey toward the head of Chessmen Canyon, which reveals spectacular views of pink cliffs and hoodoos. Walking along the rocky creek bed into the canyon is laborious, but the spectacular scenery makes the trek worthwhile. Progress into the head of the canyon is eventually blocked by large boulders.

Arch Creek Option

A red spire overlooks the confluence of Bristlecone Canyon and Arch Creek. Follow Arch Creek to the right (south) where pine trees grow from the rocky slopes. When the season is right, small waterfalls drape themselves down the south canyon walls. This creek bed, like the others, is strewn with loose gravel, cobblestones, and boulders. The stream meanders from wall to wall across a wide wash, so several fords or leaps are necessary. The trek ends at large boulders that fill the head of the canyon. Overhead are sheer cliffs and a seasonal waterfall that spills over the headwall.

Jericho Canyon Option

Narrow white and pink cliffs overlook the watercourse of Jericho Canyon. Watch for an overhanging arch on the north wall near the mouth of the canyon. The creek bed is rocky like that of the other area streams; however, the footing is a bit firmer. The slopes bordering the canyon are barren and dry, offering a forbidding landscape overlooked by ragged spires. The head of Jericho Canyon is congested with boulders.

40 Virgin River Rim

A multiple-day backpack along the south rim of the Markagunt Plateau, ending at Woods Ranch County Park, including an optional hike to Cascade Falls

Distance: 25.2 miles (40.6 km) one way
Hiking time: About 13 hours
Best season: June–September
Difficulty: Moderate east to west; moderately strenuous west to east

Water availability: Simpkins Spring is reliable, and other springs are intermittent. Water can always be had at Cascade Falls and Navajo Lake.
Topo map: Trails Illustrated
Jurisdiction: Dixie National Forest. See Appendix A for more information.

Finding the trailhead: Follow UT14 east from Cedar City to mile 32.6, where the gravel Strawberry Point Road runs southward. Follow this road for 8.4 miles, passing through a subdivision of country homes and climbing to a hilltop where a trail sign marks a pullout and the beginning of the Virgin River Rim route. The trail ends at the Woods Ranch County Park (mile 11.6 on UT 14). It can also be accessed en route via the Lars Fork Road, the Cascade Falls Road, the Navajo Lake Road, and the Webster Flat Road. GPS of start: N37° 26' 24.30"/W112° 41' 55.15"; GPS of finish: N37° 35' 38.59"/W112° 54' 58.95"

The Hike

Constructed to accommodate both hikers and mountain bikers (although motorized vehicles are prohibited), this outstanding trail links a network of former and current roadways along the southern edge of the Markagunt Plateau, featuring brilliantly colored spires along the rims and sweeping southward vistas. Motorists may access the trail from Strawberry Point, Lars Fork, Cascade Falls, Navajo Lake, and the Webster Flat Road. The numerous access points in the middle of the trail allow hikers to approach it in sections, either as day hikes or as part of one extended backpacking trip.

Upon leaving the trailhead, the path initially flirts with east-facing rims, with horizon-stretching views. As the road bends away at a hairpin turn, the trail ducks into the trees and angles downward through gladed forest. At the bottom of the grade are the grassy bottoms of Strawberry Creek, which carries no water. Travelers who

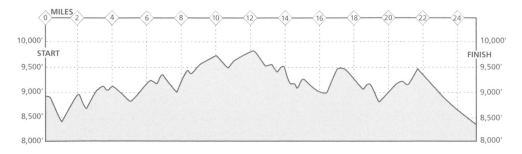

arrive in this area during the twilight hours should watch for white-tailed deer grazing at the edge of the meadows. In the midst of the vale, the path crosses the Strawberry Point Road. There are no parking pullouts in this area, so it is difficult to begin the hike at this point.

After crossing the Strawberry Point Road, the trail runs westward through a loose grove of aspens and then climbs steadily up a heavily forested hillside. Most of the trees are Douglas fir and spruce, but openings filled with ponderosa pine and manzanita indicate spots that were once burned by small lightning-caused fires. Near the top of the hill, the trail joins a dirt road, which it follows westward for a short distance. A signpost marks the spot where the trail breaks away from this road and descends into an aspen-choked gulch.

After passing through this wooded defile, the path climbs steadily, and openings in the forest allow southward views of Strawberry Point. The trail flirts with a jeep track and then makes its way to the edge of the Virgin River Rim for spectacular views. Weathered spires of pink and orange rise from the rimrock below, and hikers can see the monoliths of Zion Canyon far to the south. The tallest and most distinctive of these monoliths is the massive West Temple.

As the trail runs west along the edge of the Markagunt Plateau, the cliffs recede and are replaced by steep slopes forested in Douglas fir, Englemann spruce, and limber pine. Views to the south encompass the headwaters of the Virgin River's North Fork, highlighted by the grassy meadows of Hay Canyon. The trail descends as a new set of castellated cliffs rises ahead. These eroded walls are banded with brilliant whites and oranges that are almost blinding in direct sunlight.

After bottoming out at the mouth of a small draw, the trail works its way around to an overlook that is accessed by the Lars Fork Road. Views are even better a short distance up the trail, where it crests the ridgetop. The path then continues to climb, working inland through coniferous forests interrupted by aspen groves.

When the path finds its way back to the rims, the limestone of the Pink Cliffs takes on more muted tones, pastel oranges and lavenders. Ahead, a long finger of cliffs juts out from the edge of the plateau. The trail runs behind a hilltop and then descends to the base of this eroded backbone, where bristlecone pines grow. A narrow spur path runs onto the finger ridge for breathtaking views of the Pink Cliffs guarding the plateau's edge.

The main trail then drops steeply through the spruce-fir forest to reach the Cascade Falls trailhead on a pretty overlook. (**Option:** The spur trail to Cascade Falls makes a fascinating side trip. This 0.5-mile trail runs level across the cliffs to reach the top of a spectacular waterfall. This torrential flow originates at sinkholes in the bottom of Navajo Lake and then travels through subterranean passageways in the limestone. It emerges from a cave in the cliffs and then rushes down as a foaming cascade to form the headwaters of the North Fork of the Virgin River.)

Meanwhile, the Virgin River Rim Trail swings inland, crossing a meadowy slope as it climbs steadily to the top of a lofty hill. It ultimately turns back toward the rims,

Virgin River Rim

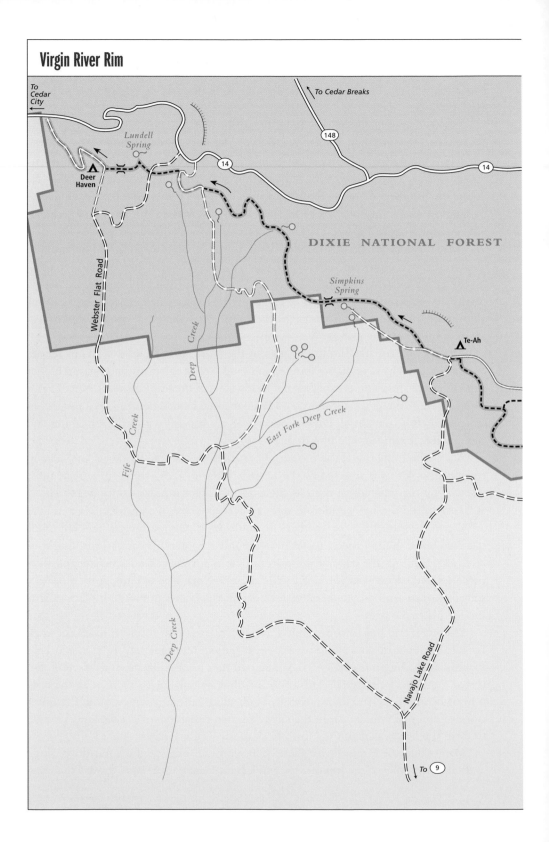

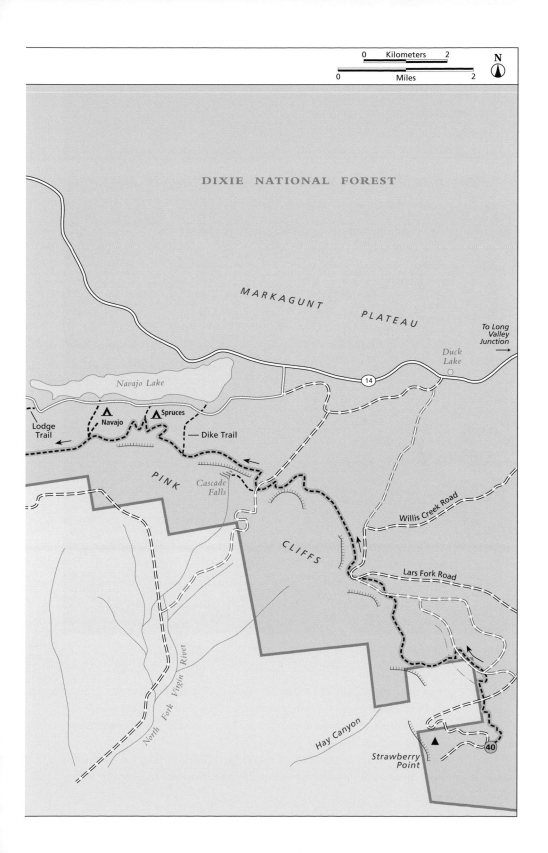

0 Kilometers 2

0 Miles 2

N

DIXIE NATIONAL FOREST

MARKAGUNT PLATEAU

To Long
Valley
Junction

Duck
Lake

14

Navajo Lake

Navajo   Spruces

Lodge
Trail   Dike Trail

PINK   Cascade
Falls

Willis Creek Road

CLIFFS

Lars Fork Road

North Fork Virgin River

Hay Canyon

Strawberry
Point   40

Limestone fins along the east end of the Virgin Rim

and short excursions to the edge yield views of the largest spires on the hike. Copses of aspen and conifers are interspersed with meadows as the trail continues westward. Views of a cliff-girt point soon unfold ahead as the Dike Trail splits away to the north on its way to the foot of Navajo Lake.

The main trail soon reaches the end of the ridgetop and doubles back to the east as it descends into a dense stand of spruce and fir. Gaps in the canopy allow glimpses of deep-blue Navajo Lake. The lake occupies a blind basin that formed when lava flowed from fissures to the north and dammed a small drainage. The path bottoms out at a low gap where a side trail runs northward to reach the lakeshore at the Spruces Campground.

The main trail then climbs through the aspens, mounting the next hill and then returning to the rimrock. The path jogs into a fold in the hilltops, and yet another spur path breaks away to the right, this time bound for Navajo Campground. The Virgin Rim trail returns to the edge of the plateau and soon reaches a point that protrudes southward from the rims. The cliffs of the Virgin River Rim stretch away in a broad arc to the east, while the distant backbone of the Pine Valley Range rises far to the west.

The trail then drops behind a hill to traverse heavily timbered slopes. As a tall hillock looms ahead, the path turns northward along the slope and runs out onto a wooded finger ridge. Atop this ridge the Lodge Trail runs northward to the head of Navajo Lake, while the main trail swings west once more. It follows the hillsides around the head of Navajo Lake, yielding fine views of the water through the trees. Watch for wild turkeys as the path descends to meet the Navajo Lake Road at a trailhead across from the Te-Ah Campground.

Follow the road westward from the Te-Ah trailhead and watch for signs for the Virgin River Rim Trail as it follows a side road that splits away to the right. After descending for a short distance, the trail breaks away from this road and traverses forested slopes below a small outcrop of the Pink Cliffs. The path then wanders westward through a forest of Douglas fir, with copses of aspen growing in the swales where groundwater is abundant. Views through the trees encompass the headwaters of Deep Creek's East Fork, with its vast aspen woodlands. Aspen are normally replaced over time by conifers, but this stand has been here since the beginning of historical time. It has likely been maintained by heavy sheep grazing throughout the last two centuries.

The path makes its way across sloping meadows, and game trails descend toward Simpkins Spring. The route then crosses through a broad gap in the hills where the aspens attain impressive sizes. As it contours across the hillsides beyond this saddle, the trail passes over rills fed by several nameless seeps. There is yet another spring just inside the conifers that rise to the west.

The path continues across the hillsides to intersect the Deep Creek Road (FR 1599), and the route follows this road westward for 1.2 miles. The trail departs from FR 1599 at Stuck Spring, where several unimproved seeps emit an unreliable trickle of water. The mountaintops have by now devolved into rounded hills that are covered by stands of mature aspen.

After crossing the Webster Flat Road, the trail climbs along a grassy slope toward a low hillock. Along the way hikers can take in views of an impressive face of orange-pink limestone rising to the east. Old rail fences and the pipe-fed trough of Lundell Spring hark back to pioneer ranching days, when this area was an important summer range for livestock.

After cresting the hilltop the trail runs along south-facing slopes to reach a fir-covered ridgetop. It then follows this ridge above a meadowy bowl to reach the Deer Haven Group Campground. As the path approaches the campground, lava flows appear on the slopes of the hills that rise ahead. The trail reaches a junction with several roads in front of the camping area; turn right on a rough forest road to complete the trek, following signs for the Virgin River Rim Trail. Straight ahead, the dusky summit of Brian Head rises above the colorful cliffs of the Cedar Breaks.

The road soon drops into the forest, weaving downward through a series of hairpin turns. The views are quite limited for the remainder of the journey to Woods Ranch County Park. The road emerges next to the children's fishing pond, just above the park's main pavilion.

Key Points

0.0   Strawberry Point trailhead

1.1   Strawberry Point Road crossing

1.8   Trail joins dirt road. Turn left along road.

2.1   Trail descends from road to the left.

3.3   Virgin River Rim

5.2   Trail crosses Lars Fork Road. Follow trail signs and bear left along the rim.

7.3   Spur trail runs south onto overlook point.

7.9   Cascade Falls trailhead and junction with the Cascade Falls spur trail. (***Option:*** Add an extra mile to your hike by taking in Cascade Falls.) Virgin River Rim Trail climbs uphill to the northwest.

9.2   Dike Trail splits away to the right, bound for foot of Navajo Lake.

10.8   Spruce Trail splits away to the right, bound for the Spruces Campground on Navajo Lake.

11.5   Navajo Trail departs to right toward Navajo Campground on the lake.

13.3   Lodge Trail departs to right for the head of the lake.

14.4   Te-Ah trailhead. Follow Navajo Lake Road westward.

14.7   Road junction. Virgin River Rim route follows road that descends to the right.

14.9   Virgin River Rim Trail splits away from road to the right.

17.1   Saddle above Simpkins Spring

19.4   Trail joins FR 1599.

20.6   Trail splits away from road at Stuck Spring.

21.2   Trail crosses Webster Flat Road.

21.5   Lundell Spring

22.6   Deer Haven Group Campground. Follow the dirt road that descends to the northwest.

25.2   Woods Ranch County Park

Bryce Canyon National Park

Every year, visitors are awed by the spectacular geological formations and brilliant colors of Bryce Canyon National Park. The towering hoodoos, spires, and natural bridges seem to deny all reason or explanation, leaving hikers gazing skyward with jaws agape in wondrous incredulity.

The forces that created Bryce Canyon are still at work today. The bedrock originated sixty million years ago, when southern Utah held a series of low-lying lakebeds. For millions of years rivers deposited sediments into these lakebeds, eventually filling them and causing the lakes to dry out. The continual deposition of rocks, clays, and silts caused these materials to be compressed and form sedimentary rock layers. Some layers contained deposits of clays and silts, while other layers were rich in lime, dolomite, and carbonates. Throughout all of these layers are iron oxides and manganese compounds, lending hues of orange and purple to the stone. Over time these sediments hardened into rock known as the Claron Formation.

These geologic processes continued unchanged until about sixteen million years ago, when powerful forces began to lift the Colorado Plateau. The stress caused by the uplift created countless joints or vertical cracks throughout the Claron Formation and caused southern Utah to fracture along several fault lines. Resulting from this uplifting force are the nine high plateaus of southern Utah. Three of these high plateaus—the Paunsaugunt, the Markagunt, and the Aquarius—contain the Claron Formation.

Bryce Canyon National Park forms the eastern edge of the Paunsaugunt Plateau. In fact, Bryce Canyon is not so much a canyon as it is a series of amphitheaters created by erosional forces of the Paria River system along the edge of the plateau. As the streams traveled eastward over the edge and down the slope of the plateau, its waters gained velocity and began to carry away bits of the Claron Formation. As this process continued, gullies cut deeply into the plateau, exposing layers of rock. These gully walls then became vulnerable to other forms of erosion, primarily through trickling water and the freeze-thaw cycle.

During warm seasons water trickles down the gully walls, slowly dissolving the carbonates that bind the sedimentary rock together. Sediment layers containing rich deposits of lime, carbonates, and dolomite are more resistant to this erosion than lime-poor

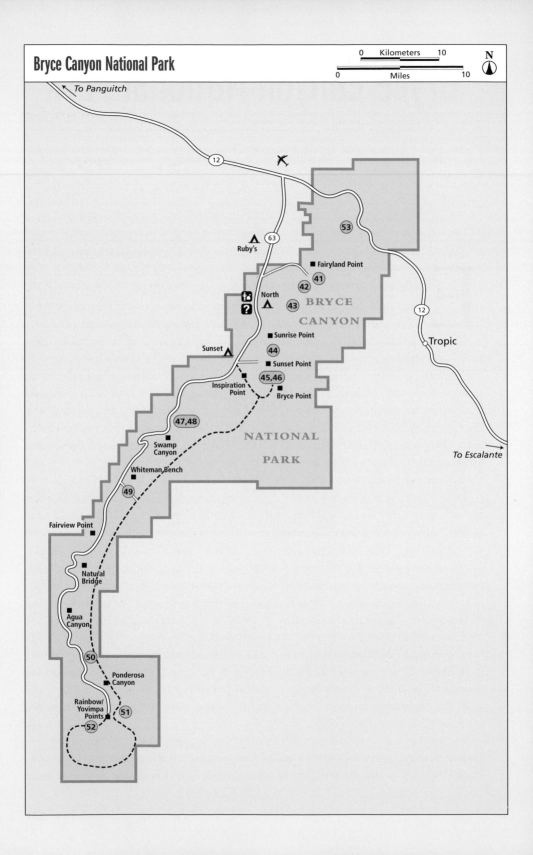

Bryce Canyon National Park

0 — Kilometers — 10
0 — Miles — 10

N

To Panguitch

12

Ruby's

63

53

Fairyland Point

42   41

North

43   BRYCE

CANYON

Sunrise Point

Sunset   44

Sunset Point

45,46

Inspiration
Point

Bryce Point

47,48

Swamp
Canyon

NATIONAL

PARK

Whiteman Bench

49

Fairview Point

Natural
Bridge

Agua
Canyon

50

Ponderosa
Canyon

Rainbow/
Yovimpa
Points

51

52

12

Tropic

To Escalante

layers of siltstone and clay. In many instances more resistant layers overlie, or cap, less resistant layers. The caprock then protects the underlying layers from further erosion, resulting in the spectacular hoodoos and spires that tower above the canyon floor.

In addition to its chemical powers, water also forms hoodoos (often pink and purple from iron and manganese) through the mechanical processes of freezing and thawing. During winter months water seeps into vertical joints and cracks in the rock layers. As temperatures fall below freezing, the water solidifies and expands. This ice-driven expansion widens the cracks and ultimately causes blocks of rock to crumble away from the vertical faces.

The end result of all these erosive forces is the natural wonder known as Bryce Canyon National Park. Understanding the processes that created this spectacle only increases a sense of awe. Visitors overlooking the canyon rim can see for themselves what time and geological forces have created, and adventurous and curious hikers can take advantage of the park's trails to experience Bryce Canyon on a more intimate level.

Because Bryce Canyon has exceptionally high air quality (protected as "pristine" under federal law) and is far from sources of light pollution, it offers world-class stargazing opportunities. Amateur astronomers will find this area to be a prime destination to set up a telescope and observe celestial events.

Day hikers and backcountry users will find numerous options to suit varying needs. Day hikes through the park range from 1-mile loops to 11-mile round-trip trails. One advantage of hiking in Bryce Canyon is that many of the trails intersect each other and can be connected to form loops. For instance, the Navajo Loop, Peekaboo Loop, and Queen's Garden trails can be combined with short excursions along connecting trails.

Bryce Canyon offers two primary trails for backcountry camping: the Riggs Spring Loop and the Under the Rim Trail. The Riggs Spring Loop makes a long day hike or a relaxed overnight trip. The 23-mile Under the Rim Trail can be traveled over two or three days or shortened by combining sections of the trail with the Sheep Creek, Swamp Canyon, Whiteman, or Agua Canyon connecting trails.

We recommend a short excursion along one or all of the short connecting trails, which do not receive as much use as other trails in the park. These short trails can be exhausting since they undergo rapid changes in elevation as they drop from the rim through scenic canyons to the floor below, but the views and solitude are well worth the extra effort.

Before embarking on any hike in Bryce Canyon National Park, hikers should make sure they carry several essential items. First and foremost is water. Bryce Canyon is extremely hot and dry during summer. Water sources below the rim are severely limited and must be treated prior to consumption. As a rule, always carry ample water to last the duration of the hike, and then some. Carry sunscreen, eye protection, and a hat to prevent overexposure to the sun's rays. Since trails in Bryce Canyon traverse steep and rocky slopes, wear sturdy boots that provide ample support and protection. Always remember that Bryce Canyon sits at a high elevation; lowland visitors must

The Pink Cliffs tower above the head of Yellow Creek (hike 46).

allow themselves time to acclimate to the elevation. Finally, do not overestimate your abilities or overexert yourself while on the trails.

Hikers who wish to take an overnight backcountry trip must obtain a backcountry permit for a fee from the Bryce Canyon Visitor Center. In efforts to minimize impact upon the backcountry ecosystem, the National Park Service has designated campgrounds along the Under the Rim Trail and Riggs Spring Loop. Backcountry campers must indicate which campgrounds they will be using on their trip and stick to their itinerary. While obtaining a permit, hikers can question the park rangers about water availability and seasonal conditions.

A shuttle runs between the shuttle area outside the park and trails in the main, upper amphitheater, which makes an excellent option to avoid crowded parking lots during busy summer weekends.

Most supplies and services can be found in the nearby town of Panguitch. However, Panguitch is a notorious speed trap: The police have been known to ticket out-of-state visitors traveling below the speed limit. If you don't have Utah license plates, we recommend steering clear.

41 Fairyland Loop

A day loop through Fairyland Canyon

Distance: 8-mile (12.9 km) loop
Hiking time: About 4 hours
Best season: April–October
Difficulty: Moderate

Water availability: None
Topo maps: Bryce Canyon; Trails Illustrated
Jurisdiction: Bryce Canyon National Park. See Appendix A for more information.

Finding the trailhead: From the Bryce Canyon Visitor Center, drive north 0.7 mile to the sign for the Fairyland Point Overlook. Head east for 1 mile and park in the designated parking zones. GPS: N37° 38' 57.66/W112° 8' 51.41"

The Hike

An enjoyable day hike, this route loops through the Fairyland amphitheater just north of Bryce Canyon. The trail can be accessed easily from a trailhead at Fairyland Point or from Sunrise Point via a short jaunt north along the Rim Trail. Since the access road to Fairyland Point is located between the park entrance and the Bryce Canyon Visitor Center, first-time visitors often drive by, missing Fairyland Point and the Fairyland Loop.

From the Fairyland Loop trailhead, follow a well-worn path of loose gravel northeast down a gradual slope. The trail quickly turns east and briefly traverses a ridgeline toward the sloped hoodoo bases and hills of Bryce Canyon. Hikers will get rewarding views of the Sinking Ship and many other grand formations as the trail approaches and then descends across scree slopes. Trees growing here include Douglas fir, juniper, and limber pine.

The trail continues to wind down the slope until it crosses a draw. The path straightens out on the draw's left bank and briefly parallels the watercourse and then follows switchbacks down again and crosses the draw a second time. Along this section the hoodoos and cliffs of Boat Mesa can be seen off to the southwest.

Beyond the draw the trail traverses a slope, crosses a wash bottom and then briefly climbs upslope before continuing its general descent. Hoodoo formations tower overhead with fantastic views to the left. A ground cover of manzanita colors the rocky

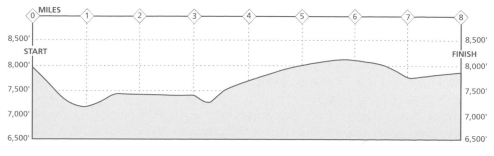

View along the Fairyland Loop SHUTTERSTOCK

slopes a verdant green. Near the bottom of the canyon, the trail passes beneath giant hoodoos surrounding Boat Mesa. To the left is the Fairyland Canyon watercourse and even more spectacular rock formations.

The trail continues down across a few more draws and then begins to switchback upward. From the first right turn of this climb, the sheer cliffs of Boat Mesa can be seen to the right, followed by close views of the Sinking Ship. The path curves around a wall of hoodoos and then descends to cross a series of small draws. Once across the draws, hikers climb through twisted specimens of juniper, ponderosa pine, bristlecone pine, and Douglas fir.

Just above the mouth of Fairyland Canyon, the trail ascends via a series of long switchbacks and then runs along the rim of a small mesa. Views of the surrounding canyon are limited here. The climb soon tops out and the trail continues toward Boat Mesa. It then begins a gradual descent along a somewhat narrow ridgeline. The trail soon heads out onto a slope and continues its descent into the western portion of the canyon.

After several meanderings the trail makes switchbacks down to the Tower Bridge Trail. The Tower Bridge formation is visible from the switchbacks of the Fairyland Loop. However, a short excursion along this 200-yard path will offer closer views near the base of Tower Bridge.

Once beyond the Tower Bridge junction, the Fairyland Loop traverses two draws and begins a steady ascent to the Chinese Wall. The path levels off at the base of the

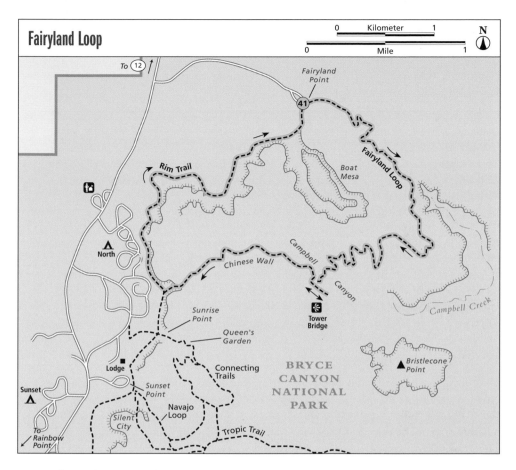

Fairyland Loop

wall and then parallels its foot for about half the length of the formation. It then cuts up through a gap in the hoodoos before making the steady ascent back to the rim of the canyon.

At the rim the path connects with the Rim Trail. Hikers have two options at this point: Take the Rim Trail south to Sunrise Point, or take it north toward Fairyland Point to complete the loop. The portion of the Rim Trail heading back to Fairyland Point is vegetated with juniper, manzanita, and Douglas fir and offers fine views. From the trail junction the path continues a steady ascent for about 1.5 miles. The trail then gradually descends to Fairyland Point.

Key Points

- **0.0** Fairyland Point trailhead; walk this loop clockwise.
- **3.2** Junction with the Tower Bridge Trail. Bear right.
- **3.7** Chinese Wall
- **4.6** Junction with Rim Trail. Continue right (north) to return to Fairyland Point.
- **8.0** Trail returns to Fairyland Point.

42 Rim Trail

A popular trail above Bryce Canyon that connects all the scenic overlooks from Fairyland Point to Bryce Point

Distance: 5.5 miles (8.9 km) one way
Hiking time: About 3 hours
Best season: April–October
Difficulty: Moderate
Water availability: Water is provided at various park restrooms.

Topo maps: Bryce Canyon, Bryce Point; Trails Illustrated
Jurisdiction: Bryce Canyon National Park. See Appendix A for more information.

Finding the trailhead: From the Bryce Canyon Visitor Center, drive north 0.7 mile to the turnoff for Fairyland Point and park in the designated area. From the parking area walk east to the rim at Fairyland Point and follow the stone path south. The Rim Trail is also accessible from Sunrise, Sunset, Inspiration, and Bryce Points. GPS of start: N37° 38' 57.66/W112° 8' 51.41"; GPS of finish: N37° 36' 14.50"/W112° 9' 24.00"

The Hike

This very popular path runs along the rim of Fairyland Canyon and Bryce Canyon. Many park visitors hike the Rim Trail since it is accessible from the park road at various lookout points and provides spectacular views of the spires and canyons below. Travelers can choose to hike the entire trail by starting from Fairyland Point or Bryce Point or break the hike up into smaller segments. Most of the pathway between Sunrise and Inspiration points is either paved or so well worn that portions are wheelchair accessible. However, steep gradients and uneven surfaces may make wheelchair access to some areas difficult.

From Fairyland Point follow the well-worn gravel path southward as it winds upward through a forest of juniper, ponderosa pine, Douglas fir, and bristlecone pine. For about a mile the path intermittently leaves the rim to pass along the westward slopes of hills, blocking views of Fairyland Canyon to the east. The trail emerges into a lightly forested area burned by the Park Service in fall 1995 as a controlled management burn. The path levels off along the rim and then turns southwest into the burn area.

Continuing westward, the trail descends across another slope, moving away from the rim. It eventually winds east to round the hill and emerges once again at the rim of the canyon. Northward views from this

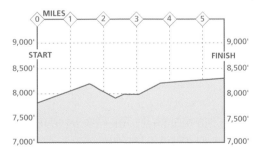

Looking down on the Wall of Windows from the Rim Trail

location encompass Boat Mesa and the Aquarius Plateau. Bristlecone Point, Canaan Mountain, the Kaiparowits Plateau, and Navajo Mountain can be seen to the east.

From here the path briefly levels out along the rim before ascending westward around another hill. Bristlecone pines grow from the barren, rocky slopes here. The trail eventually starts to descend, looping around to the northeast and again emerging at the canyon rim. From here the trail begins a gradual descent through a dense forest of conifers. The path levels off briefly and then begins to climb along the rim.

Next the path gradually descends toward a junction with the Fairyland Loop. At this junction turn left to begin the Fairyland Loop, or bear right to continue along the Rim Trail, which traverses an eastward-facing slope that overlooks the canyon. The trail then leaves the slope and descends to Sunrise Point, 0.25 mile south of the Fairyland junction. Views of the Sinking Ship and Boat Mesa present themselves on the final approach to Sunrise Point. As the trail climbs a gradual slope to Sunrise Point, it meets the Queen's Garden Trail. Bear right to remain on the Rim Trail. Sunrise Point provides spectacular views of the Bryce Canyon amphitheater below.

Sunset Point is encountered about 0.5 mile south of Sunrise Point. Follow the path as it continues along the rim, providing excellent views of the south rim of Bryce Canyon. A juniper-pine forest with a ground cover of manzanita grows to the west of the trail. Wooden benches at various points along the path give visitors opportunities to relax and enjoy the wondrous scenery.

As the trail nears Sunset Point, northward views once again reveal Boat Mesa, the Sinking Ship, and the Aquarius Plateau. A junction with the Navajo Loop lies just north of Sunset Point. Thor's Hammer lies directly below the rim to the left (north) of the Navajo Loop.

From Sunset Point visitors can look down to see a small portion of the narrow rift called Wall Street. After taking in the view, follow the paved path southward. The numerous rifts and caverns of the Silent City await, directly below the rim to the

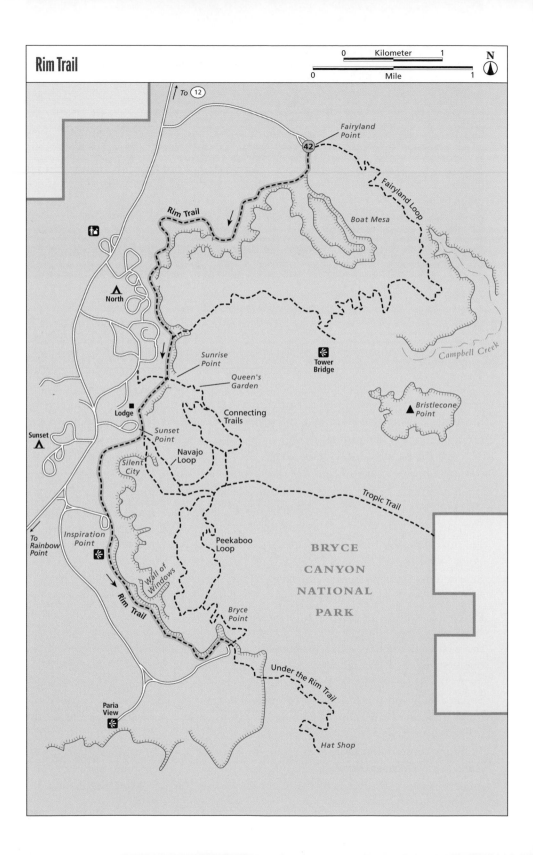

Rim Trail

0   Kilometer   1

0   Mile   1

N

To 12

Fairyland Point

42

Fairyland Loop

Rim Trail

Boat Mesa

North

Campbell Creek

Sunrise Point

Queen's Garden

Tower Bridge

Bristlecone Point

Lodge

Connecting Trails

Sunset Point

Sunset

Navajo Loop

Silent City

To Rainbow Point

Inspiration Point

Tropic Trail

Peekaboo Loop

Wall of Windows

BRYCE

CANYON

NATIONAL

PARK

Rim Trail

Bryce Point

Under the Rim Trail

Paria View

Hat Shop

south of Sunset Point. Across the canyon the Peekaboo Loop can be seen as it winds around the base of The Cathedral.

The Rim Trail soon meets a spur trail leading to Sunset Campground. Bear left and follow the Rim Trail as it leaves the rim and climbs a moderate grade. Below the trail to the west is a pine forest dominated by ponderosas but including limber pine as well. The trail levels off and quickly returns to the rim with the Silent City to the north and The Cathedral and Wall of Windows to the southeast.

The trail quickly winds around another small hill and returns to the rim once more before undertaking the steady climb to Inspiration Point and its three overlooks. As the trail approaches the first overlook, the Wall of Windows can be seen to the left (southeast). The northern horizon opens up dramatically as the trail continues to gain elevation. After a steady climb to the second Inspiration Point overlook, hikers can observe the bottom of Bryce Canyon and study the drainage pattern that flows eastward into Bryce Creek. The third Inspiration Point overlook is located on a spur trail at the top of the ascent. From this point one can see the Wall of Windows to the northwest and the town of Tropic in the opposite direction.

Returning along the spur back to the Rim Trail, through hikers should look for a trail sign that indicates the direction to Bryce Point. The trail now becomes a narrow, unpaved path. The path traverses a ridgeline, passing precariously steep cliffs and crossing a draw. Beyond the draw the narrow path winds up through a pleasant conifer stand. This stretch of trail overlooks the Wall of Windows and grotto formations in the canyon walls. The trail then leaves the rim and begins a gradual descent through a loose growth of conifers. It eventually approaches the rim just above the Wall of Windows and bends southward. Hikers can see more grottos and caverns in the rim wall below Bryce Point, to the southeast.

Once again the trail briefly leaves the rim and then returns to it and descends a series of switchbacks. At the bottom of the grade, the trail levels out and continues a gradual descent until it overlooks a draw. From here it makes a steady climb to Bryce Point. The final approach to Bryce Point is along a steep, westward-facing slope.

Before reaching its terminus at the two Bryce Point overlooks, the trail meets a spur trail to the Bryce Point parking lot. Turn left to reach the overlooks. These two vantage points provide excellent views northwest into Bryce Canyon, north toward the Aquarius Plateau, and northeast toward the Kaiparowits Plateau.

Key Points

0.0	Fairyland Point
2.2	Junction with Fairyland Loop. Bear right.
2.5	Sunrise Point
3.0	Sunset Point
3.8	Inspiration Point
4.3	Wall of Windows Overlook
5.5	Bryce Point

43 Queen's Garden Complex

A short trail descending below the canyon rim

Distance: 0.9 mile (1.4 km) one way
Hiking time: About 0.5 hour
Best season: April–October
Difficulty: Moderate
Water availability: None

Hazards: Steep slopes, loose gravel
Topo maps: Bryce Canyon, Bryce Point; Trails Illustrated
Jurisdiction: Bryce Canyon National Park. See Appendix A for more information.

Finding the trailhead: From the Bryce Canyon Visitor Center, drive south 0.4 mile to the turnoff for Sunrise Point. Follow road signs to Sunrise Point and park in the designated area. From the parking area walk southeast along well-worn paths to the Queen's Garden trailhead. GPS: N37° 37' 47.61"/W112° 9' 46.90"

The Hike

The Queens Garden Trail is a short, 0.9-mile route that drops about 320 feet below the canyon rim. Although the trail is not a loop, hikers can loop back up to the rim by combining a connecting trail with either branch of the Navajo Loop. Interesting rock formations along this popular path include Gulliver's Castle, the Queen's Castle, and Queen Elizabeth herself.

From the trailhead the trail descends along a slope below Sunrise Point. The path briefly traces a ridgeline but soon returns to a northward-facing slope. Early views include Boat Mesa, the Sinking Ship, and the Aquarius Plateau to the northeast; Bristlecone Point, Canaan Mountain, the Kaiparowits Plateau, and Navajo Mountain show themselves in the east.

The trail continues along this slope until it bends to the south and descends a series of switchbacks. At the bottom of the grade, the path straightens out onto a ridgeline with Bryce Canyon below to the south and a conifer-filled draw to the north. The trail soon descends another set of switchbacks and levels off along a slope with the Aquarius Plateau and the Sinking Ship to the northeast. It then bends right and comes to a junction with the Tropic Trail; bear right to continue the Queen's Garden Trail.

The trail continues to descend via a series of short switchbacks to a tunnel cut through a wall of hoodoos. Beyond the tunnel ragged spires tower over the trail, which continues along the base of the formations, passes between two hoodoos, and again descends via switchbacks. The path straightens out above a draw and

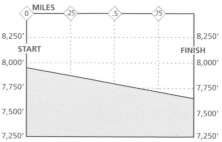

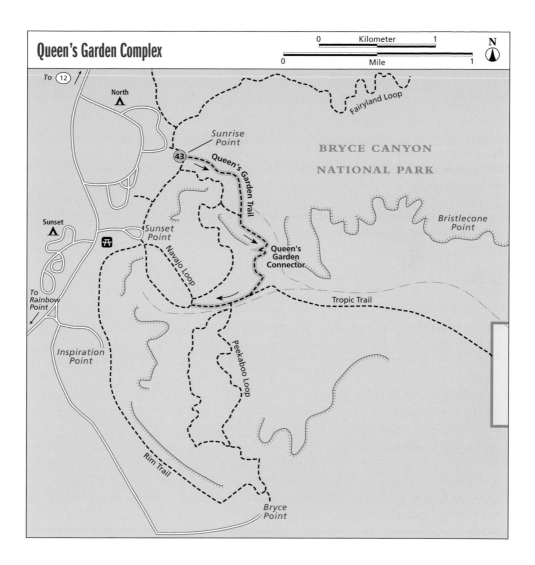

Kilometer

Mile

N

To 12

North

Sunrise Point

43

Queen's Garden Trail

BRYCE CANYON

NATIONAL PARK

Fairyland Loop

Sunset

Sunset Point

Navajo Loop

Queen's Garden Connector

Bristlecone Point

Tropic Trail

To Rainbow Point

Inspiration Point

Peekaboo Loop

Rim Trail

Bryce Point

passes through another tunnel. Beyond the tunnel the trail bends south and traverses along the slopes overlooking another draw. The trail bends right, passes through a third tunnel, and joins the Navajo Loop Connecting Trail at the bottom of the canyon. Bear left to reach the Navajo Loop, or right to continue the Queen's Garden Trail.

The Queen Elizabeth formation and the end of the trail rise 50 feet west of the junction.

Key Points

0.0 Queen's Garden trailhead at Sunrise Point

0.8 Junction with connecting trail to the Navajo Loop. Bear right.

0.9 Queen Elizabeth formation and end of trail

44 Navajo Loop

A loop from Sunset Point down to the floor of Bryce Canyon and back again

Distance: 1.4 miles (2.2 km) overall
Hiking time: About 1.5 hours
Best season: April–October
Difficulty: Moderate

Water availability: None
Topo maps: Bryce Point; Trails Illustrated
Jurisdiction: Bryce Canyon National Park. See
Appendix A for more information.

Finding the trailhead: The trail departs from a signpost at the central overlook point at Sunset
Point. GPS: N37° 37' 25.21"/W112° 10' 1.86"

The Hike

This popular trail makes a short one- to two-hour loop from the rim at Sunset Point down to the floor of Bryce Canyon. The trail visits favorite hoodoo formations such as Wall Street, Twin Bridges, and Thor's Hammer.

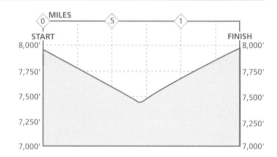

From Sunset Point the trail immediately descends along a paved path with safety railings along the edges. After about 100 feet the railing ends and the path splits, with two trails heading off to the right (south) and one trail heading off to the left (east). The left-hand path is the eastern leg of the Navajo Loop; it will be discussed later in this description. The two right-hand paths consist of an upper and a lower trail.

The upper trail is a short spur to a window looking through a hoodoo wall down into the west portion of Bryce Canyon. The lower trail is the first leg of the Navajo Loop; it begins a rapid descent along a series of long and short switchbacks down to the canyon floor. At the bottom of the switchbacks, the trail straightens out and makes a gradual descent through Wall Street, where two towering Douglas firs have been growing in the depths of the rift for more than 750 years.

Upon emerging from Wall Street, hikers follow a wide pathway bordered by manzanita, juniper, and ponderosa pines. The end of the south leg of the Navajo Loop is identified by trail signs for the Peekaboo Loop Connecting Trail and the Queen's Garden Connecting Trail. Hikers can make a hard left turn to complete the remaining 0.6 mile of the Navajo Loop back up to Sunset Point, or connect with one of these other paths for a longer hike.

Douglas firs soar within Wall Street, along the Navajo Loop. ▶

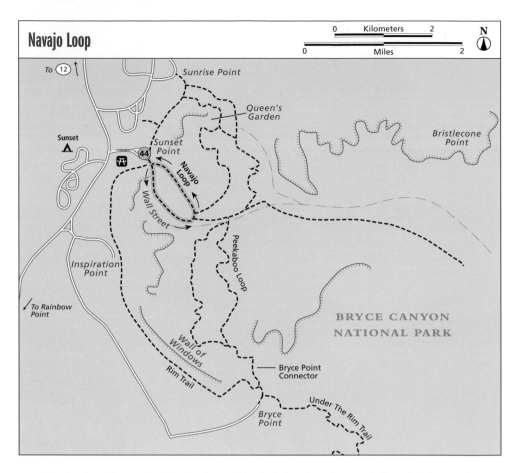

Navajo Loop

0 Kilometers 2
0 Miles 2
N

To (12)
Sunrise Point
Queen's Garden
Bristlecone Point
Sunset
Sunset Point
Navajo Loop
Wall Street
Peekaboo Loop
Inspiration Point
To Rainbow Point
BRYCE CANYON NATIONAL PARK
Wall of Windows
Rim Trail
Bryce Point Connector
Bryce Point
Under The Rim Trail

Continuing along the Navajo Loop (the left-hand path noted above), hikers gain enjoyable views of large hoodoo formations flanking both sides of the path. One such formation, Twin Bridges, is located on the right side of the trail at mile 1. Beyond Twin Bridges the path ascends a series of switchbacks to return to the rim. Look for Thor's Hammer to the north along this final section of trail.

Key Points

0.0 Navajo Loop trailhead at Sunset Point

0.4 Wall Street

0.6 Junction with Peekaboo Loop and Queen's Garden Connecting Trail. Turn left to complete the Navajo Loop.

1.0 Twin Bridges formation on north side of trail

1.4 Trail returns to Sunset Point.

45 Peekaboo Loop

A loop for hikers and horses through the pink limestone formations below the rim of Bryce Canyon

Distance: 5.5 miles (8.9 km) overall
Hiking time: About 3 hours
Best season: April–October
Difficulty: Moderate

Water availability: None
Topo maps: Bryce Point; Trails Illustrated
Jurisdiction: Bryce Canyon National Park. See Appendix A for more information.

Finding the trailhead: From the Bryce Canyon Visitor Center, drive south 1.6 miles to a turnoff for Inspiration and Bryce Points. Follow road signs to Bryce Point and park in the designated area. The Bryce Point trailhead is at the north corner of the parking lot. GPS: N37° 36' 14.50" / W112° 9' 24.00"

The Hike

A short connector begins at Bryce Point and descends below the rim to connect with the Peekaboo Loop, a hiker and horse trail that winds around hoodoo formations below Inspiration Point and Bryce Point. Views along this trail include the popular Wall of Windows, The Three Wisemen, The Organ, and The Cathedral as well as eastward views beyond the canyon toward the Aquarius Plateau, Canaan Mountain, and the Kaiparowits Plateau.

The trail departs from the north corner of the Bryce Point parking lot. From the sidewalk follow the trail as it descends southeast along a slope below the parking lot. The trail soon meets a junction with the Under the Rim Trail; bear right to follow this trail toward The Hat Shop formations.

To reach the Peekaboo Loop, turn left and follow the trail as it descends northeast along a gravel path. Bristlecone and limber pines grow along the trail as it heads down a series of short switchbacks. At the bottom of the grade, the trail straightens out along a slope beneath towering white cliffs of limestone. Northward views here include Bryce Canyon, below, and Boat Mesa rising in the distance.

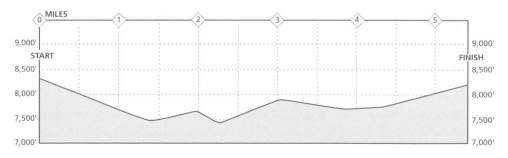

The trail drops until it reaches a man-made tunnel. Beyond the tunnel the pathway levels off and continues northwest beneath Bryce Point overlook and several grotto formations. Rockfalls commonly make the path extremely narrow and rocky, making for unstable footing.

Continuing northwest, the trail passes a large hoodoo wall and begins another gradual descent. The Wall of Windows lies to the west of the trail as it turns a switchback and then bends to the right. Hoodoos directly below this portion of the trail provide good examples of resistant, lime-rich layers capping the formation and protecting the weaker layers below from erosion. The trail winds down the slope and traverses beneath these caprock formations.

Just beyond the hoodoos the trail comes to a junction with the Peekaboo Loop. Turn left (west) at the junction to quickly reach the Peekaboo Loop horse corrals and pit toilets. Then turn right and follow the trail as it heads down a switchbacked slope, passing bristlecone and limber pines along the way. The trail straightens and continues to drop gradually along the west side of a draw. Pink hoodoos line the draw's sides as ponderosa pine, juniper, and manzanita grow in the bottom.

The path eventually traverses northwest across the draw and begins a slow ascent across a series of washes and then follows switchbacks up to a tunnel cut into the ridgetop. Beyond the tunnel the trail bends left and continues up the opposite (north) slope of the ridge. Hoodoos decorate the ridgetops as the trail levels off and winds along the slopes. Other views include Bryce Point and grotto formations to the south of the trail.

The trail eventually makes a short ascent and cuts between two hoodoo formations. At the top of the climb, the rifts and caverns of the Silent City can be seen ahead to the north. The trail begins to descend at the base of The Cathedral. It then straightens out and follows the upper left side of a draw, with Boat Mesa rising on the northern horizon.

Another set of switchbacks drops hikers down into the draw. From here the trail goes down the draw to a junction with the Navajo Loop Connecting Trail. Bear right to reach the Navajo Loop; turn left to return to the Bryce Point trail via the Peekaboo Loop.

The main route heads up a gradual slope here, providing overlooking views of a washbed and the Navajo Loop to the right (west). The path ascends steadily along slopes until it passes through a small cavern. Afterward it levels off somewhat and begins to wind around pink limestone formations above the canyon floor.

After several small ascents and descents, the path passes through a man-made arch and into a small grotto with large hoodoo walls towering above. The trail descends through this cavern via a series of short switchbacks. At the bottom of the switchbacks, it emerges from the cavern with a close-up view of the Wall of Windows to the right. The trail briefly traverses the base of the Wall of Windows. Looking up at the canyon rim from here, hikers can see grottos in the cliffs.

Beyond the Wall of Windows, the trail descends to the canyon floor, where a horse corral and pit toilets are located (this is the only trail in Bryce Canyon where

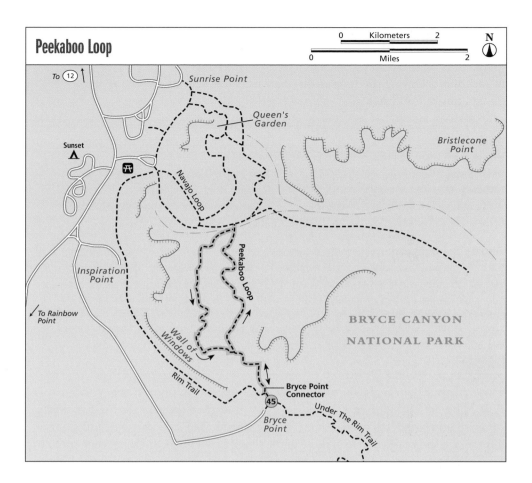

Peekaboo Loop

Kilometers

Miles

N

To (12)

Sunrise Point

Queen's Garden

Bristlecone Point

Sunset

Navajo Loop

Peekaboo Loop

Inspiration Point

To Rainbow Point

Wall of Windows

BRYCE CANYON

NATIONAL PARK

Rim Trail

Bryce Point Connector

(45)

Under The Rim Trail

Bryce Point

pit toilets are provided along the route). The junction with the Bryce Point Trail, which will take you back to your starting point, is located slightly uphill from the horse corral.

Key Points

0.0 Trailhead at Bryce Point

0.1 Junction with the Under the Rim Trail. Turn left.

1.0 Junction with the Peekaboo Loop. Turn right.

2.2 Junction with the Navajo Loop Connecting Trail. Turn left.

2.5 The Cathedral

3.1 The Wall of Windows

3.6 Horse corral

4.0 Return to Bryce Point Trail. Turn right.

5.0 Junction with the Under the Rim Trail. Turn right.

5.5 Bryce Point

46 Under the Rim Trail

A backpack following the foot of the Pink Cliffs through the southern reaches of Bryce Canyon National Park

Distance: 23 miles (37 km) one way
Hiking time: About 12 hours
Best seasons: April–June, September–October
Difficulty: Moderately strenuous*
Water availability: The Right Fork of Yellow Creek and Ponderosa Canyon, Iron, and Birch

Springs carry water except during drought conditions.
Topo maps: Bryce Point, Tropic Reservoir, Rainbow Point; Trails Illustrated
Jurisdiction: Bryce Canyon National Park. See Appendix A for details.

Finding the trailhead: From the Bryce Canyon Visitor Center, drive south on the park road for 1.6 miles to reach the turnoff for Inspiration Point and Bryce Point. Follow the paved road southeast for 0.5 mile, bearing left at the junction to reach Bryce Point. The trail begins from the east side of the parking lot. GPS of start: N37° 36' 14.50"/W112° 9' 24.00"; GPS of finish: N37° 28' 29.99"/W112° 14' 25.77"

The Hike

The Under the Rim Trail is the premier backpacking route in Bryce Canyon National Park. Although it seldom strays more than a few miles from the park road, its position below the rimrock lends it a backcountry-like solitude. The hoodoos and cliffs along this trail are less spectacular than those in the heavily traveled northern reaches of the park, but those who hike here will seldom run into other visitors. Several connecting trails link this route with the road, allowing backpackers to select a route of almost any conceivable length. For overnight trips travelers must register in advance for one of the designated campsites that appear on the map accompanying this description. Once set, you cannot change your itinerary (written on your permit).

After departing from Bryce Point, the trail wanders across barren hilltops where scattered conifers provide dappled shade for clumps of manzanita. Watch for chipmunks as the path makes its way to the upper rim of Merrill Hollow. From here hikers will have distant views of the Tropic Valley and the Aquarius Plateau beyond it.

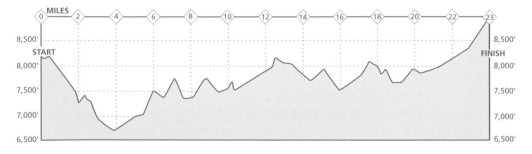

Nearer at hand, observe how winter gales have whipped the ponderosa pine, limber pine, and Douglas fir into twisted forms. Weathered rock spires crowd the head of the hollow, bathed in oranges, reds, and purples. These brilliant colors are derived from iron and manganese oxides within the bedrock.

The trail runs down a finger ridge and then drops below the cliffs to cross the head of the drainage. Taller conifers disappear here, replaced by Utah juniper in an arid scrubland. The path soon runs onto a sinuous ridgetop overlooking the Right Fork of Yellow Creek. The slope to the south is covered with a pinnacle formation known as The Hat Shop. The slope is formed of a loose conglomerate that melts away quickly with summer rains; isolated boulders of more resistant stone have protected some of the conglomerate from erosion, forming slender spires below the telltale caprock.

After passing The Hat Shop, the trail descends toward the Right Fork valley floor, passing a layer of resistant sandstone along the way. At the bottom of the grade, the trail arrives at the Right Fork Camping Area, situated in a grove of enormous ponderosa pines. A reliable flow of water has carved a deep gully into the valley floor here, and the path follows this wash downward through the brush. The valley ultimately opens onto sage-juniper flats where the Right Fork joins the main channel of Yellow Creek, which flows in from the southwest.

From here the path bends around the toe of the ridge and begins a gradual ascent toward the source of Yellow Creek. The Yellow Creek Group Camp occupies a clearing in the Gambel oak woodland a short distance up the drainage. Farther on, gaps in the scrub trees reveal tantalizing glimpses of the multicolored pinnacles that form the headwall of the valley. This is arid country; watch for desert shrubs and barrel cacti among the junipers.

The Yellow Creek Camping Area occupies a grove of tall pines near the head of the drainage. Soon after passing it the trail zigzags briskly up a grassy slope that affords expansive views in all directions. To the east gray cliffs of shale rise above blood-red badlands of sandstone.

Upon cresting a high saddle near the base of the Pink Cliffs, the path runs southward through an open pine woodland where bright green clumps of manzanita dot the forest floor. This gentle descent is followed by a steady climb to the divide overlooking Pasture Wash. The trail then traverses the high country for a time before beginning a vigorous descent to the valley floor. Superb views of the Pink Cliffs accompany hikers during the descent, featuring gabled walls and squared-off towers.

Once on the valley floor, the path heads toward a massif of reddish stone that is crowned with needle-shaped spires. The trailbed is badly eroded in places; watch for cairns where the route becomes faint. After crossing Pasture Wash, the trail ascends a side draw and then climbs to a saddle overlooking the Sheep Creek valley. Colored cliffs stretch away in an unbroken line to the south, while Swamp Canyon Butte and Mud Canyon Butte stand apart from the main mass of limestone. As the path descends into the eroded hill country of upper Sheep Creek, dagger-shaped pinnacles unveil themselves to the west.

Soon after crossing the Sheep Creek wash, the Under the Rim Trail intersects the Sheep Creek Trail. Continue westward as the trail climbs gently through a low pass and then drops into the Swamp Canyon bottoms. Cold air from the top of the plateau flows down into this area and pools in the lowlands, creating a climate suitable for aspen.

Upon passing the Right Fork Swamp Canyon Camp, the trail swings southwest to a junction with the Swamp Canyon Connecting Trail. This spur trail climbs to the park road atop the plateau. Turn left as the Under the Rim Trail climbs a gentle but steady incline, following Swamp Canyon. Swamp Canyon Butte and Mud Canyon Butte slide by to the east as the trail climbs to the top of the plateau.

After passing a small amphitheater filled with eroded spires, the trail reaches Swamp Canyon Camp, perched on a wooded terrace high above the floor of the canyon. Just beyond the camp the Whiteman Connecting Trail departs on a westward bearing toward the road. The Under the Rim Trail bears southward through a broad gap, where a pine and aspen woodland is interspersed with grassy glades. A steady descent leads into the upper basin of Willis Creek, which is forested in tall ponderosa pines. Ahead, a jagged formation of orange limestone juts into the basin like the prow of a sinking ship.

The trail makes its way across the high country beneath the eastern edge of this landform to reach a sandy saddle where dunes and blowouts have been partially stabilized by patches of manzanita. On the descent into the next basin, look westward for an unobstructed view of Natural Bridge, which stands apart from the base of the Pink Cliffs. On the basin floor the trail reaches Natural Bridge Camp in a grove of pines. Campers can see some cliffs from here, but Natural Bridge itself is not visible from this point.

The path continues, crossing an open meadow crowded with wildflowers that explode into a profusion of yellow blossoms during late summer. Upon returning to the forest, the route follows the wash of Agua Canyon toward its headwaters. Follow the cairns where the pathway becomes faint or washed out. Near the head of the drainage, travelers are faced with a long slog up a north-facing slope. A full-grown forest of Douglas fir provides shade for most of the climb, but the trees thin out near the top and allow panoramic views to the north and west. At the top of the climb, gnarled piñon pines grow from the ridgetop amid a scattering of boulders and outcrops. Here, the Agua Canyon connecting trail takes off to the west.

The Under the Rim route carries travelers down into the basin to the south, which is overlooked by a brightly colored cliff. This portion of the trail was poorly maintained at the time this book was written; expect some underbrush and occasional washouts at streamcourse crossings. As it crosses the basin, the path surmounts several finger ridges. It then charts a level course along the edge of the amphitheater. Water can often be found in the main wash of Ponderosa Canyon, and there is a small campsite at Iron Spring.

The trail climbs onto the slopes of the long ridge that bounds the basin to the south. The grade is gentle but constant, and views encompass the orange walls that

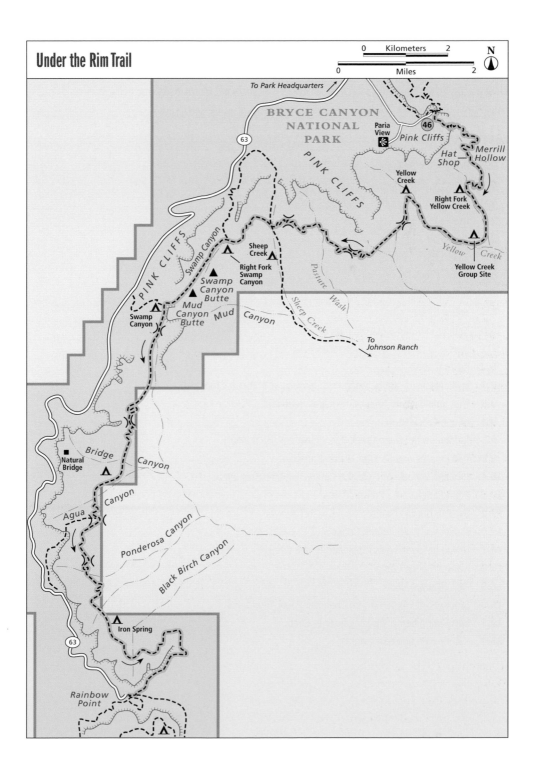

Under the Rim Trail

0 Kilometers 2
0 Miles 2

N

To Park Headquarters

BRYCE CANYON
NATIONAL
PARK

63

Paria
View

Pink Cliffs

Hat
Shop

Merrill
Hollow

P I N K   C L I F F S

Yellow
Creek

Right Fork
Yellow Creek

Yellow Creek
Group Site

Yellow   Creek

P I N K   C L I F F S

Swamp Canyon

Sheep
Creek

Right Fork
Swamp
Canyon

Pasture   Wash

Sheep Creek

Swamp
Canyon
Butte

Mud
Canyon
Butte

Mud   Canyon

Canyon

To
Johnson Ranch

Swamp
Canyon

Bridge   Canyon

Natural
Bridge

Agua   Canyon

Ponderosa Canyon

Black Birch Canyon

Iron Spring

63

Rainbow
Point

stretch northward all the way to Bryce Point. When the trail rounds a corner onto east-facing slopes, the gradient increases, presenting a grueling climb. At the top the path runs onto the spine of a narrow ridge that overlooks the nearby pinnacles and alcoves of the Pink Cliffs. The path then enters a subalpine forest for the final ascent. Bear right at all trail junctions to reach the Rainbow Point parking area, where the hike ends.

Key Points

0.0 Bryce Point trailhead

0.2 Junction with Peekaboo Loop. Turn right.

1.4 Head of Merrill Hollow. Trail begins descent.

2.3 The Hat Shop

3.0 Right Fork Camp

3.5 Right Fork wash crossing

4.0 Yellow Creek Group Camp

5.2 Yellow Creek wash crossing

5.4 Yellow Creek Camp

5.9 Saddle into nameless drainage

7.1 Pass into Pasture Wash watershed.

8.2 Pasture Wash

8.7 Trail crosses divide between Pasture Wash and Sheep Creek.

9.3 First junction with Sheep Creek Trail. Bear right.

9.4 Sheep Creek wash

9.5 Junction with Sheep Creek Connecting Trail. Bear left.

9.9 Trail crosses saddle into Swamp Canyon.

10.4 Junction with Swamp Canyon Connecting Trail. Stay left.

10.5 Right Fork Swamp Canyon Camp

12.2 Swamp Canyon Camp

12.3 Junction with Whiteman Connecting Trail. Bear left.

14.7 Divide between Willis Creek and Bridge Canyon

15.6 Natural Bridge Camp

16.3 Agua Canyon wash

16.9 Junction with Agua Canyon Connecting Trail. Bear left.

19.5 Iron Spring Camp. Trail begins final climb.

23.0 Rainbow Point parking area

47 Sheep Creek

A day hike from the Bryce Canyon rim down to the canyon bottoms and, if desired, outside the park into national forest

Distance: 3–5 miles (4.8–8 km) one way
Hiking time: About 1.5–2.5 hours
Best season: April–October
Difficulty: Easy heading east; moderate heading west

Water availability: None
Hazards: Loose gravel
Topo maps: Bryce Point; Trails Illustrated
Jurisdiction: Bryce Canyon National Park. See Appendix A for details.

Finding the trailhead: Drive 5 miles south from the Bryce Canyon Visitor Center and park in a small parking area. A trailhead sign for the Sheep Creek and Swamp Creek Connecting Trails is located at the parking area. GPS: N37° 35' 15.30"/W112° 12' 47.41"

The Hike

This 3- to 5-mile route encompasses the Sheep Creek Connecting Trail, a short stretch of the Under the Rim Trail, and the Sheep Creek Trail proper. The trail leaves from a small parking area 5 miles south of the Bryce Canyon Visitor Center. The first mile of the trail stays above the rim, traversing the uplands of the Paunsaugunt Plateau. The trail then follows the Sheep Creek draw south as it descends below pink limestone cliffs to visit the canyon bottoms.

At the trailhead a confusing array of trails presents itself. Follow the path leading from the trail sign downhill to the left (north). Continue downhill to reach a second trail sign that indicates the junction of the Sheep Creek and Swamp Canyon Connecting Trails.

Follow the Sheep Creek Connecting Trail to the left (north). The path here is narrow and consists mostly of bare soil. The trail heads north for approximately 0.8 mile, paralleling the park road. The path begins in a meadow but soon approaches a pine-juniper woodland and travels along the edge of it. A small draw lies to the left (west) of the trail.

After about 0.8 mile the trail joins an old dirt road that follows the draw as it turns southeast. The draw soon passes a bare saddle with a forest of juniper and pine occupying the hillsides to either side. Limestone hoodoos rise into view to the southeast as the trees open up.

Just before beginning a descent along the Sheep Creek wash, hikers pass

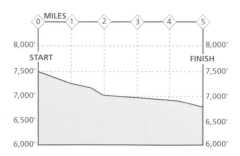

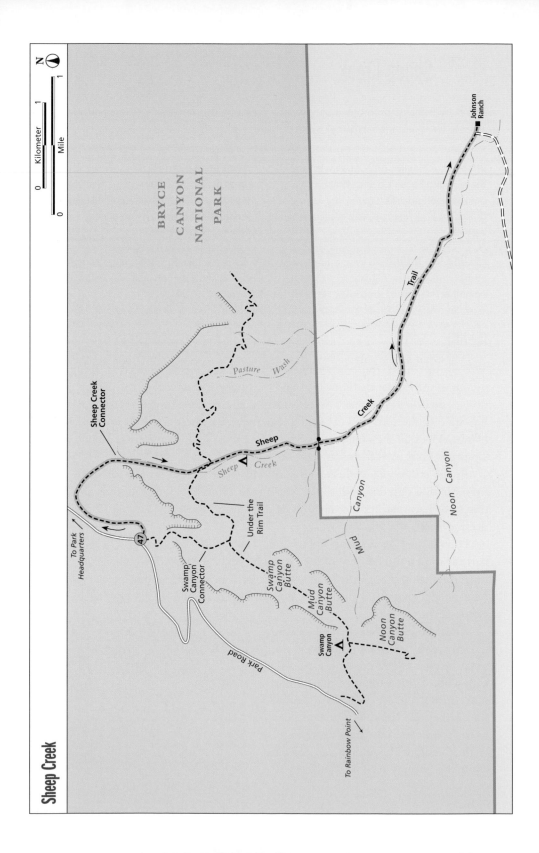

Sheep Creek

N

Kilometer
0   1

Mile
0   1

BRYCE
CANYON
NATIONAL
PARK

Johnson
Ranch

Trail

Noon Canyon

Sheep   Creek

Pasture   Wash

Sheep Creek
Connector

Sheep

Sheep   Creek

Under the
Rim Trail

Mud   Canyon

Noon
Canyon
Butte

Mud
Canyon
Butte

Swamp
Canyon
Butte

Swamp Canyon
Connector

Swamp
Canyon

To Park
Headquarters

47

Park Road

To Rainbow Point

a USGS elevation marker to the right of the trail. Beyond the USGS marker the path turns southward and gradually descends through a gap in the cliff walls. Pink cliff formations can be seen ahead to the left and right as the trail sinks below the rim. The trail continues down toward the canyon floor until it intersects with the Under the Rim Trail.

Follow the Under the Rim Trail left (south) about 0.1 mile to its junction with the Sheep Creek Trail. Bear right and follow this trail as it traverses south along the Sheep Creek wash through a forest of juniper and pine. Take time to enjoy the intermittent backward views of the rim. The Sheep Creek Campground lies 0.5 mile from the junction. The campground is surrounded by ponderosa pine and Gambel oak and offers views of Swamp Canyon Butte to the west.

Another 0.5 mile beyond the campground lies the park boundary, where there is a padlocked gate and barbed-wire fencing. A hikers' gate is not provided along this section. Beyond the park boundary lies Dixie National Forest land. This area is used to graze cattle. Hikers who wish to continue traveling along Sheep Creek can choose one of several cattle and horse paths through the area. The landscape here consists of arid scrubland dominated by juniper, sagebrush, and Gambel oak. The watercourses have beds of sand, cobblestone, and gravel. A cattleguard and fence indicate the national forest boundary line, beyond which the route enters private property.

Key Points

0.0 Trailhead for Sheep Creek and Swamp Canyon Connecting Trails

0.1 Sheep Creek Connecting Trail splits from Swamp Canyon Connecting Trail. Bear left.

2.0 Junction with the Under the Rim Trail. Turn left (south).

2.1 Junction with the Sheep Creek Trail. Bear right.

2.6 Sheep Creek Campground

3.1 National park boundary

5.0 National forest boundary

48 Swamp Canyon Connecting Trail

A trail connecting the park road and the Under the Rim Trail near Swamp Canyon Butte to the Right Fork Swamp Canyon Campground

Distance: 1 mile (1.6 km) one way
Hiking time: About 0.5 hour
Best season: April–October
Difficulty: Easy heading south; moderate heading north

Water availability: None
Topo maps: Bryce Point; Trails Illustrated
Jurisdiction: Bryce Canyon National Park. See Appendix A for more information.

Finding the trailhead: From the Bryce Canyon Visitor Center, drive south 5 miles to a small parking area with a trailhead sign for the Swamp Canyon and Sheep Creek Connecting Trails. The hike begins here. GPS: N37° 35' 15.30"/W112° 12' 47.41"

The Hike

This 1-mile trail makes a quick descent of 500 feet to drop below the rim and connects with the Under the Rim Trail. Many confusing paths lead from the trailhead sign; follow the path that heads downhill to the left (north). Continue heading downhill to the left until you come to a second trail sign indicating the junction of the Sheep Creek and Swamp Canyon Connecting Trails.

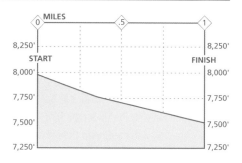

From this junction the Swamp Canyon Connecting Trail turns right (south) and immediately descends along a draw between limestone cliffs to the east and west. Below the rim the trail winds southwest along the wash through an area vegetated with Gambel oak, Douglas fir, ponderosa pine, juniper, and manzanita. The cliffs of the rim appear to the northeast and northwest of the trail. Once the path reaches the junction with the Under the Rim Trail, hikers will see Swamp Canyon Butte jutting up into the sky to the south.

Key Points

0.0 Trailhead
0.1 Junction of Swamp Canyon and Sheep Creek Trails
1.0 Junction with Under the Rim Trail

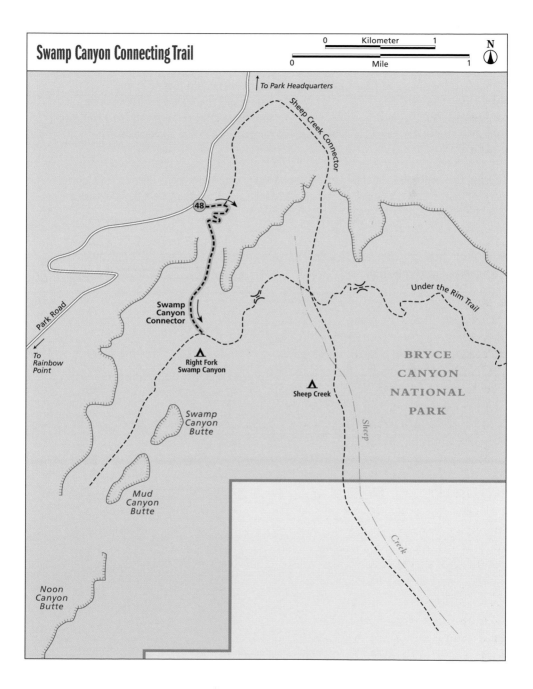

Swamp Canyon Connecting Trail

0   Kilometer   1

0   Mile   1

N

To Park Headquarters

Sheep Creek Connector

48

Park Road

Swamp
Canyon
Connector

Under the Rim Trail

To
Rainbow
Point

Right Fork
Swamp Canyon

Sheep Creek

BRYCE
CANYON
NATIONAL
PARK

Swamp
Canyon
Butte

Sheep

Mud
Canyon
Butte

Creek

Noon
Canyon
Butte

49 Whiteman Connecting Trail

This trail connects the park road with the Under the Rim Trail near Swamp Canyon Campground and Noon Canyon Butte.

Distance: 0.9 mile (1.4 km) one way

Hiking time: About 0.5 hour

Best season: April–October

Difficulty: Easy heading west; moderate heading east

Water availability: None

Topo maps: Bryce Point; Trails Illustrated

Jurisdiction: Bryce Canyon National Park. See Appendix A for more information.

Finding the trailhead: From the Bryce Canyon Visitor Center, drive along the park road to mile marker 9 and turn left into the small parking area on the east side of the road. The hike begins here. GPS: N37° 33' 49.77"/W112° 14' 20.35"

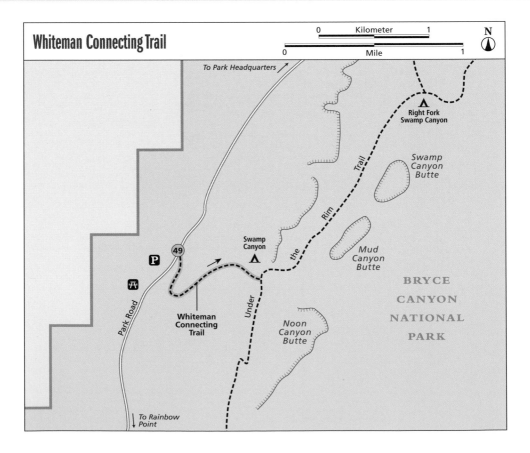

The Hike

From the parking area the trail heads south, briefly paralleling the park road. The trail continues generally south through a juniper-pine forest until it reaches a dry wash. From here the path turns northeast and follows the wash downhill. The path follows the wash until it intersects with the Under the Rim Trail near the Swamp Canyon Campground.

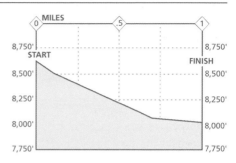

Key Points

0.0 Trailhead

0.9 Junction with Under the Rim Trail

50 Agua Canyon Connecting Trail

A trail connecting Ponderosa Point with the Under the Rim Trail

Distance: 1.8 miles (2.9 km) one way
Hiking time: About 1 hour
Best season: April–October
Difficulty: Moderate
Water availability: None

Hazards: Steep pitches and loose rocks
Topo maps: Tropic Reservoir, Bryce Point; Trails Illustrated
Jurisdiction: Bryce Canyon National Park. See Appendix A for more information.

Finding the trailhead: From the Bryce Canyon Visitor Center, drive south on the park road for 13.7 miles to the Ponderosa Point parking area. The trail departs from a signpost on the northwest side of the parking area. GPS: N37° 29' 52.15"/W112° 15' 31.65"

The Hike

From the trailhead sign this connecting path climbs northwest up a small hill into a forest of fir and pine. The trail parallels the park road in a northerly direction for about 0.5 mile, emerging into a shallow valley draw. It then begins a gradual north-easterly descent through stands of fir trees.

For the next 0.4 mile, views of hoodoo formations are obscured by the dense forest canopy. As the path progresses downward, the forest opens to reveal splendid views of the cliffs to the north as well as aerial views of the canyon below. A stand of bristlecone pines grows along the rocky cliff tops bordering the trail. This portion of the route calls for caution; it traverses steep slopes covered with loose gravel.

The path soon narrows and makes switchbacks down an open slope that is sparsely populated with bristlecone pine, Douglas fir, and white fir. Views into the canyon accompany travelers along this open slope. This section of path is poorly maintained, and several rockfalls make for unstable footing.

The trail ultimately emerges onto an open slope below the rim and passes beneath pink limestone cliffs. From here hikers can gaze northward at the multicolored cliffs

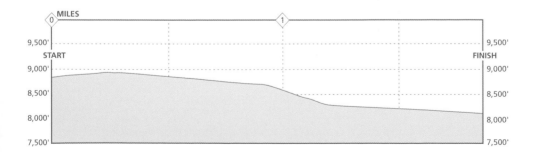

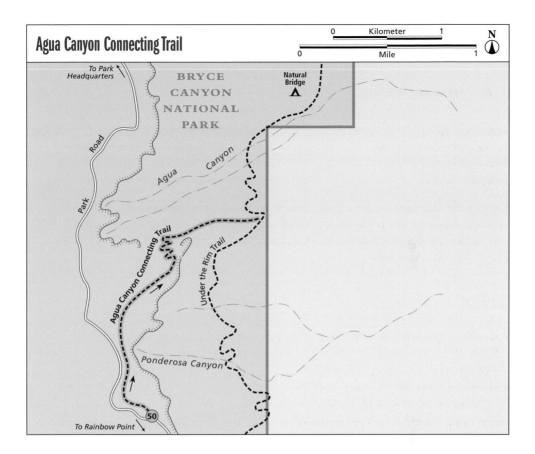

of Agua Canyon. Travelers with keen eyesight might spot Natural Bridge to the north across Agua Canyon and Bridge Canyon. The path continues down along this slope until it ends at a junction with the Under the Rim Trail. The junction commands northward views of the Pink Cliffs, Agua Canyon, and Natural Bridge. Rainbow Point rises above the horizon to the south.

Key Points

0.0 Ponderosa Point trailhead

1.1 Top of the switchbacks

1.4 Bottom of the grade

1.8 Junction with Under the Rim Trail

51 Bristlecone Loop

A short loop trail above the rim at Rainbow Point

Distance: 1 mile (1.6 km) overall
Hiking time: About 0.5 hour
Best season: April–October
Difficulty: Easy

Water availability: None
Topo maps: Rainbow Point; Trails Illustrated
Jurisdiction: Bryce Canyon National Park. See Appendix A for more information.

Finding the trailhead: From the Bryce Canyon Visitor Center, drive 16.8 miles south to Rainbow Point. Follow the sidewalk to the southeast side of the parking lot to the Bristlecone Loop trailhead sign. An additional trailhead sign is located to the left of the restrooms. GPS: N37° 28' 29.46"/W112° 14' 25.34"

The Hike

This short loop stays entirely above the canyon rim as it traverses a subalpine fir forest. The trail is named after the bristlecone pine, which is found more frequently along this trail than along other trails in Bryce Canyon National Park. Bristlecone pine can be identified by the foxtail tufts of needles growing at the tips of its limbs. It can survive on

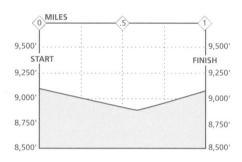

high, windy ridges and can weather prolonged periods of drought. Due to its tenacity the bristlecone pine has a tremendous lifespan. A California specimen has been dated at more than 4,000 years old.

From the trailhead the path winds southeast through dense stands of white fir, Douglas fir, and ponderosa pine. The path loops out to the cliffs and the canyon rim. Bristlecone pines grow atop the open, windy cliffs along the rim. As the trail returns to Rainbow Point, it intersects the Under the Rim Trail. Trail signs along the route direct hikers back to the starting point.

Key Points

0.0 Rainbow Point trailhead. Follow the path south.
0.1 Junction with Riggs Spring Loop
0.8 Junction with the Under the Rim Trail. Follow trail signs for Rainbow Point to return to the trailhead.
1.0 Trail returns to Rainbow Point trailhead.

Bristlecone Loop

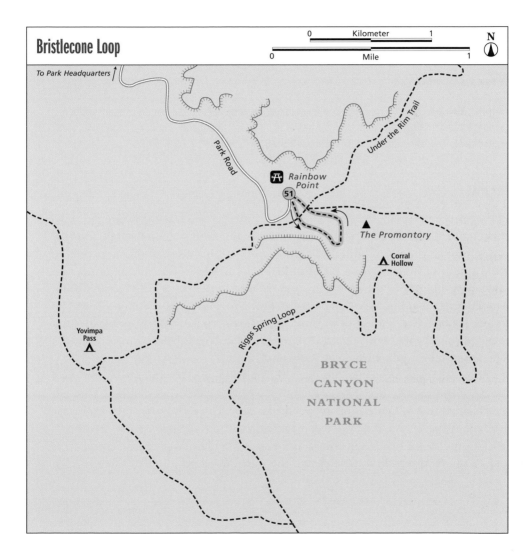

0 Kilometer 1

0 Mile 1

N

To Park Headquarters

Park Road

Under the Rim Trail

Rainbow Point

51

The Promontory

Corral Hollow

Riggs Spring Loop

Yovimpa Pass

BRYCE

CANYON

NATIONAL

PARK

52 Riggs Spring Loop

A loop traversing above and below the Pink Cliffs at the southern edge of Bryce Canyon National Park

Distance: 8.8 miles (14.2 km) overall
Hiking time: About 4.5 hours
Best season: April–October
Difficulty: Moderate
Water availability: None

Topo maps: Podunk Creek, Rainbow Point; Trails Illustrated
Jurisdiction: Bryce Canyon National Park. See Appendix A for more information.

Finding the trailhead: From Rainbow Point follow the sidewalk on the southwest side of the parking lot toward Yovimpa Point. Look for trailhead signs for Bristlecone Loop, Yovimpa Pass, and Riggs Spring. The hike starts here. GPS: N37° 28' 29.46"/W112° 14' 25.34"

The Hike

Hikers can complete this 8.8-mile loop as a day hike or as a relaxing overnight back-packing trip. There are three park backcountry campgrounds along the trail. The trail passes through country south of Rainbow Point, crossing some of the more remote backcountry of Bryce Canyon National Park. The northwestern portion of the trail stays above the rim of the Pink Cliffs and traverses a pleasant subalpine forest until it reaches the Yovimpa Pass Campground. From Yovimpa Pass the trail follows the Lower Podunk Creek wash down from the canyon rim to Riggs Spring. Beyond Riggs Spring the trail skirts the base of pink limestone cliffs before climbing around The Promontory and returning to Rainbow Point.

From the Riggs Spring trailhead sign, the trail goes westward along the park road for 200 feet. The path then splits away from the road and descends southwest through a subalpine forest of Douglas fir and ponderosa pine. The early parts of the trail as far as Yovimpa Pass are marred by a steel pipe that rises from the soil at various points.

The trail soon bends southward and passes through an area of charred trees and brush. As the path winds through the burn, it carries the hiker to the edge

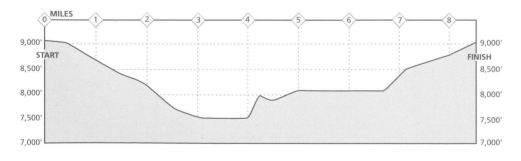

Leaves turning in the fall near Riggs Spring SHUTTERSTOCK

of the Pink Cliffs, providing views of the valleys and hoodoo formations below. The trail then leaves the cliffs and continues down through blackened forest, eventually reaching an opening at the Yovimpa Pass Campground. This meadow is bordered by aspen and ponderosa pines, and down-valley views feature Molly's Nipple and No Man's Mesa. The scenery is somewhat tainted, however, by a gravel road beside the campground and a National Park Service pump station just downhill from the campsite.

A gravel road west of the campground heads northwest toward Yovimpa Pass and offers a pleasant side trip. This road passes through an aspen-pine forest that eventually opens up into a grassy meadow. Continuing on, the road splits into left and right forks. The left fork ends at the national park boundary.

From Yovimpa Pass Campground, the Riggs Spring Trail descends along Podunk Creek. The trail zigzags over the wash several times before heading southeast. Hoodoo cliffs rise to the right along this portion of the trail. As the path continues downward, it passes through a forest of ponderosa pine, piñon pine, aspen, Douglas fir, and manzanita. The path crosses the creek a few more times before heading southeast toward Riggs Spring.

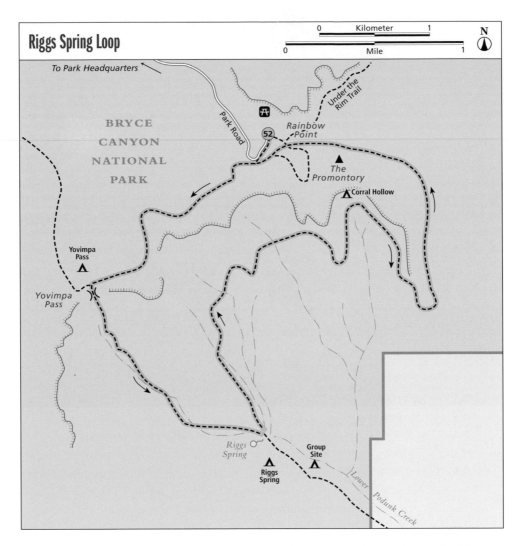

Along the way, the trail runs through a stand of juniper, ponderosa pine, and white fir. The Pink Cliffs tower above, but views are limited as the path travels through dense forest. The trees eventually open up into the small meadow where the trail reaches Riggs Spring, the Riggs Spring Campground, and a spur trail to the Riggs Spring Group Campsite. Riggs Spring is enclosed by a wood rail fence to the west side of the trail.

The trail leading to the group campground appears to be a former dirt road that continues past the campground toward the park boundary. Vegetation along this stretch includes ponderosa pine, Gambel oak, juniper, and Douglas fir.

To continue along the Riggs Spring Loop from Riggs Spring, follow the trail marked under the rim trail. This path crosses Podunk Creek and heads north on a low hillock between two other washes. The Pink Cliffs rise into view as the trail climbs westward toward the plateau. The trail winds through a forest of ponderosa pine, juniper, Gambel oak, and white fir to the east of the foothill that rises above Riggs Spring and then begins a northerly trek toward the cliffs.

The trail then turns northeast and crosses several washes as it follows Mutton Hollow. After leaving Mutton Hollow the trail climbs for 0.5 mile and then descends to the south and loops around a small foothill. As the trail turns north again, it travels through a small grove of maple trees. Just beyond this stand is the Corral Hollow Campground. Through gaps in the trees, hikers gain excellent views of the cliffs to the north.

Beyond the campground the overall scenic quality of the trail improves dramatically. The path traverses numerous open slopes, providing unobstructed views of the valleys to the east. The trail continues southeast along the west side of The Promontory, staying relatively level until it drops via switchbacks and crosses several draws. These draws offer intermittent views of the white and pink cliffs that rise above.

The trail eventually rounds the southern end of The Promontory and begins a long and steady ascent up the eastern slopes of the foothills. Near the end of the trek, a trail sign indicates a junction with the Under the Rim Trail, as well as the direction to return to Rainbow Point.

Key Points

- **0.0** Rainbow Point trailhead
- **0.1** Trail splits from Bristlecone Loop. Turn right.
- **1.8** Yovimpa Pass Campground and trail. Turn left.
- **3.4** Riggs Spring and trail to Riggs Spring Campground. Turn left and bear northward.
- **5.7** Corral Hollow Campground
- **8.8** Trail returns to Rainbow Point.

53 Mossy Cave

A short hike at the northeastern end of Bryce Canyon National Park

Distance: 0.4 mile one way
Hiking time: About 0.25 hour
Best season: April–October
Difficulty: Easy

Water availability: Water Canyon typically holds water.
Hazards: Slippery stream crossings
Topo maps: Tropic Canyon; Trails Illustrated
Jurisdiction: Bryce Canyon National Park

Finding the trailhead: Drive UT 12 east from the junction with UT 63 to a marked pull-off on the south side of the road, 1.2 miles west of the park's east entrance. GPS: N37° 39' 55.59" / W112° 6' 36.09"

Bridge on the Mossy Cave Trail SHUTTERSTOCK

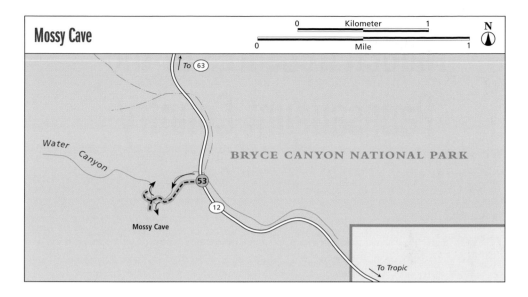

The Hike

This trail offers a short stroll into the reddish pinnacles of Bryce Canyon from UT 12, offering a smaller-scale sampler of the grandeur to the south for travelers who do not wish to make the side trip into the main part of the park. The stream flows found here are not natural; pioneering settlers diverted water from the Sevier River into Water Canyon via a series of canals to feed croplands around Tropic.

The trail begins by following Water Canyon up into the breaks, with a wall of impressive pinnacles rising to the west. Soon the path reaches the first of two stream crossings. The crossings are usually easy rock-hops, but they can be tricky during spring runoff. Near the upper crossing look up to view the natural arches and window walls in the cliffs to the west. Once the second crossing is made, a short climb leads to a T-intersection. To the right a short stroll leads to a 10-foot waterfall. To the left a brief but steep climb leads to Mossy Cave itself. This spacious alcove has been chiseled out by groundwater seeping through weaknesses in the bedrock. In winter the seeps feed impressive icicle gardens, while in summer the water provides sustenance for a vivid growth of mosses.

Hidden Treasures of the Paunsaugunt Country

Though Bryce Canyon National Park receives hundreds of thousands of visitors each year, it occupies only a tiny corner of the vast Paunsaugunt Plateau, rimmed with rugged country that falls largely within the public domain. Countless hidden nooks and crannies here offer outstanding scenery, whether the view features the eroded red hoodoos of the uplands or the

Sugar Knoll, a butte of Navajo Sandstone along the Elkheart Cliffs (hike 57)

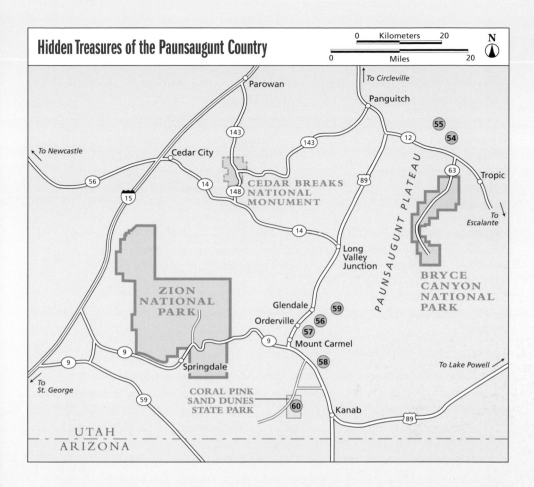

spectacular white cliffs of the Navajo Formation that gird the plateau's lower reaches. Most of these areas are known only to locals and receive very low levels of visitation. It is here that travelers are most likely to avoid crowds and experience the wild solitude of a primeval landscape.

The Paunsaugunt Plateau is a long, narrow upland that is bounded on either side by deep valleys. "Paunsaugunt" derives from the Paiute Pa-unco-a-gunt, meaning "Place of the Beavers." (The local beavers were subsequently killed off during the height of the fur trade.) The highest elevations are at its north end, where freshwater limestones of the Claron Formation have eroded into the fantastic pillars and hoodoos that are showcased within Bryce Canyon National Park. Neighboring canyons within Dixie National Forest also offer day-hiking opportunities through these eroded forests of stone. The north plateau area is dominated by unbroken forests of ponderosa pine, which are maintained by periodic wildfires. At the highest elevations spruce and fir dominate a landscape that is locked in deep snow throughout the winter months.

54 Red Canyon Loop

A day-hiking route through Red Canyon encompassing portions of the Cassidy, Rich, and Ledge Point Trails in Dixie National Forest

Distance: 4 miles (6.4 km) round-trip
Hiking time: About 2 hours
Best season: April–October
Difficulty: Moderate
Water availability: None

Hazards: Steep slopes, rocky surfaces
Topo maps: Wilson Peak; Casto Canyon
Jurisdiction: Powell Ranger District, Dixie National Forest. See Appendix A for more information.

Finding the trailhead: From US 89 drive east on UT 12. Continue 1 mile east from the Red Canyon Visitor Center to a paved turnoff for the Cassidy trailhead on the north side of UT 12. A parking area, horse corral, information board, and pit toilet are located at the trailhead. GPS: N37° 44' 41.357"/W112° 18' 3.540"

The Hike

This moderate route is pieced together with portions of the Cassidy, Rich, and Ledge Point Trails, making a loop through Red Canyon. These trails are also used by horse parties from April through October. Hikers who encounter horses on the trail should step aside and yield the right-of-way.

The route begins at the Cassidy trailhead at the northwest end of the parking lot. The path heads north, paralleling a wash through an arid landscape of ponderosa pine, limber pine, manzanita, and juniper. The terrain is rugged; pink limestone scree slopes border the wash. Like those of Bryce Canyon and the Cedar Breaks, the formations visible through Red Canyon are predominantly white and pink limestone from the Claron Formation. About 0.5 mile up the wash, the first pink limestone hoodoo formations come into view.

About 0.8 mile from the trailhead, hikers reach a first junction with the Rich Trail. Bear right, staying on the Cassidy Trail. The trail continues along the streamcourse to a confluence of several washes. Here the trail turns left and heads up a gradual-to-moderate slope to surmount a small hill. The path briefly follows the ridgeline. As you make upward progress, notice the resistant rock formations along the ridges to the left and right. Douglas firs grow in these higher elevations.

While still up in the high country, the Cassidy Trail reaches a second intersection with the Rich Trail. Break from the Cassidy Trail and follow the Rich Trail to the left (south). This portion of trail goes through a saddle and then descends along a draw that lies just west of the ridge that bears the Cassidy Trail. Along the descent the trail passes by The Gap, a wash between two resistant buttes.

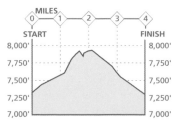

Along the Cassidy Trail

Beyond The Gap the trail ascends partway up another wash and then cuts across to another saddle, heading toward the Ledge Point Trail. The Ledge Point Trail is a horseshoe loop that intersects with the Rich Trail at two points. The loop brings hikers to Ledge Point, a picturesque overlook of the Red Canyon area with UT 12 visible below and to the south.

Follow the right (east) leg of the horseshoe loop back to the Rich Trail. Turn right and descend a slope that passes under cliffs of variegated sandstone above a watercourse. This portion of the trail is quite rocky, with gravel and cobblestones. The trail briefly parallels the wash below and then descends rapidly to the streambed via a series of steep switchbacks. Along this portion of the trail are good examples of pink hoodoos and alcoves that border the wash. At the end of the draw, the path rejoins the Cassidy Trail. Backtrack southward along this portion of trail to return to the trailhead.

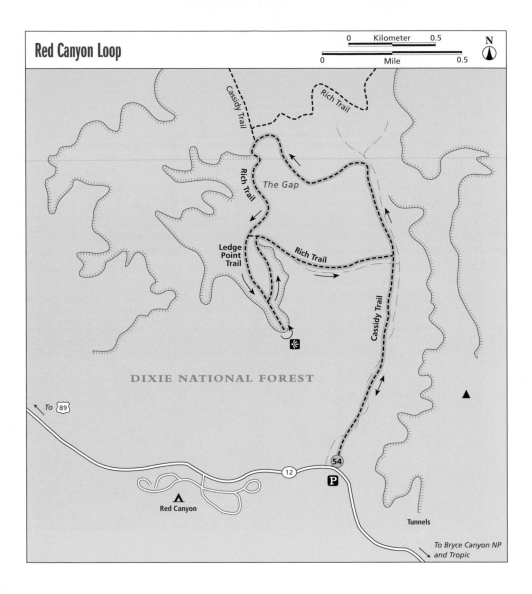

Red Canyon Loop

| 0 | Kilometer | 0.5 |
| 0 | Mile | 0.5 |

N

Cassidy Trail

Rich Trail

Rich Trail

The Gap

Ledge
Point
Trail

Rich Trail

Cassidy Trail

DIXIE NATIONAL FOREST

To 89

12

54

P

Red Canyon

Tunnels

To Bryce Canyon NP
and Tropic

Key Points

0.0 Trailhead

0.8 Junction with the Rich Trail. Stay right on the Cassidy Trail.

1.7 Second junction with the Rich Trail. Turn left onto it.

2.1 Junction with the Ledge Point Trail. Turn right for a spur loop.

3.2 Junction with the Cassidy Trail. Turn right.

4.0 Trailhead

55 Losee Canyon

A day hike through Losee Canyon in Dixie National Forest

Distance: 3 miles (4.8 km) one way
Hiking time: About 1.5 hours
Best season: April–October
Difficulty: Moderate
Water availability: None

Topo map: Casto Canyon
Jurisdiction: Powell Ranger District, Dixie National Forest. See Appendix A for more information.

Finding the trailhead: From US 89 drive 1.9 miles east on UT 12 to Casto Canyon Road. Head north on Casto Canyon Road 2 miles to a parking area and trailhead sign on the east side. A parking area, horse corral, and pit toilet are located at the Losee Canyon trailhead area. GPS: N37° 46' 10.80" / W112° 20' 4.21"

Hoodoos along the Losee Canyon Trail

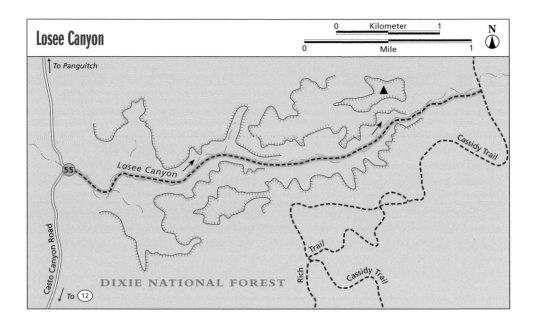

Losee Canyon

0   Kilometer   1
0   Mile   1

N

↑ To Panguitch

Casto Canyon Road

55

Losee Canyon

Trail

Rich

Cassidy Trail

Cassidy Trail

DIXIE NATIONAL FOREST

↓ To 12

The Hike

The trail travels the bottom of Losee Canyon through a rocky, arid landscape of pine and juniper trees. This easy path visits numerous pink limestone hoodoos and alcoves in the canyon walls.

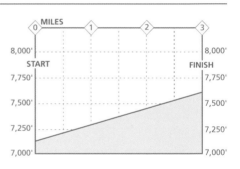

From the trailhead the trail parallels the Losee Canyon wash through an open, thirsty terrain populated sparsely by ponderosa pine, limber pine, juniper, and manzanita. During the first half of the trek, the trail stays to the left side of the wash, visiting cliffs and hoodoo formations that line the north side of the canyon. Southward views along this portion of the trek are intermittent and consist primarily of scree slopes.

The remainder of the trail stays generally level along the wash bottom, with no major changes in elevation. The path continues up the wash, visiting pink and orange hoodoos and alcoves. The trail ends at the Cassidy Trail junction and horse corral, from which visitors can retrace their steps or go on to more elaborate circuit hikes in the Red Canyon area.

Key Points

0.0 Trailhead
3.0 Junction with Cassidy Trail

56 Red Hollow

An out-and-back wilderness route up a short, picturesque canyon

Distance: 2 miles (3.2 km) round-trip
Hiking time: About 1 hour
Best season: April–October
Difficulty: Easy
Water availability: None

Hazards: Some scrambling over uneven surfaces, flash flood danger
Topo maps: Orderville; Glendale
Jurisdiction: Bureau of Land Management, Kanab Field Office. See Appendix A for more information.

Finding the trailhead: Follow US 89 to Orderville. Turn east on 100 East Street at the Centennial School. Turn left (north) on Red Hollow Drive. Drive 0.15 mile to a sand/gravel road. Follow the sand road 0.3 mile to a small turnout where a cement reservoir atop a small foothill should be in view. The hike begins by heading into the opening of a small canyon that is overlooked by pad-mounted transformers and a cement reservoir. GPS: N37° 16' 16.57"/W112° 37' 46.83"

The Hike

As the route enters the mouth of the canyon, a high bank presents itself on the left side. It soon gives way to red cliffs that extend down to the canyon floor. The canyon soon splits into two short branches, each of which invites further exploration. Both branches are wooded with Gambel oak, juniper, and ponderosa pine. Hikers should not attempt to climb onto the sloping canyon walls; they may be easy to ascend, but they are almost impossible to get back down.

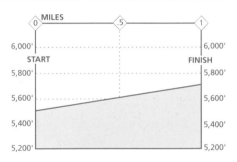

The south branch of the canyon breaks away to the right and has a somewhat narrow watercourse. Sheer cliffs of red sandstone form the walls of this side canyon. Cobblestones and sand line the narrow watercourse, making for easy traveling. At the end of this branch are some interesting natural arch formations overhanging the wash. At the very headwall of the canyon, a freestanding leaf of stone has been carved out of the cliffs by erosion.

The main branch is called Red Hollow. Heading up it, hikers will find crimson walls that slant into the canyon floor on the left, while overhanging walls with solution holes rise on the right. The walls of this branch narrow abruptly to a width of 6 feet or so and become impassable after a distance of 0.8 mile from the parking area. This is the end of the trek; travelers must now retrace their route.

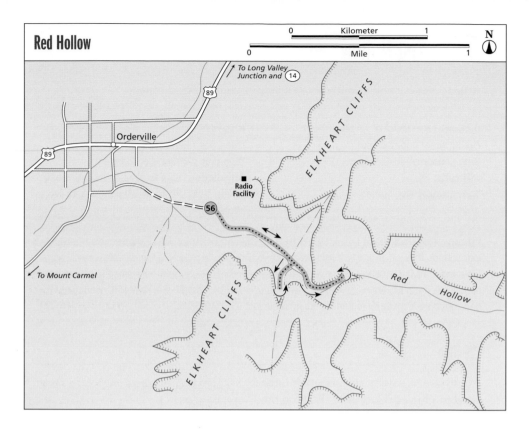

Red Hollow

Key Points

0.0   End of improved road
0.7   Confluence with wash coming in from the right (south)
0.9   Headwall of southern canyon
1.0   End of main canyon and turnaround point

57 Sugar Knoll

A day hike to Sugar Knoll with an option to Red Cave

Distance: 2.1 miles (3.4 km) to Sugar Knoll; 1.8 miles (2.9 km) to Red Cave, one way

Hiking time: About 1.5 hours one way to either destination

Best season: March–November

Difficulty: Moderate

Water availability: The potholes within Red Cave always contain murky water.

Hazards: Extreme flash flood danger within Red Cave

Topo map: Mount Carmel

Jurisdiction: Bureau of Land Management, Kanab Field Office. See Appendix A for more information.

Finding the trailhead: From Orderville drive south on US 89 to the historic schoolhouse at mile 83.5. Park here and hike north along the highway for 0.2 mile to a dirt road that runs eastward to the river. This road is the beginning of the hike. GPS: N37° 14' 55.33" / W112° 39' 46.66"

The Hike

This route offers several manageable day-hiking options, visiting the spectacular high country at the base of the Elkheart Cliffs. These destinations are well-known to local residents but receive little attention from others, so these hikes offer a fairly good opportunity for solitude. The Sugar Knoll route travels right to the base of the Elkheart Cliffs, while the Red Cave route visits an impossibly narrow slot canyon carved into red sandstone.

The hike initially follows a dirt road that runs eastward across the Long Valley. It soon makes an ankle-deep ford of the East Fork of the Virgin River. On the far bank the road swings north along the river for a time and then jogs east again to reach a corral and gravel pit at the base of the hills. The route then follows a jeep track that rounds the corral on a northward heading and soon climbs to the top of a low plateau. Along the way are fine views of the Long Valley's fertile bottomlands.

Once the jeep road reaches the top of the plateau, a scrub forest of juniper allows only brief glimpses of the bone-white Elkheart Cliffs to the east. These cliffs, which are of the same Navajo sandstone as Zion Canyon, guard the edge of the Paunsaugunt Plateau. The jeep trail meanders through the scrub and breaks out onto a sagebrush flat just before reaching the Bureau of Land Management land boundary.

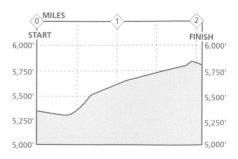

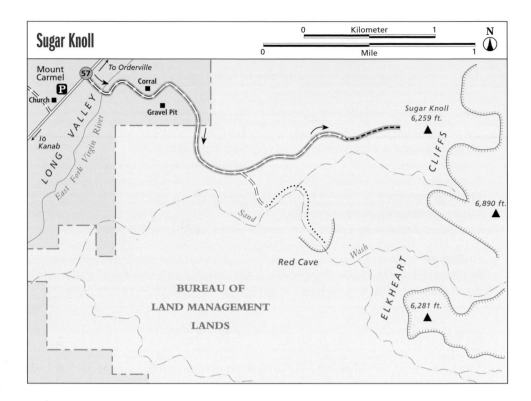

The track then makes its way to the edge of a steep bluff. Far below, a sandy wash issues from the red rock layers that underlie the Elkheart Cliffs. This arroyo is known as Sand Wash, and at its head is the slot canyon known locally as Red Cave. A second jeep trail soon drops away to the right to begin a journey up this canyon (see Red Cave Option, below).

Bear left at the fork for Sugar Knoll as the main jeep trail continues to climb gently toward the base of the cliffs. After 1.4 miles the jeep road ends and a rough trail bears east–northeast toward a red rock hoodoo. Follow this trail as it climbs across the slickrock to reach an overlook that offers a sweeping view of Sugar Knoll, with the Elkheart Cliffs providing a stunning backdrop. The junipers fall away as the trail drops onto sand dunes that have been stabilized by a growth of sagebrush, manzanita, and Gambel oak.

Expect sandy hiking conditions as the trail covers the remaining distance to the base of Sugar Knoll. Here, beneath a small blowout cave in the bedrock, the path splits into a tangle of sandy avenues that entice further exploration along the base of this striking butte of wind-sculpted sandstone.

Key Points

0.0   Dirt road departs US 89.

0.2   Road fords the East Fork of the Virgin River.

0.4   Gravel pit. Follow jeep trail to the north.

1.1   Jeep trail enters BLM lands.

1.2   Jeep trail splits; bear left. (***Option:*** Turn right for the 0.6-mile trail to Red Cave.)

1.8   Jeep trail ends. Follow rough path to the northeast.

2.1   Base of Sugar Knoll

Red Cave Option

This moderate trail adds about 1.2 miles round-trip to your hike. From the bluff-top junction of jeep trails, follow the track to the right (southeast) that descends steeply into the valley of Sand Wash. As its name implies, the wash is a wide avenue of sand that has been deposited by eons of flash flooding. Traveling is easy as the route follows the wash upward toward its source, an impossibly narrow declivity in the red lower layers of Navajo sandstone. This is the slot canyon called Red Cave, and hikers can penetrate it for only a short distance without vigorous climbing.

Deep pools of water form in the floor of the cleft and are always cold—wear a wetsuit for extended exploration. Whorled walls rise up to block the sky, and the canyon floor is only wide enough to admit travelers in single file. This narrow chasm is a death trap when waters reach flood stage, since hikers have no way to climb upward. Visitors should carefully monitor the weather conditions and enter the slot canyon only if cloudless skies are a certainty.

When you return to the main trail, take a right for Sugar Knoll or turn left to return to the trailhead.

Fluted walls in Red Cave

58 Dianas Throne

An out-and-back day hike along jeep trails

Distance: 2.1 miles (3.4 km) round-trip
Hiking time: About 1 hour
Best season: March–May
Elevation Gain: 342 feet
Difficulty: Easy
Water availability: None

Hazards: Extremely hot and dry
Topo map: USGS Mount Carmel
Jurisdiction: Bureau of Land Management, Kanab Field Office. See Appendix A for more information.

Finding the trailhead: Take US 89 west from Kanab or east from Mount Carmel to mile 76.4, just west of the highway's summit. Drive north on a gravel road to a junction with the old highway bed, now a gravel road. Park here; the hike begins on the gated jeep trail (marked 106P) that runs north from this junction. GPS: N37° 10' 51.71" / W112° 38' 4.78"

The Hike

Dianas Throne is a majestic tower of white Navajo sandstone that rises at the southern tip of the Elkheart Cliffs. This often sandy hike follows jeep trails that remain open to vehicle travel, so you may encounter motorized users along the route.

The hike begins with a sandy uphill through piñons and junipers, bearing for the western face of Dianas Throne. After a short climb you will meet a powerline; turn left onto jeep trail 106L. Follow this route up a gentle grade to a saddle, then turn right onto 106Q, which you will follow for the remainder of the hike.

The trees thin out now for unobstructed views of Dianas Throne, as well as the stone temples of Zion National Park on the western skyline. The understory here is a mixture of old sagebrush, rabbitbrush, and Mormon tea grown large in the absence of fire. The sandy jeep trail rises gently beside the west face of Dianas Throne and then curves into the alcove behind it. Upon striking a wash, it climbs briskly eastward to reach the end of motorized travel. From here, you can hike north up a ridgelet of pink sand to view the yellow- and rose-colored sandstone at the base of the Elkheart Cliffs. Note the contrasting diagonal bedding of the sandstone, known as "cross-bedding," indicating that the sand was deposited in the form of wind-blown dunes before it solidified into rock.

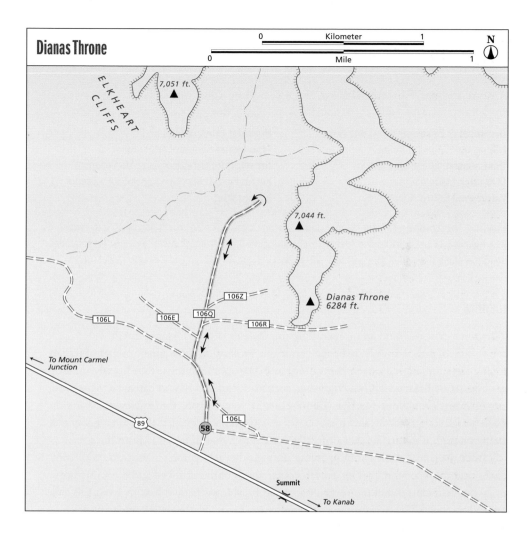

Dianas Throne

ELKHEART CLIFFS

7,051 ft. ▲

7,044 ft. ▲

106Z

106E 106Q

106L

106R

Dianas Throne
6284 ft. ▲

To Mount Carmel
Junction

89

58

106L

Summit

To Kanab

Key Points

0.0 Begin hike. Hike north along jeep trail 106P.

0.1 Route reaches powerline at junction with jeep trail 106L. Turn left.

0.3 Junction. Turn right onto jeep trail 106Q.

0.4 Junction with jeep trail 106E. Continue straight ahead.

0.5 Junction with jeep trail 106R. Continue straight ahead.

0.6 Junction with jeep trail 106Z. Continue straight ahead.

1.0 Jeep trail ends. Hike north to top of ridge.

1.1 End of hike

59 White Tower

A route through Fourmile Hollow, ending at White Tower

Distance: 6.1 miles (9.8 km) one way
Hiking time: About 4 hours
Best season: April–May
Difficulty: Moderate
Water availability: None

Hazards: Extremely hot and dry
Topo maps: Glendale; White Tower
Jurisdiction: Bureau of Land Management,
Kanab Field Office. See Appendix A for more
information.

Finding the trailhead: From Mount Carmel Junction drive 8.8 miles north on US 89 to Glendale. Turn right (east) on UT 300 North (Bench Road) and drive 4.3 miles to Threemile Hollow. Parking can be found along the side of the road near the wash. GPS: N37° 17' 55.98" / W112° 32' 12.62"

The Hike

This route traverses land administered by the Bureau of Land Management and crosses the fringes of private land as well. Since Fourmile Hollow and the upper reaches of Kanab Creek are administered by the Bureau of Land Management, the area is heavily used by grazing cattle. Evidence of heavy grazing, such as disturbed soil and damaged vegetation, are obvious throughout the trek. Because cattle contaminate the waterways, drinking from water sources along this route is not recommended, even if the water is filtered. Bring enough water to last the entire hike without having to take any from the stream.

After the initial challenge of tiptoeing through the cow patties, hikers can travel fairly easily over this open terrain. The uneven cobblestones of the washbed and the sandy horse trails can be awkward but are certainly manageable. However, it is best to avoid this area after a heavy rain. The disturbed soil and cow droppings make for an extremely muddy and practically impassable mess when wet.

Despite these unpleasantries, Fourmile Hollow and upper Kanab Creek offer wonderful landscapes of Navajo sandstone. Hikers are rewarded with a spectacular view of the ominous White Tower at the conclusion of the trek after a gradual, barely perceptible loss of elevation.

Follow a dirt path to the right (west) of the hollow to an opening in barbed-wire fencing where the path intersects a dirt road. Take the dirt road leftward (east) toward the hollow. After a short trek follow a cobblestone path that angles down a slope into the hollow. This is the most convenient way to begin the trek. Downstream from the cobblestone path, the cliffs of the hollow grow steep, making a climb down into the hollow at a later point a dangerous proposition. (*Option:* From Threemile Hollow you can climb down into the wash immediately from Bench Road and

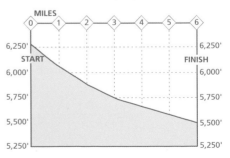

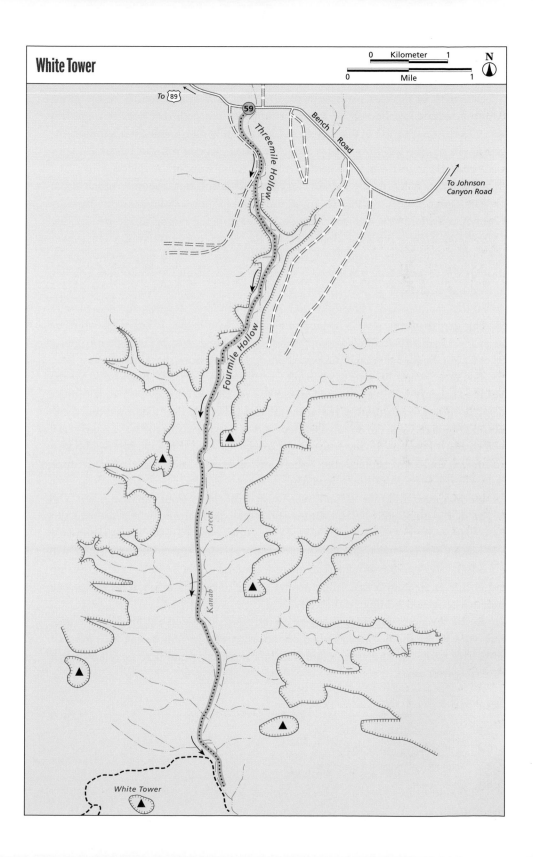

White Tower

Kilometer
0   1

Mile
0   1

N

To 89

59

Bench Road

To Johnson Canyon Road

Threemile Hollow

Fourmile Hollow

Kanab Creek

White Tower

follow the wash from there—although Threemile Hollow gets narrower before it gets wider, and the narrows are choked with brush and may be extremely muddy.)

Just south of the first main wash on the right is a small waterfall and its pool. Climb down beside the falls, or follow an intermittent path that goes through this area. Hiking this portion of the route is not aesthetically pleasing due to the high concentration of cow and horse manure scattered everywhere. You can best make your way through the patties along a path on the left (east) bank of the hollow.

This is the worst of the manure, and beyond it the trek becomes much more pleasant. Hikers are now free to enjoy the peaceful surroundings, highlighted by Gambel oaks, junipers, and towering ponderosa pines growing inside the hollow. Cross-bedded cliffs and scree slopes border the watercourse, offering a spectacular geologic counterpoint to the trees. Watch your footing in this part of the canyon, though; the terrain along this stretch is unevenly strewn with loose boulders, cobbles, gravel, and sand.

At the confluence of Threemile and Fourmile Hollows, step over the barbed-wire fencing that spans the wash. The area south of the confluence is heavily trodden by livestock. Despite the trampled condition of the washbed, this area is made intriguing by the cross-bedded cliffs and ponderosa pines growing from the stony slopes.

The White Cliffs become a dominant feature to the south of Cottonwood Spring Wash, as canyon walls begin to widen and rise up to a height of 400 feet. Unfortunately, as in earlier portions of the hike, this area is heavily disturbed by cattle. Continuing on, hikers will encounter a barbed-wire fence that spans the watercourse. You will need to crawl under the fence to get across. Beyond this fence the washbed is an uneven jumble of cobblestones. Follow any of several sandy paths, typically stock trails, along the banks of the watercourse.

Upon approaching the second main wash that enters from the east, hikers will begin to see black cliffs on the southeastern side of the canyon. The walls of this mesa represent the Kayenta and Moenave sandstones, which were deposited during the Jurassic Period, 140 million years ago. With the mesa still to the east, hikers will encounter a deep, narrow gully cut into the middle of the washbed. The wash on either side of the gully is wide and open with little or no vegetation. It is easy to walk here without descending into the gully.

As the wash gets wider and the mesa on the east falls away, the White Tower comes into view to the south. This striking monolith is composed of the same Navajo sandstone that makes up the White Cliffs. Hikers can turn around here or follow a trail that runs westward.

Key Points

- **0.0** Trailhead at Threemile Hollow
- **0.4** Confluence with Fourmile Hollow
- **3.2** Fourmile Hollow joins Kanab Creek.
- **6.1** White Tower

60 Coral Pink Sand Dunes

A day-hiking loop onto the ridges overlooking the dynamic Coral Pink Sand Dunes, returning through the dunefields themselves

Distance: 2.5 miles (4 km) overall
Hiking time: About 2 hours
Best season: April–November
Difficulty: Moderately strenuous
Water availability: None

Hazards: Steep slopes with uneven footing
Topo map: Yellow Jacket Canyon
Jurisdiction: Bureau of Land Management, Kanab Field Office; Coral Pink Sand Dunes State Park. See Appendix A for more information.

Finding the trailhead: From Mount Carmel Junction drive south on US 89 to a sign marked CORAL PINK SAND DUNES. Turn right on CR 1850 and drive 9.3 miles to a large, open area used for four-wheel-drive recreation on the left (east) side of the road. GPS: N37° 4' 2.13" / W112° 42' 17.61"

The Hike

More than half of the Coral Pink Sand Dunes are administered by the State of Utah as a state park. A state park campground and fee area are located in the southern section of the dunes. The dunes are used frequently by off-road vehicles. Hikers are also welcome but should exercise caution with this in mind.

The Coral Pink Sand Dunes offer an infinite array of possible route choices. The dunes occupy a long, narrow valley overlooked by sandstone hills to the east. As a result of prevailing winds, the dunes are oriented along an east-west axis. Travel is easiest along the axis of the dunes; hikers on a north-south heading will face numerous up and downs. A few loosely defined jeep tracks trace the edges of the dunes, but the heart of this miniature Sahara is essentially trailless. Our route climbs onto the ridges west of the dunes for an aerial view before descending into the heart of the dunes for the return trip.

From the parking area head southeast over the sand dunes toward the sandstone hills bordering the valley. These hills are wooded in an open scrub of ponderosa pine and juniper. Wherever possible stay on the four-wheel-drive tracks as you walk for easiest traveling. This will spare the delicate vegetation growing on the unstable slopes of the dunes. Watch the undisturbed surface of the sand for animal tracks and patterns made by the wind.

As you gain elevation and approach the sandstone foothills, notice that the dunes are partially stabilized by populations of ponderosa pine, sagebrush, yucca,

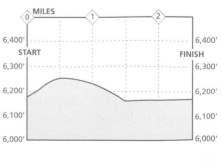

In the midst of the Coral Pink Sand Dunes

and a variety of small desert plants. As the route climbs into the hills, limber pine, Gambel oak, and manzanita populations become prevalent.

Once up on the sandstone, head south along the foothills toward a gorge that penetrates the rock. This portion of the trek provides an excellent vantage point from which to look out over the dunes and study their patterns. Just before the gorge a few shallow washes head southward. Explore these, but proceed with caution—the washes end abruptly with a rapid descent into the gorge.

Descend into the dunes, choosing a route slightly north of the gorge. Investigate your route before beginning a descent in order to avoid thickets of Gambel oak and manzanita. Spending a few minutes studying the east-west pattern of the dunes will help you end your descent within a trough or on the crest of a dune. The trough or crest can then be followed back toward the parking area.

Sagebrush flats and a barbed-wire fence guard the western border of the state park. Angle northwest to encounter this fence and follow it north through the sage-brush to return to the parking area.

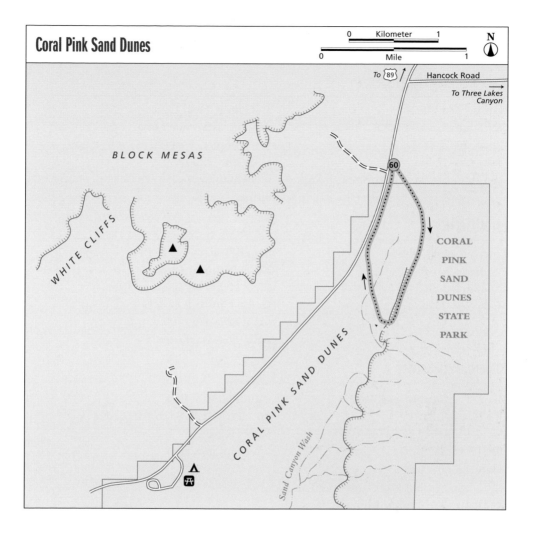

Coral Pink Sand Dunes

0   Kilometer   1

0   Mile   1

N

To [89]

Hancock Road

To Three Lakes
Canyon

BLOCK MESAS

WHITE CLIFFS

60

CORAL
PINK
SAND
DUNES
STATE
PARK

CORAL PINK SAND DUNES

Sand Canyon Wash

Key Points

0.0   Parking area

1.3   Deep gorge through the sandstone hills. Turn west and descend into the sand dunes.

2.5   Route returns to the parking area.

Appendix A: Managing Agencies

Bureau of Land Management

Kanab Field Office
669 South Highway 89A
Kanab, UT 84741
(435) 644-1200
www.blm.gov/ut/st/en/fo/kanab.html

St. George Field Office
345 East Riverside Drive
St. George, UT 84790
(435) 688-3200
www.blm.gov/ut/st/en/fo/st__george
.html

Forest Service

Powell Ranger District
225 East Center
Panguitch, UT 84759
(435) 676-9300

Supervisor
Dixie National Forest
1789 North Wedgewood Lane
Cedar City, UT 84721
(435) 865-3700
www.fs.usda.gov/dixie

National Park Service

Bryce Canyon National Park
PO Box 640201
Bryce Canyon, UT 84764-0201
(435) 834-5322
www.nps.gov/brca

Zion National Park
Springdale, UT 84767-1099
(435) 772-3256
www.nps.gov/zion

Cedar Breaks National Monument
2390 W. Highway 56, Suite 11
Cedar City, UT 84720
(435) 586-9451
www.nps.gov/cebr

State of Utah

Coral Pink Sand Dunes State Park
PO Box 95
Kanab, UT 84741-0095
(435) 648-2800
www.utah.com/stateparks/coral_pink.htm

Appendix B: Hiker Checklist

Most hikers realize the importance of a good checklist once they are on the trail: What you have forgotten to pack may turn out to be only an inconvenience, or it may pose a serious problem. A good checklist will help you remember the essentials.

The list below is only a suggested list. Use it to create your own, based on the nature of your hike and personal needs. Items will vary depending on whether you are day hiking or backpacking into remote country. If you are carrying supplies on your back, select items judiciously, with weight in mind.

Clothing

- ❑ dependable rain parka
- ❑ wind-resistant jacket
- ❑ wetsuit (for canyon wading in cold weather)
- ❑ thermal underwear
- ❑ shorts
- ❑ long pants
- ❑ cap or hat
- ❑ wool shirt or sweater
- ❑ warm jacket
- ❑ extra socks
- ❑ underwear
- ❑ lightweight shirts
- ❑ T-shirts
- ❑ wool gloves

Footwear

- ❑ comfortable hiking boots
- ❑ lightweight camp shoes
- ❑ water shoes or sandals

Bedding

- ❑ sleeping bag
- ❑ foam pad or air mattress
- ❑ pillow (deflating)
- ❑ ground cloth (plastic or nylon)
- ❑ dependable tent

Cooking

- ❑ 1-quart plastic water containers
- ❑ 1-gallon collapsible water container
- ❑ backpack stove with extra fuel
- ❑ funnel or pour spout for fuel
- ❑ aluminum foil
- ❑ cooking pot
- ❑ bowl or plate
- ❑ spoon, fork, knife, spatula
- ❑ butane lighter or matches in a waterproof container

Food & Drink

- cereal
- bread and/or crackers
- trail mix
- margarine
- powdered soups
- salt, pepper, spices
- main-course meals
- snacks
- coffee, tea, hot chocolate
- powdered milk
- drink mixes

Photography

- camera
- film
- accessories
- dry bag

Miscellaneous

- maps, compasses
- wading staff
- toilet paper and PVC "poop tube"
- small trowel or shovel
- toothbrush and toothpaste
- water filter or purifier
- first-aid kit
- survival kit
- pocket knife
- insect repellent
- flashlight, with spare batteries and bulb
- candles
- extra plastic bags to pack out trash
- biodegradable soap
- towel/washcloth
- waterproof covering for pack
- binoculars
- watch
- sewing kit
- this hiking guide

Index

About the Authors

Erik Molvar discovered backpacking while working on a volunteer trail crew in the North Cascades of Washington. His experiences led him to choose a career in the outdoors, and he soon found himself studying wildlife biology at the University of Montana. His studies there were followed by a master of science degree from the University of Alaska, Fairbanks, where his groundbreaking research on the behavior and ecology of moose was published in several international journals. Erik is currently a professional conservationist in Laramie, Wyoming. His other FalconGuides include *Hiking Arizona's Cactus Country, Hiking the Bob Marshall Country, Hiking Colorado's Maroon Bells–Snowmass Wilderness, Hiking Glacier and Waterton Lakes National Park, Hiking the North Cascades, Hiking Olympic National Park, Hiking Wyoming's Cloud Peak Wilderness,* and *Wild Wyoming.* He also is the author of *Scenic Driving Alaska and the Yukon* (Globe Pequot Press) and *Alaska on Foot: Wilderness Techniques for the Far North.*

Tamara Martin holds a bachelor of science degree in environmental health from Westchester University in Pennsylvania. After graduation she began her professional career as an environmental consultant in southeast Texas. In pursuit of her dreams, she took a sabbatical to spend a summer hiking in Denali National Park in Alaska. She has also worked as a ranger at Moran State Park in Washington and as a part-time sea-kayaking guide in the San Juan Islands.

American Hiking Society

Because you
hike.
We're with you
every step of the way

As a national voice for hikers, **American Hiking Society** works every day:

- Building and maintaining hiking trails
- Educating and supporting hikers by providing information and resources
- Supporting hiking and trail organizations nationwide
- Speaking for hikers in the halls of Congress and with federal land managers

Whether you're a casual hiker or a seasoned backpacker, become a member of American Hiking Society and join the national hiking community! You'll enjoy great member benefits and help preserve the nation's hiking trails, so tomorrow's hike is even better than today's. We invite you to join us now!

American Hiking Society

www.AmericanHiking.org • info@AmericanHiking.org